Douglas Stewart was born in New Zealand in
1913 and moved to Australia in 1938. He was literary
editor of the *Bulletin* from 1940 to 1961, then literary
advisor and editor at publishers Angus & Robertson
until 1973, and did a great deal to encourage
Australian poets and writers. His own output
included many books of poetry, verse plays, such as
The Fire on the Snow, as well as prose works including
Norman Lindsay: A Personal Memoir and the autobiography *Springtime in Taranaki.* He married artist
Margaret Coen in 1945, the union lasting until his
death in 1985. His last book *Garden of Friends* was
published posthumously in 1987.

THE SEVEN RIVERS

Douglas Stewart

DUFFY & SNELLGROVE
SYDNEY

Published by Duffy & Snellgrove in 2001
PO Box 177 Potts Point NSW 1335 Australia
info@duffyandsnellgrove.com.au

First published by Angus & Robertson in 1966

Distributed by Pan Macmillan

ACKNOWLEDGMENTS
'The Fish That Got Away', 'The Seven Rivers', 'A Pool in the Waingongoro',
'The Town Creek', 'The Pleasures of Poaching', 'Bulls', and 'Swordfish Waters'
were first published in the *Bulletin*; 'Brindabella' in *Meanjin*; 'The Badja' in
Blackwood's.

Illustrations by Margaret Coen
Cover design by Alex Snellgrove
Typeset by Cooper Graphics
Printed by Griffin Press

ISBN 1 875989 99 4

visit our website: www.duffyandsnellgrove.com.au

CONTENTS

Introduction *vii*

Foreword *xiii*

1 The Fish That Got Away *1*

2 The Seven Rivers *15*

3 Pool in the Waingongoro *29*

4 The Town Creek *41*

5. The Pleasures of Poaching *51*

6 The Awakino *63*

7 North to Kawhia *89*

8 The Country of the Wild Pigs *115*

9 Bulls *133*

10 Once at Taupo *147*

11 The Duckmaloi *163*

12 Brindabella *193*

13 The Badja *207*

14 Swordfish Waters *235*

15 Prosser's *249*

16 The Snowy *273*

INTRODUCTION

PERHAPS IT was because he cast with such con-
summate skill, the thick green line with fine leader
flicking surely to and fro above the river before it landed
his fly exactly over the nose of an invisible trout. Perhaps
that's why my father could always catch a fish. On days
when it was too baking hot to be on the river, while
others were tramping the tussocks to no avail, when the
only sensible thing would be to find a good shady tree
and lie under it or, as my father's great fishing mate
David Campbell did once when the fishing was utterly
hopeless, sit in a willow with a book of poetry, my father
could still pull a trout from the Moonbah.

I was ten, turning eleven, the first time he took me
trout fishing. I had been on fishing holidays before. A
magical summer on the Badja when I was very small my
father even forsaking fishing to look after me and build
mermaid's houses out of river stones, so my mother
could paint. But I hadn't fished with him. That first year
at Kiandra I used a rod with a spinning reel and, so I
could hold my head up with trout fishing cognoscenti,
a dry fly kept afloat by a plastic bubble half-filled with

water. I caught nothing and had to be rescued from a marshy ledge because I became so absorbed in casting my bubble across a long deep pool that I failed to notice my gumboots – dangerous footwear for trout fishing – had filled with water and I was about to disappear into a bog.

I fished with him nine summers in row after that. My mother came with us but never fished, though once when she was painting, my father flipped a tiny trout out of the river into her lap. My parents had a pact. He fished, she painted, and we stayed somewhere she didn't have to cook or do housework. After my first Kiandra summer we fished at Kosciuszko. We stayed, until it was drowned as part of the Snowy Mountains Hydro-Electric Scheme, at a celebrated trout fishing lodge called the Creel, on the Thredbo River out from old Jindabyne. The Creel had what my father described as a *slither* of trout about it. A notice board which recorded every trout over three pounds caught hung in the dining room and intent men in khaki fishing gear stomped up and down the veranda floor boards at the crack of dawn and late into the night.

I did one more year with the bubble, I think, before I graduated to a neat silver fly reel. My fibre glass rod wasn't quite as long as my father's slender tipped split cane, which dismantled into three pieces, and it never quite made the same swishing sound as it waved back and forwards in the air. Nor did it have such a delicious wobble to its tip. But I cast happily, hooking briars, tea-tree bushes and gum tree branches high overhead, from which there was no chance of saving either fly or leader, and occasionally I managed to place my fly reasonably near a fish.

We went scrambling down hillsides, the sun bright

on our backs, and he told me about Judith Wright's summer's bubble-sound of sweet creek-water. When we reached the Snowy, the Thredbo, or whatever river we were making for, it was like poetry: shaded green–black pools with bright little runs of water that ended in bubbled eddies on which tea-tree blossom floated white as the specks of broken water.

He taught me how trout fishing was as much about being there, as catching fish. About being with the river and often, those Kosciuszko January days, we were nearly waist deep in its refreshing chill, and enjoying the minutia of life on it. Observing a lizard or lichen on a granite boulder was as crucial as knowing whether to choose a Royal Coachman fly, or doing 'battle' with the rapids as David Campbell so loved. My father also instilled in me patience; patience, above all, after lunch when trout are sluggish and hide from glaring mid-afternoon heat. Come the end of day, he reminded me, and the evening rise, a river that has seemed devoid of fish will suddenly resound with the excited splashing of young fish in a feeding frenzy, and the gentle plopping of older, less-hurried trout rising.

There was the intriguing paraphernalia, never quite as all-important to me as it was to the male guests at the Creel. You could never start fishing without putting on your snake armour, the stiff canvas leggings and boots. Your boots were meant to have soles which wouldn't slip on treacherous river stones and weed slime. Boots with felt soles were supposed to give the best grip. My father, with great expectation, once sent away for a pair imported, I think from Scotland, which turned out to be so heavy he could never wear them at all.

After you'd made up your rod, a fly had to be selected from a hinged plastic box with separate little containers for each type of fly … March Brown, Hardy's Favourite, Tup's Indispensable. The infallible Tup's Indispensable! My father took, or lost, all his biggest fish, he said, on a Tup's. I always liked fly boxes. Years later when my mother was old and dying I kept the daily doses of her multitude of pills carefully set out in one of dad's old fly boxes.

I liked, too, the rich, steady chirring of a reel unwinding, especially my father's mellow Hardy's Perfect, the rhythmic rasp when you wound back in, the high-pitched tone as the line ran out with a trout. It wasn't only on the stream you heard these sounds. Old hands used to string their wet silk lines out round special pegs on the veranda that ran the length of the guests' bedrooms. In the morning after they'd had a cup of tea with, in some cases, a shot of rum or whisky, you'd hear the rasp of reels as they wound up lines that had been carefully re-greased in readiness for a fresh day's casting.

I never caught a great many fish. Usually I was so excited when a trout did rise at my fly, I would strike too early and jerk the fly out of its mouth. I never had my own net. My father either helped me land those trout I did catch, shouting out instructions as he rushed to assist, unfurling his net with a quick deft wrist movement, or stood looking appalled as somehow the fish stayed hooked while I lifted it out of the water, netless.

So ten summers of fishing with my father passed. I stopped trout fishing when I was twenty. I had a job. I had boyfriends who did not fish. I went away overseas, I came back. I was busy doing things other than fishing. But then in my early thirties I joined him again. He was older and frailer, content to fish in a more leisurely manner.

Even so, he could unerringly lure out a lazy old brown lurking under the nearest overgrown bank, giving lie to the doctrine he had so energetically espoused in seasons past, that the fishing is always better Further On. My own casting had improved out of sight. Now I really could send the line right across a pool, or almost. I caught my biggest fish. Not a three-pounder, it wouldn't have made the Creel's notice board, but big enough, and after several summers my father presented me with a net, the final symbol of being a trout-fishing person in my own right. I had my own net. I could fish without him now.

For him just putting on the gear, even doing up the buckles on his leggings, was an effort that year, likewise slowly fitting together his rod, threading the line through its guides, tying on his fly and anointing it with dressing. Each step and almost every breath exhausted him, and he had to rest after walking less than twenty-five metres to the stream. But still he cast cannily.

He settled on a February date, later than usual, for our next trip to Kosciuszko. On New Year's day he finished hand-writing (typing was too strenuous for him) his last book, *Garden of Friends*. He was sicker than he admitted, or we knew. During the early part of January he deliberated as to whether we should or shouldn't keep our fishing date, whether he felt strong enough to go. Reluctantly, he decided against it.

Instead of quietly fishing a pool of the Moonbah, he came down with pneumonia. He was four days in hospital. My mother was to visit in the afternoons, I could come in the evenings, he said. He wanted no other visitors. Unthinkably, he had no interest in reading. Who knows where his mind skimmed? I would like to think it was filled with summer's bubble-sound of

sweet creek-water; that still and fast water mingled cool-
ingly as he waded up dappled streams; and that after a
perfect cast, a spritely rainbow leapt out at his Tup's,
sending his reel racing and green line shooting through
his brown fingers. At least, that's what I wish him.

And it probably would have been too hot for any
decent fishing that February, anyway. Except for him, of
course.

Meg Stewart
Sydney, 2001

FOREWORD

THOUGH there is a chapter about swordfish in this book, another about snapper, and even a piece about pig-hunting, it is mostly a book about trout-fishing in Australia and New Zealand, and mostly meant for fishermen. It contains very little expert advice, for I don't claim to be an expert. I wrote it simply for the pleasure of going fishing again in retrospect along my favourite rivers.

It is also perhaps a kind of nature book, since you do meet a lot of interesting birds, beasts, bugs, and human beings when you are walking up the trout streams; and it is also a kind of autobiography ... but only of those parts of my life which I consider really important and significant, such as catching a lot of kahawai at Kawhia, or losing that ten-pounder in the Badja.

D.S.

1

THE FISH THAT GOT AWAY

OF COURSE it is always the biggest and best fish that get away; and anyone who maintains otherwise and disbelieves an angler when he says he has lost a trout of half a ton knows not the running streams and the wiles of their inhabitants.

They get away simply because they are so big, these monsters that haunt our dreams. They leap, and the hook tears out. They race for rapids and waterfalls, down from one pool to another fifty yards away, and the frail cast breaks when you try to check them. They are old and cunning and live among snags from which no angler can extricate them. They have been hooked before and know the perfect procedure for circumventing you.

Or do they? Certainly it seems so. At Fred's on the Badja – Fred's is the name of a pool; and the Badja is near Cooma – a fine big rainbow who knew exactly where he was going rushed straight under a submerged rock-ledge, instantly cut the cast, and left me sorrowing to this day. I hooked a three-pound brown trout in the

Tangatara in New Zealand long ago and he dashed upstream from his pool and climbed a fallen tree. Nobody can tell me he did not know it was there. He knew precisely what to do. When hooked, climb a tree. Sea fish, it seems, do not have such good memories. At the mouth of the Awakino where the river curves through the black sands to meet, past the headland, the creaming breakers of Taranaki's west coast, I caught a kahawai (the fish miscalled 'salmon' in Australia), and in a little rock-pool I had half a dozen live herring, themselves apparently little disturbed by their recent transfer from the river, swimming about for bait. These are the kahawai's natural food; and when I caught my kahawai and put him in the pool he at once, obviously without a thought for the experience of taking a hook, being dragged ashore and travelling a hundred yards or so over the sands, set about chasing those herrings up and down and around the pool until he had gobbled the lot.

Apparently the one thought in his fishy brain, if it can be called a thought, was that kahawai eat herring. I had to knock him on the head and operate on him to retrieve my bait. And I got from him, for good measure, an extra supply of bait in the shape of three or four more herring which he had previously devoured in the ocean.

Of course any fish of the ocean is but a poor relation of the trout, coarser in habit, dimmer in wit. There are trout, sometimes, that seem to be similarly short-memoried; but if trout have no recollection of having been hooked, how is one to explain the conduct of those titans which have clearly grown too wise to rise to a bait?

There were four or five wonderful brown trout, six-pounders each of them, if not more, at which, when

I lived in New Zealand, we used to gaze from the road-bridge over the Kaupokonui every Sunday on our way out to fish the more generous waters of the Tangatara, the Mangahume, or the Waiau. Nothing, when we tackled them, would induce those fish to move: no fly, dry or wet, no spinning Devon or Wisden, no 'creeper' from under a stone, not the fattest worm from the fowlyard.

Had they been hooked a hundred times and become utterly scornful of all the clumsy mechanisms of fishermen? Could they instantly detect in their dim underworld the sheen of an all-but-invisible gut cast, the shaft of the tiniest brown hook? Was it, as I am more inclined to believe, that we never tried them with the right bait at the right time? Or was it, since they lived immediately below the Kaponga dairy factory and fed on curd — a deplorable habit of Taranaki trout — that they were so bloated with this degenerate diet that they were never interested in anything else?

One answer is as good as another; but there they remained for years, those colossal, shadowy fish in their pool below the cliff, sombre, mysterious, and uncatchable.

And how they do haunt the mind, these fish that were never landed! In fishing it is as in any other art: mankind demands a conclusion to its dramas so that, at least within the limited area selected for the battle-ground, the universe may make sense. The hero and the heroine of the romantic novel must be married; the master criminal must be caught and, offstage, hanged; even Hamlet must kill the king at last: and the fish, if he is not to wander for ever in limbo, floating loose to the surface of dreams, must be brought to the net; and, I think, for we partake of the nature of the cat — not to say the lion — must be not merely grassed but brought home to be admired and devoured by the spouse and the children.

Even a sea fish, if it is large or lost in circumstances sufficiently bizarre, haunts the mind like an unfinished symphony, like 'Kubla Khan', with romantic unfulfilment.

I remember a gigantic coral-cod, twenty pounds, perhaps, or sixty for all I know, which my stepmother, Anne Stewart, from our tourist launch rocking in the swell off an outcrop of the Barrier Reef, heaved up inch by inch until, just as it was near enough to the surface for us to glimpse, it straightened the hook and, ghostly and gigantic, sank back to the depths again like the Old Man of the Sea.

I remember some fish unknown, a kingfish I always hoped, for I have never caught one of that noble tribe, which, superbly powerful and heavy, raced away with my line through the blue waters off Red Head at Russell until it reached that point I dreaded where (to my eternal shame) there was a tangle on the reel; and, straining prodigiously on the line for a moment while I waited for the inevitable to happen, snapped the strong cuttyhunk and away. I remember a Thing, lolling in the surf near Lake Cathie, on the New South Wales north coast, too big to reel in; and the hook, at last, pulling out.

I remember a stout snapper at Kawhia, not an outsize fish for those waters but a twelve or fourteen-pounder all the same, which, when it broke free and swirled back into the ocean, came near enough to taking me with it ...

Round the point from the Beacon at Kawhia was a tiny bay, sheltered by rocks from the tide, and there, filling in time till slackwater at the heads, I hooked my snapper. The deep water, where an occasional fish would wander past on its way to the harbour mouth, lay over a steep sandbank; and in the excitement I hardly noticed that my hand-line was cutting deeper and deeper into the sand as I pulled one way and the snapper the other. It cut in so deep at last that it stuck fast, just where the topmost of my three hooks was tied. The fish was anchored to the sandbank.

I could see it weaving in the green water, huge and pale. Instead of giving it some slack line, when I daresay it would have pulled itself clear, I heaved on the line till I broke it at the point where the hooks began. I said goodbye to that fish; but there he still was, incredibly, swirling about on the bottom hook, still anchored to the sandbank. I rushed waist-deep into the water, plunged my hand down to grab the line bristling with hooks, wrenched it free of the sand, and for a moment stood holding the fish on the line at the edge of the bank. He looked enormous; it was like holding a wild horse.

Then with a mighty flurry, wrenching at the line in my grasp, he straightened the hook out and disappeared into the green depths; and it was only then, or afterwards recapturing him on the edge of sleep, that the interesting possibility occurred to me that if he had heaved just a fraction harder, making the line slip in my hands where I grasped it between the top hooks, he might well have hooked me too; and both of us could have gone together from the sandbank.

How you would fight your way back to the shore, hooked to a twelve-pound snapper in deep water, I don't quite know; but like some of the big-game fishermen who have occasionally got themselves tangled with a swordfish at Russell – it would have been a great catch for the fish.

But if a snapper or a potential kingfish, hooked by blind chance in the obscure immensity of the ocean, can thus sometimes make himself memorable, how much more so is the solitary trout, whose capture, if you are not just insipidly dangling a worm, is the drama of one man against one fish, seen rising or feeding in his clear element and fished for with all the skill and finesse at your command – scared by a single rash movement, the stumble of a foot, the shadow of the rod, a crinkle of the cast or the tiniest splash of the fly upon the surface; capricious in his choice of food; needing infinite care, in the midst of all the excitement, to bring to the net with your light tackle; never safe even then, until he is lifted clear out of the water without fumbling or clumsiness, then unhooked with a firm grip in his gills well up the bank away from the rushes through which he can still wriggle back to the river ... always notable in his capture and doubly so if you lose him.

What is the most harrowing way in which you can lose a trout? One that caused me quite exceptional agony was a fish that simply rose once to look at the bait and then was seen no more. It was in the Tangatara one golden morning; and it was the hugest fish that ever I lost. It was so big that I don't even believe in it myself. And yet I saw it.

I dropped my worm that morning into the head of a small pool, just above the shallows where the cattle crossed; and, as I watched the bait go slowly turning in the current to where the pool deepened against the yellow clay bank, something so enormous rose up, floated up, loomed up leisurely from the bottom, with mouth agape, with brown fins gently wavering on the vast pale spotted body, that I could hardly believe it was a trout. Ten pounds, twelve pounds, I could not have denied that it was a twenty-pound fish – such things are possible. And as it rose, steadfast and unbelievable, there was no doubt whatsoever that it meant to take the bait.

Somehow I moved. I twitched the rod with the slightest involuntary movement; the worm twitched with it, just the slightest jerk away from the mighty jaws that were even then closing upon it; and down, slowly down, without flurry as befitted his dignity, but irrevocably down and down, fading out of sight again, sank that great fish for ever.

I cast again and again. I crept upstream and – reputedly an infallible device – simulated a flood by stirring mud into the current, down which I let my worm float as if newly washed in from the bank. I tried what flies I had; I tried the minnow. But never again that day or any other day could I rouse that titan from the depths.

But can you really claim to have lost a fish that you never even hooked? It is a point that adds to the agony.

Perhaps one has more right to be grieved by those fish that go further than this vision of the Tangarakau and, momentarily before you lose them, take the worm, the fly, or the spinner, and calmly spit it out again; or, hooked for one wild second, break free in the first leap: like that delectable rainbow I lost high up the Awakino, the day I caught a six-pounder.

I do not, I am relieved to say, claim this fish to have been a twenty-pounder. But whether he was two pounds lighter than my six-pounder or, as I swore at the time in the first agony of losing him, two pounds heavier, he was a notable fish; and the way he appeared and vanished makes him a peculiarly poignant memory: for, away up there among the ranges, wading down the silver waters through the bush, I floated a locust lightly down the current and, just where the stream divided at a big rock, bang went the locust, high in the air behind the rock as the reel screamed leapt the beautiful shining trout – and that, as he tossed the hook out, was the end of him … A four-, a six-, optimistically an eight-pounder, silver and rosy as the rainbow from which he took his name, who looked at me once over the top of a rock: so I remember him.

Again, there are the fish, whether large or merely respectable, that you lose in freakish circumstances: like the three-pound brown which Fin Maslin hooked with a bee from the bridge high above the huge green pools of the Maunganui and which he lost most lamentably, for no visible reason, after he had played it from the bridge and clambered down the cliff into the water to

lead it upstream to a landing-place; and like the three-pounder I myself lost in the Tangarakau when it raced downstream in a swirling, flood-yellowed rapid and dived through a barbed-wire fence.

And again, it is quite satisfactorily painful, up to a point, to lose someone else's fish for him through some folly in beaching or netting: like the four-pounder in Pound Creek, which lies so heavily upon my conscience, for it was David Campbell's fish and I knocked it off his line for him.

Pound Creek, running flat and shallow and tiny between its tussocks to join the Badja at Countegany, was supposed to be teeming with trout. Perhaps at times it was, if the fish came up it from the river to spawn; or perhaps that was only a legend born of the fact that one quite uncatchable six-pounder was always to be seen in the first pool you came to, while another big fish, about four pounds, also utterly immune from temptation, invariably leaped clean out of the water, half a dozen times during the day, from the gleaming round reedy pool which was the next you encountered.

The stream, so far as my experience goes, never lived up to its promises; but there was one pool, far downstream across the boggy flats and broken-down granite spurs, where I have taken, on occasion, a few pretty fish: and it was there, where the long pool lay under the high red bank, sandy at the run-in and wide among reeds and watercress at the tail, that David Campbell hooked his four-pounder. So far as I remember when, perched above the stream on a tall granite boulder, he brought it flapping to the backwater beside his rock and asked me to net it for him, I simply scooped it into the net and then tipped it out again. Well, I always did think that was 'my' pool.

At any rate, out went the trout; and, grieving for his loss, down with a mighty splash, waist-deep into the water, leapt the poet. I did myself once catch a trout in New Zealand by sitting on it – I fell over when trying to beach it with my foot – but exactly what Campbell hoped to accomplish by jumping on his four-pounder in deep water I have never been able to determine. However, it was a memorable sight, like a waterspout ... I take it as one of the noblest acts of forgiveness in human history that all Campbell remarked when at length, dripping like a grampus he emerged from the depths, was, 'Oh well, I was getting a bit sorry for that fish, anyhow.'

But far sadder than lost fish that belong to some-one else – most grievous and most beautiful of all except for the occasional glimpses of a dream-fish like the monster in the Tangarakau – are the really big fish you lose after you have fought them long enough to be reasonably hopeful of landing them.

I do not know which of the two fish – David Campbell's in the long pool where Micalong Creek meets the Goodradigbee at Wee Jasper, or my own in the vast glittering circle of Fred's in the Badja – was really the bigger (mine, I trust): but Lord, what fish they were!

Never shall I forget David Campbell, purple with cold, elated with a defeat that was infinitely more worthwhile than most victories, wading back to the bank and the rum after (with brief intervals for food and sleep) two whole days in the icy waters of that moun-tain stream pursuing a single trout. It was – all fair-minded men must admit – at least an eight-pounder. And fish were scarce that time at Wee Jasper. He spotted it beside a rock, far out in waist-deep water,

and for those two whole days he fished for it. He tried
it with every fly in his box — as I, lower down the
stream, was trying every fly I had on a modest three-
pounder, until at last, late on the second day, it took a
March Brown. And so, too, at last, did Campbell's big
one rise to a fly, and leapt, and flashed in the afternoon
sun, and raced up the pool and circled and leapt and
raced again; and then, for no good reason and when its
capture seemed fairly sure, broke free and was gone.

I had not fished for my own immortal giant in Fred's for
two solid consecutive days; but I had known him longer
than that, and so lamented him all the more.

I knew his habits. I had watched him feeding along
the fringe of waterlilies by the shore, or at the top of the
pool where the stream rippled out from the overhanging tea-tree and suddenly widened into a waterhole
shining and enormous. I had fished for him before —
with never the remotest sign of interest from him — following him and trying to anticipate his rises as he
cruised along the lily-bank. I suspected that he lived
on water-beetles. I knew he was a big fellow — though

who could have dreamed, who could have dared to
dream he was as big as all that?

I fished for him that last bright morning, seeing no
rise but knowing where he ought to be. I crept up to
the edge of the backwater and dropped my Tup's Indispensable over the lilies; and with one almighty swirl he
took it – and there he was racing across the pool, that
magnificent seven-pound rainbow, only a few ounces
lighter than David Campbell's if that; leaping, surely an
eight-pounder if not more – six times in all he leapt,
with my heart in my mouth each time for fear I should
lose him; rushing away out over the perilous submerged
rocks, across to the far bank where the dangerous wattles dipped their branches into the water, back to the
centre of the pool with such a weight and drag on the
line that I was certain the cast would never stand it; leaping again with his gigantic body silver over the blue
water, racing off once more until there was barely ten
feet of line left on the reel – and I had no backing.

Slowly he began to come in, inch by inch, ounce
by ounce – I really do think he may have been up to ten
pounds, but hardly more. I was afraid of the snags near
the edge – nasty-looking submerged logs; I was afraid of
the waterlilies; I wondered how ever I could fit him into
the net.

But I needn't have worried about any of those
things; for when he was so close that I could see him
plainly, swimming in about six feet of water, a colossal
shadow, dark-backed and silver-flanked, suddenly the
line went slack.

And that was my fatal mistake. I thought he was
off, and he wasn't. He had taken a sharp little run
towards me, incredibly swift and sudden, and when I
swung back the rod to pull the fly out of the water he

was still on. But one wag of his head, with the grip of the hook loosened by that momentary slackening, and he was gone indeed. I sat on the bank and I shook.

If only I had not let the line go slack — if only I had allowed for his great power and speed even when he was coming to the net ... But the sun shone on the white sally-gums and the wide blue pool; and was I so sorry after all that he had got away? He was the most wonderful fish I have ever lost; and roughly, I should say, a twelve-pounder.

2

THE SEVEN RIVERS

BETWEEN Eltham, where we lived in New Zealand, and Opunake twenty-four miles away on the coast, seven clear rivers tumbled from the mountain to the sea.

Their names were a tangle of Maori polysyllables, wild as the ferns and blackberries that clung to their yellow clay banks, sweet as the water that bubbled over their stones: the Waingongoro, the Mangatoki, the Kapuni, the Kaupokonui, the Tangatara, Mangahume, and Waiau.

They were all trout streams and it would have been hard indeed to have lived in that country and not to become a fisherman; though a few lost souls, such as my father and his brother Geordie (when he was over staying with us from Australia) contented themselves with cricket in Taumata Park ... and, as these great men did one memorable day, made 116 runs between them. Fifty-six not out was my father's score; and Geordie made sixty. My uncle further distinguished himself by hitting a historic 'six' clean out of the cricket-ground, high over the road and into the yard of the dairy factory. No mightier stroke was ever struck in Eltham.

But those of us who knew better, fished: Fred Vincent the jeweller, my uncle Maurice FitzGerald the County Engineer, Caleb Maslin the carrier, Sam Pepperill the joiner and undertaker, Bert Thomas from the garage, George Batchelor who worked for Peebles the grocer, Bert Williams the Ranger who had the inestimable advantage of being able to take his rod with him when he went to inspect the farms for blackberry and ragwort, Pip Connell whose father was an artist and photographer and did some excellent pastels of the mountain; a fine, democratic fraternity among whom, and all the rest who fished, I never knew a scoundrel except for one dreadful youth whom, the day before the season opened, while I was exploring the Waingongoro to spot where a fish might lie, I caught sneaking with his rod over the very water I intended to fish next morning.

If ever there was a poacher who aroused my indignation it was that awful boy; and the worst of it was that he was too well-connected in Eltham, where everybody knew everybody, for anything to be done about him. The other poachers, farmhands who were rumoured to prowl the Waingongoro by night with torch and three-pronged spear and who were sometimes stalked over the dark countryside by Constable Townsend, seemed too far-off, too heroic and romantic for complaint. If they speared any fish on those wild expeditions they deserved them.

Sometimes I fished the seven rivers with Bert Williams, for I was then working for the Eltham *Argus* and could get away early in the afternoon, as soon as we had gone to press, to join him while he inspected the farms for weeds or the rivers for trout; but mostly I fished them with Fin Maslin, the carrier's son, a short, stocky, humorous youth as he was then, black-haired and black-eyed, in whose company, as the world first burst upon us like a great rushing river full of girls, trout, hares, wild pigs and bottles of Speight's beer, I explored, always with amusement and delight, quite a variety of waters …

Those were the heroic days when to be up before dawn, leaping out of bed to the clangour of the alarm-clock in my cherished private bedroom where the rock-wallaby-skin rug from Kawau Island, the rabbit-skins from the Waikato and the goat-skin from Moeroa bore witness to other great expeditions, seemed the most natural thing in the world. Of course you must be on the water before sunrise! – it was then that the trout took the worm most freely: and the worm, I confess with all proper shame, was our favourite bait in those days.

Up in the dark house where the family still slept; cooking that noble breakfast of tea and bacon and eggs or bacon and tomatoes; out to the garage where the little red two-seater Austin sports-car (appropriated from my father the day he bought it 'for economy') lay waiting in faithful slumber; backing past the coalshed and that awkward turn round the drainpipe; down the long drive, past the silver-birch at the gate, and along the dark silent streets to Fin Maslin's, where, after he had finished his own breakfast, we dug up the little red worms in his fowlyard by torchlight while the indignant turkey-cocks cried gobble-obble-obble, gobble-obble-obble … and so we were away, through sleeping Eltham and over Burke's Hill to the seven rivers.

We had, of course, passed the Waingongoro, for the lure of distant waters was upon us, and the Waingongoro was our home stream, crossed by a bridge just out of the town and running at that point not very salubriously between the bacon factory and a rubbish dump – the things that people do to rivers! So there in its temporary disrepute we left it, curling in its willows at the foot of the hill; and, through the steel-grey glimmer of a world neither in night nor daylight, with the boxthorn hedges crowding close upon the road and the mountain vast and ghostly on the skyline, on and on we drove to the Mangatoki, the Kapuni, the Kaupokonui, the Tangatara, the Mangahume or the far and broad Waiau.

How the blackbirds and the thrushes, English birds long become native to Taranaki, sang on those clear cold mornings! – perched on the topmost twigs of the hedges or, as once I saw them, six or eight of them together, singing in chorus or competition with each other from neighbouring stumps and fenceposts.

And how incredibly cold must those rivers have been, running their swift courses from Mount Egmont to the sea, as, racing to put our rods together and be first in the stream, we plunged straight into the water without waders, nothing but our boots and socks between our feet and its icy tongue!

Such is the hardihood of youth, or such the human capacity for forgetting discomfort and remembering only delight, that I do not recall ever feeling very cold in the water, though it steamed with frost-smoke around us; but I do remember how gloriously the daybreak came when the first rays of light turned the huge snowy shoulder of the mountain a rosy pink and, one morning in particular, on the Tangatara, swept in shaft and ripple of gold over a green hillside and the pale sand where birds, even earlier to the water than ourselves, had left their three-pronged footsteps. That must have been a great morning's fishing, too, for when the sun came over the hill, I was frantically turning over dried cowpats in a search for worms – we had already run short of bait.

How good it was, nevertheless, after that freezing fishing, to fish our way back to the car at about eight or nine o'clock – we would fish the downstream waters first, then later work our way up towards the mountain – and drink hot coffee from the thermos. My mother used to make for us the most superb bacon-and-egg pies and we ate great chunks of them then for a second breakfast.

Sometimes, on the fierce mornings from October to December – for Taranaki's summer is a precarious thing; never really settled until January and liable to burst in storms and floods in February – the dawn was a wilder phenomenon, glaring red and angry at us over Rawhitiroa and Mangamingi as we glanced back from the top of Burke's Hill. Then, by the time of the second breakfast, or long before it, we had rain and hail and wind upon us; and, sometimes in oilskin overcoats but usually without, we fished on regardless till the rivers grew hopelessly swollen and muddy. Then we would drive back to Eltham and play at fishing in the cleaner little pools of the Town Creek.

One day before the rain began – when Caleb Maslin, Fin, and my brother Neil and I had gone north of Eltham, away from the seven rivers to a big stream named the Waitara – my brother caught his first trout: a five-pounder, no less, on the totally inadequate tackle of a boy's rod and reel. The storm began to pelt as he wrestled with it, floodwater poured down the river, and by the time he had landed that superb and solitary trout, all fishing in the Waitara was finished: a most notable capture it was, out of the jaws of the flood. We drove to a river that had escaped most of the downpour and I landed a most interesting little trout, which, foul-hooked in the side, fought like another five-pounder. Fat enough to seem reasonably impressive on the bank (it was about two pounds) it seemed to melt on the way home. A very pale, silvery trout, though a brownie, its lie was near a dairy factory and it must have been full of curd.

It was on another day of rain, though made mysterious because the storm was falling high up on Egmont and I was in sunshine, that, while playing a trout, I watched the Waingongoro swell up and swirl with sticks and leaves and floodwater all in a flash as if a tidal wave were sweeping down it: and broke my rod-tip in my haste to land my fish and get out of it, and had to walk miles beside the wild torrent before I found a bridge to cross back to the car.

The wildest and wettest day of all was on the Waiau. It rained, it blew, the mountain was lost in blackness; and then, while we still clung to the last of the fishing, such a fury of enormous hailstones pelted down on us that we had to run for our lives from them, clutching our oilskins over our heads as we rushed over the wide bare paddocks looking in vain for shelter; and found in the end the most valuable and inexplicable hole in a clay bank, just big enough for both of us to put our heads in; and, like a pair of half-drowned ostriches, but stretched full length on the ground, lay with our heads in the hole and roared with laughter and delight while the icy fusillade pelted down on our backs.

But even in Taranaki it did not always rain.

No day since the world began ever sparkled more freshly with sunshine than that lovely afternoon when Bert Williams and I pushed our way up the Kapuni further than I had been up any of the streams, until we were into the gorges of the mountain itself; in the secrecy of rock and fern where, melting from the snowfields, all the rivers first began to be rivers ... 'A savage place, as holy and enchanted/As e'er beneath a waning moon was haunted' ... only it wasn't any woman wailing for her demon lover who haunted it that afternoon but the bright sunshine, bathing naked like a naiad.

It was a wonder how sun or naiad or fisherman or the water itself ever got into that gorge. The bush had closed in upon the Kapuni, rimu, tree-fern and stiff-leafed totara. The colossal rock-mass of the mountain, surging a mile into the sky, had shut it into a cleft so steep and narrow that we could not skirt the pools but must wade straight through them, waist-deep in ice that had only just changed into water. Bracken, blackberry, and gorse, the weeds and scrub that lined the banks in the open country, had changed to ferns and moss; and, startling among the ferns, lay the mountain's first footprints of snow. Yet, golden through the green bush, the light sifted down; the pools, where a shaft struck them, sparkled like crystal; and there, when we peered over the top of a huge grey boulder into a pool where a waterfall made further fishing impossible, swam in solitary, unexpected splendour, a three-pound brown. Williams stalked him over the edge of the boulder; hooked him; and, I am glad enough to say, though he would have been a memorable prize, lost him.

Sunlight gladdened the land, too, on that other great day of exploration when Fin Maslin and I pursued

the Mangahume up into the mountain gorges, through
that most curious country where the plains were studded with hummocks as big as haystacks, as if, under the
grass, the earth was slowly boiling. I never knew
whether they were great blobs of lava hurled out of
Egmont in prehistoric eruptions or whether they were
little, subsidiary volcanoes that in some inconceivable
convulsion had heaved themselves up from the earth.

Through all that savage country we fished our way
up into the forest glades once more; and, deep in the
wilderness, we came upon a huge bearded sawmiller
whom we had last known, in all the trim respectability
of his profession, as a solicitor in Eltham. He looked as
clean and brawny as any tree or rock and made
sawmilling seem a much finer life than that of the dank,
musty legal offices where my father still spent his days
(when he couldn't escape to cricket or the golf-links)
and from which, by plunging into journalism for the
Argus, I had so narrowly escaped myself ...

It would be hard to say which of those seven rivers,
in sun or in rain, gave us the most joy. They were all
essentially the same kind of river; rapid and pool and
rapid; clear water, rounded pebbles, little beaches of sand
and shingle, a music of bubbles and boulders; and they
all had plenty of trout. And, threading that general
resemblance, each had its cherished particularities ... the
Waingongoro so many of them, where it was not cor-
rupted by the bacon factory and the rubbish dump,
that it deserves a chapter to itself. Yet even the rubbish
dump provided, in our extreme youth, one day of rap-
turous excitement when, after Wilkinson's hardware
store burnt down, and the debris was cast on the river
bank, we picked up such treasures as fireblackened
tin-openers, padlocks that wouldn't open, and even

pocket-knives with the bone handles burnt off. And once, but once only, we did fish the waters below the bacon factory; where there were many fish, very many fish, but very hard to catch. Which may have been because the river there was exceptionally clear and shallow; or may have been because murky things came floating down it, which the trout ate.

The Mangatoki was too narrow, deep-gorged and overhung with blackberries for us to bother with from the road; but, when I crossed the paddocks to it higher up with the ranger, we had one memorable day when (arguing most incongruously at intervals about Mrs Simpson and the Duke of Windsor; whom I supported and the ranger did not) I caught a couple of unexpected two-pounders and then could catch no more though every fish in the river began to rise. They were coming up head and tail, 'nymphing', scorning worms for the hatching larvae of the stoneflies.

The Kaupokonui was where we fished so often in vain for the enormous trout under the road-bridge, fattened on curd from the dairy factory and never to be persuaded to look at any other bait. The rest of the stream, being reserved for fly-fishing, terrified us. But one evening when I did fish it, after I had advanced to the fly, I saw as exciting an evening rise – and as maddening; for I couldn't find what they were taking – as ever I saw anywhere: trout rising by the dozen, quietly ringing the surface or leaping into the sunset, until the whole river seemed alive with them. It was in the Kaupokonui, I think, that Maurice FitzGerald and Fred Vincent, really expert anglers, caught forty-six trout one Sunday … and told all their rival anglers in Eltham that it was in the Kapuni. And the next weekend, while everybody flogged the Kapuni, they went back to the

Kaupokonui and caught another twenty or thirty good fish.

The Kapuni, upstream, gave us the mountain gorges; but downstream, too, in the more docile dairying country, it also had its moments; and one sunny afternoon, in a little pool not far down from the bridge, I came upon one of those curious 'pockets' of trout that sometimes so signally reward the angler's patience, and caught five of them one after another, smallish fish, but takeable. What they were doing there, why they were congregated, I know not. But five trout out of one pool, when three or four out of a whole river was normally a fair day's bag for Taranaki, was good fishing.

The Tangatara we fished more often than any of the other rivers. There were big fish there, plenty of three and four-pounders, and it was a fine wide but manageable river running through rich green dairy farms where the axe and the plough had still left scrub and willows along the banks. That was where the most enormous trout I ever saw rose up and looked at my worm, turned away, and sank for ever out of sight; and where, short and dark in his black-and-white striped New Plymouth Boys' High School blazer, Fin Maslin plunged waist-deep into the rapid to try to disentangle my three-pounder from the barbed-wire fence into which it had fought, and lifted it up for one glorious moment in his net, then somehow dropped it out again.

The most furious and majestic of all the Jersey bulls that so much enlivened our days came down to the Tangarakau to talk to us. And there, one day when Caleb and Fin and I basked in the sun on the bank, we met a most diverting poacher who strode along the riverside, tall and lean and sly, and told us he had taken his five nice trout 'on the Coachman'. He did have a fly at the

end of his cast; but, protruding guiltily from his pocket, was a lump of illegal, of scandalous, of altogether unmentionable curd … I tried it myself once but did no good with it.

We caught big fish in the Waiau, too, as well as hailstorms, travelling far up its winding course towards the mountain and, on the day I remember best, swinging the 'minnow' (a little spotted artificial fish, finned with hooks that caught in your trousers, your coat, your net, and all the bushes) over its long pools.

I used to feel strangely ill-at-ease, as if I was trespassing, fishing the Waiau, for it ran very close to Opunake and was sacred to my most distant childhood when we took a beach cottage there and, on days of great adventure, clambered and ran round the rocks to the Waiau's mouth. I saw a trout fisherman near the mouth, in those far-off days, catch two fat spotted 'butterfish' – so, whatever they were, he called them – using green willow leaves for bait: a most exotic performance as he dropped the leaves to them where they lay clearly visible under the cliff and hauled them unresisting across the shallows.

The Waingongoro, the Mangatoki, the Kapuni, the Kaupokonui, the Tangatara, the Waiau – of all the seven rivers along that road between the mountain and the sea I think I loved best the tiny Mangahume. It was so clear, so gentle a little stream, hardly more than eight feet wide between its grassy banks, shortest of all in its journey from the snow to the beach at Pihama, so manageable to explore and to fish, and so very, very plentiful with trout.

They were, it is true, exceedingly small fish, nearly all about a pound, with an occasional two-pounder for a rare prize in the bigger pools downstream. And they were, it is also true, exceedingly hungry fish – they bit all the time, and at anything. It seemed rather like cheating to catch them.

But then, fishing is a gentle art; and when we had proved our hardihood sufficiently in the gorges of the Kapuni or the more strenuous waters of the Tangatara and the Waiau it was pleasant indeed to fish this happy little stream where the sun, so far as I remember, always shone, where the bulls were harmless as heifers, where the water was always warm – and you never needed to wade more than knee-deep anyhow – and where the fish were so very, very plentiful. For it is surely pleasant occasionally, when fishing, to catch fish; and in the Mangahume there must have been a fish for every pebble. In the lamplight from the bridge at dusk, where sometimes we fished for them with moths, they swarmed like a shoal of herring; and that best of all days, when I drove out alone from Eltham after hastening the *Argus* to bed at three in the afternoon, I came home in the evening with ten trout – ten, no less – bulging in my canvas fishing-bag. They were small, to be sure; and taken on the wicked minnow; but nevertheless, ten trout …

3

A POOL IN THE WAINGONGORO

THE VERY NAME of the Waingongoro is enough, as Rilke says somewhere of some other river, to fill all my consciousness with sparkling water … though I suppose you would need to have been born in Eltham to be able to pronounce it – Wy-nong-oro, with the accent on the second syllable.

It means 'Snoring Water' and is supposed to have been so named because at the mouth, near Hawera, twelve miles away from my own territory, Turi, the ancient Maori navigator, camped a night there with his canoe the *Tainui* and, semi-mythological hero though he was, snored. But it is not its history that endears the name to me; it is the sound; it is a bubbling, shingly, boulder-rumbling, altogether rivery sort of word, and even when we shortened it in boyhood to the useful monosyllable of 'the Wong' it still had a pleasant, deep, plonking sound, like a stone dropped in a pool … The Wong!

And the Wong, the long-rippling Waingongoro, was indeed a bubbling, shingly, boulder-rumbling, plonking, altogether rivery sort of river. It was shaded with willows. It was thronged with watercress and clean green sharp-smelling mint. It was a small stream, clear, steadily running, perpetually winding round low cliffs or tall clay banks into pools and shallow rapids, and pool and rapid again round the next bend, all the way down through the green paddocks from Mount Egmont to the sea. The willows spread their fibrous red roots into the runnels; ferns and the dark-green glossy leaves of the tutu-scrub glimmered in the water-lights on the cliffs; sand and shingle lay golden in the pools and grey on the beaches. It tasted of snow, earth and sunlight. I wish now, for the satisfaction of knowing every inch of it, that I had tracked it to its source somewhere high up on that gigantic pyramid of forest and stone and snow that filled the western sky; or at least that I had fished it as close to the mountain as I fished the Kapuni and the Mangahume; but if I never knew precisely in what enchanted wellspring it first bubbled through the stones below the hanging ice, in what white cascade it fell headlong through the bush to the plain of Taranaki, nor in what tiny pools and rapids among the gorges where snow still lay upon the moss it first began to be fishable, I knew that sort of country well enough; and once it fairly became a river, wandering out near Stratford to turn south for Eltham and the coastline near Hawera, I did indeed know every pool of it, almost every willow and every pebble: the deep water, silent under willows, south of the town where George Batchelor and Fin Maslin used to catch the six-pounders; the shallows upstream near Stratford, down the bank of which I sometimes walked all the way home to Eltham when I was a reporter on the Stratford *Evening Post*; and, above all, that exquisite midway water, neither too large nor too small, from Chiselhurst to Finnerty Road, where our picnic pool was.

That stretch would be, I suppose, about three miles
of the winding river. Something memorable must have
happened along every yard of it ... as when, on the
sunlit pebbles, when we were eeling, Ian Wylds and I ate
the bait; something that still strikes me as irresistibly
comic, though all we did was to cook and devour the
piece of scrapmeat we had got from Alf Ware the
butcher.

For more serious eeling we would go to the Black
Creek, where, in useful proximity to the septic tank, the
dark, slimy creatures flourished in profusion. But these
eels from the Black Creek we despised as fodder. We
called them yellowbellies and took them home only to
be cooked for the fowls: and an indescribably foul smell
they made, too, boiling in the big iron pot on the
kitchen stove.

For eels to eat ourselves, we favoured the silverbel-
lies from the clean Waingongoro, and on that day Ian
and I must have intended to cook and eat them on the
spot, for we took no lunch with us; and, while the meat
on our hooks bled white in the water, we grew hungrier
and hungrier; and looked avidly upon the bait, and
smelt it − and it smelt very richly − and debated it
and, in such an ecstasy of nausea and Rabelaisian delight
as only small boys can know, ate it. Dimly I see us still,
two brown, small boys rolling on the stones with roars
of disgust and joy while the smoke from our fire of
willow-twigs drifted across the river in the sunlight.

A mile or so downstream from the picnic pool, on
a grassy and willowy flat where a low ridge sloped down
to meet dark water swirling against a cliff, we camped
one time for a summer holidays, my sister Jean and I and
the Carter girl and boy, Wray and Desmond ... of which
glorious adventure I can remember only how startled

we were one night when our parents drove down to see how we were getting on and interrupted our comparatively innocent but enthusiastic good-night embraces with the girls – a ritual which had not been provided for in the parental programme; and how white, like naiads or like fish, the girls looked when wickedly one afternoon we peered through the tutu-scrub at them while they were bathing naked; and how tremendously Jean and I quarrelled one day, over Lord knows what, when either she attacked me or I attacked her with the toasting-fork and I ran home to Eltham and had to be ignominiously driven back to the camp by my mother.

In that same pool of the holiday camp, Fred Vincent gave me my first lesson in trout fishing. It should have been the supreme occasion of my life, but, alas, I remember it as an anticlimax.

A great and most ardent fisherman was Fred Vincent, and a most kindly soul, too, with grins of encouragement covering his round, weather-beaten face as he taught a small boy how to assemble his rod and tie his cast, how to put on his lead-shot to take the bait to the bottom, how to find a 'creeper' under a stone and, disregarding its justly indignant pincers, impale it on the hook; how to cast out gently where the current ran deep there against the edge of the cliff and where – 'By jove, now! Look at that now, Alec!' (to my father) – a fine trout was rising just at that moment.

It was too much for Fred. He grabbed my rod and fished for it himself. And, although a rising trout had no business to be taking a creeper, got a tug from it, too. Having since taught a novice or two myself, I can now understand how overwhelming was the temptation to which he submitted; and I take this belated opportunity

– years ago he fell over a cliff into the sea, snapper-fishing at Urenui, and died of pneumonia – of forgiving him …

Then there was the day when, wandering through the last patch of native bush left at Chiselhurst for shelter for the cattle or the few old ewes that were sometimes imported to these dairying pastures to have their last lambs, I heard among the ferns, the supplejack vines, the mossy stumps, and the ancient, storm-beaten white pines the blackbirds making that high-pitched, furious commotion which is their warning signal of a cat or a weasel in the neighbourhood – 'jennetting', Nigel Connell the painter-photographer used to call it; 'a jennetting blackbird' – and suddenly, when I was investigating, a monstrous great yellow hare sprang from her form on a cushion of moss and raced to safety down the trail the cattle had trodden through the undergrowth. And in that same patch of bush one howling day of July – for I used to prowl the river winter and summer alike – I saw a new-born lamb that made itself into a poem for me; so glistening white like the frosts it would still have to endure before the buds on the bare willows turned into the first green leaflets; so frail against the darkness of that stormy Taranaki dusk.

Somewhere along that sparkling stretch of the river was the cliff where the wild duck had the nest to which she returned season after season, where her eggs clustered like pebbles of jade in their hollow of grass and down from the mother's breast. Once on a misty grey dawn when I was fishing below that cliff the most curious shapes, like water-rats, raced past my legs in the water: the wild duck and her ducklings swimming underwater to evade me.

And just round the bend from the wild duck's nest

was the run where my winter explorations paid a most rare and excellent dividend.

It was a place where the stream ran fast and a fairly big rock divided it into two. Not more than four or five feet deep at most, a ragged bit of water unfishable under the willows, it was a place that normally you would just have passed by. But, clambering round the bare trunk of a willow one sunny winter's afternoon, I discovered exactly where the trout lurked in that awkward spot: in the lee of the rock, safe from the currents on either side and, with both rock and willow to protect them, pretty well safe from a fisherman. Like fish in a crystalline spring, a nest of whirlpools and bubbles isolated from the flowing waters, I could see them there nuzzling the golden sand; the dark-brown backs, the flash of a tawny speckled side as they turned, three or four most noble trout – so far as trout in that reach of the Waingongoro went, which was never above three pounds at the outside, and mostly about a pound and a half.

The only way to fish for them, if it were possible at all, would be to scramble through the willow-branches as I did then, hang out over the stream at the great risk of scaring them, and just drop the worm or the creeper on top of them, as if you were fishing for mere simpletons of fish, like eels or cockabullies in a rock-pool. And come the spring, and the first faint green of the breaking buds on the bare twigs of the willows that hung like harp-strings over that swift-running water, I did thus insinuate myself through the branches, and poke my rod out before me, and drop a creeper weighted with lead-shot, down into that bubbling whirlpool; and instantly got a strike and, playing my fish with I know not what wild excitement around the rock and in the current while I balanced as best I could on branches that dipped into the water, landed a fine two-pounder. Such are the rewards of constancy.

But now when I think back on those delectable miles of the Waingongoro from Egmont to the sea, from Ngaere down to Chiselhurst, it all seems to coalesce, to crystallize, in that one little central pool where we had our family picnics.

It was an insignificant pool, one among a thousand; but like the dusty cavern under the veranda at home where you could crawl to search for pennies dropped through the cracks between the planks, like the fort we made of an old tin washtub among the loganberries at the far end of the fowlrun, like some of the little pools of the Town Creek, it was one of those places, as vital and intimate as the solar-plexus, where the whole existence of boyhood finds its centre.

It was there, on some infinitely remote day of my boyhood, that I discovered I could swim; 'walking' along the pebbles on my hands and suddenly finding that, if you lifted your hands for a second or two and dog-paddled, there was no real need to sink to the bottom. It was there that, having mastered the dog-paddle, I learned how thrilling it was to wade into the current at the head and race down with it into the pool, partaking of its swiftness as if you were part of the water yourself.

It was there that – though for more serious blackberrying we would go to Cheal Road, where the bushes grew man-high over the tree-stumps of the Ngaere swamp – many a day we filled the fire-blackened picnic billy with those glistening fruits, eating as we picked and staining purple our hands and our mouths. It was there that one notable day I dragged a nettle across the back of my father's hand as he lay dozing under the willows

… I take it as a remarkable example of his courtesy that, though he jumped to his feet with a roar, he took no further action, while I stood poised for flight over the paddocks, but merely apologized for the roar, saying mysteriously that he thought it was the kind of nettle that stung. It was.

It was there that, on I don't know how many glorious Saturdays and Sundays (a multitude of them) we boiled the billy with a stick floating in it 'to draw the smoke', and ate such marvellous foods as tomatoes stuffed with salmon, and savoury-eggs each in its leaf of lettuce … and sunbaked on the warm sand, and swam and fished for eels, and climbed the trees for birds' nests and looked under stones for the odd creatures that lived there; and lived like water-creatures ourselves, the two active boys, the three graceful girls, and our parents at ease in the green shade of the willows.

Under the big stone that jutted into the pool from the far bank, to whose grey side we so often clung when we desperately dog-paddled the full five yards of the river and from whose sunny top we so often dived our first splashing 'belly-busters', lived, as afterwards we found out to our consternation, the father of all the eels, a monstrous great slimy creature five feet long, twenty-two pounds in weight, sixteen inches round the girth – how these proud statistics do glitter in the memory! – which, though not in the tranquillity of a family picnic, was to provide me with the most hilarious adventure, and the most perilous, which the Waingongoro ever offered.

There still exists in the family albums a photograph of Ian Wylds and myself, its captors or at any rate its successful claimants, holding up this gigantic brute outside my bedroom window when we had got it home, Ian

with his bandy legs, batlike ears and grin of tough triumph, and myself, always diminutive, precisely the
height of the eel; and I remember, as an outstanding
example of the vitality of its tribe, that, when we put it
under the hose-tap at the back of the washhouse for
some mysterious purpose – probably to revive it and
preserve it as a pet – the beast, which had been gaffed
and dragged to shore, severely damaged with stones,
hauled across the countryside, hidden under a bed and
at last triumphantly bicycled home in a sugar-bag, came
dramatically to life again and began to weave its way in
the stream of the tap-water slowly towards the shrub-
bery in the back garden. It was eventually boiled for the
fowls, and kept them happy for days.

I have told the story of its capture, pretty well as it
happened, in a short story, so cannot legitimately do
more than summarize it here: how, eeling ourselves, we
found the boy Ewans, from the neighbouring farmhouse, stocky and tow-haired, squatting like some kind
of water-haunting gnome on the big stone over the
swimming pool; how – he spoke in his father's Cornish
accent – he showed us the 'girt big yule' he was fishing
for; how we all three dangled our worms before its huge
head, clearly visible in the still water under the rock,
without its taking the slightest interest; how a kindly
trout fisherman came along in his rubber gumboots,
tried to gaff the eel and disturbed it; how we found it
again for him downstream a bit, just before the rapid
began, and he gaffed it successfully this time and
dragged it ashore for us; how, when we decided to go
home with our prize, after duly admiring its magnificent
proportions, that kindly trout fisherman said sharply,
'You leave that eel alone!' and we realized he meant to
steal it from us …

And then how, when his back was turned, we somehow snatched it up and raced across the river with it and yelled defiance and insult from the clifftop at that lean, dark, nasty-moustached man and, when he came pounding and splashing after us across the river with his ugly great gaff outstretched, fled in terror to Ewans's house and hid quaking under the bed with the bed-fluff and the porcelain chamberpot while Mrs Ewans rocked with uncontrollable Rabelaisian mirth – 'Under the bed with the po!' – and Mr Ewans, that stolid man from Cornwall whose thick lip was stained yellow with his pipe, poured scorn upon our adversary for chasing after 'a dirty great yule that only a Maori would eat'.

It was only many years afterwards that I realized that there was perhaps some substance in the fisherman's claim that it was not so much the looting of the eel as the cheek we gave him from the clifftop that had sent him so furiously chasing us, even to the door of the farmhouse; and if, making this allowance, I still think the hound was after our eel – what a rage he must have been in! – it does strike me as a weakness in our case that it was not our eel at all, if priority in discovery was to count, but belonged to Master Ewans. Very likely, as small-boy gangsters from the town, we had cowed that rustic youth out of his rightful claim to it and were in our own way quite as unscrupulous as the fisherman. Anyhow, we got that eel.

But these were indeed desperate doings. Never was the seclusion of the picnic pool, shadowy and sparkling between the cliff and the willows, shattered with such violence before or since. Even Ewans's bull, who sometimes entertained us with his uproar from his paddock below the ford, knew better than to leap the fence and burst into that sacred retreat. No other picnickers ever came there, it was ours, inviolably. And it is thoroughly in keeping with the spirit of that happy place that the supreme experience I enjoyed there should be an event from our own family life: a small thing, nothing, everything. It was no more than the sight of my uncle Maurice FitzGerald, one sunny afternoon when we were all picnicking there, coming round the bend from upstream in his canvas waders, with his rod in his hand and his canvas bag on his back — tall, straight-backed, Roman-nosed, with a clipped, reddish moustache; the very picture of a fisherman — and, in the bag, when he displayed his catch to us, two beautiful speckled brown trout, wrapped in fragrant green mint.

I do not recollect that in all the years after that flash of inspiration, when I must instantly and with my whole being have decided that trout-fishing was the joy of life, I ever caught anything very impressive in the Wong. I did catch the trout whose lair I discovered in winter; and a small fish after dusk one evening which made an occasion of singular triumph because my father, a sea-fisherman but not interested in trout, had made one of his rare excursions to the river to see me catch it; and a splendid three-pounder on the Coachman when it was rising in the late afternoon in the rapid where Maslins had their stone-crusher; what else I know not.

But I fished that stretch from Ngaere to Chiselhurst far more often than any other water in Taranaki — almost every evening of the season when I was working for the Eltham *Argus* — not for its trout but for its magic. To this day I have only to crush a sprig of mint in my hand and the whole Waingongoro comes bubbling and sparkling into my mind and, the image of the art of fishing, my uncle Maurice, with two speckled trout in his bag, wades round the bend to the picnic pool.

4

THE TOWN CREEK

THE LOVE of rivers which leads to the love of fishing must, like the rivers themselves, somewhere in
time and place have its small far source; and for me,
before I got to know the Waingongoro, it was the Town
Creek. If the Town Creek was not very far, at least not
far from Eltham, it was certainly small enough; so
modest that, for yards at a time, it was practically invisible as it flowed under its encroaching masses of
pale-green watercress; and the art of fishing it, when I
progressed so far, was to drop your fly in a runnel no
more than a foot in width, yet to do that from a distance
where you could not be seen, and then, somehow, pull
your fish from under the weed and land him over the
top of it.

The Town Creek, so far as I ever knew, was too
humble to have any other name.

Sometimes I used to believe, never having properly
tramped its course downstream, that south of the town
it became that dark and sluggish rivulet called the Black
Creek, or Taipo Creek, meaning the Devil's; but that,

though a famous place for eels, where my father, trying
out a new cuttyhunk line, thin and immensely strong,
once pulled out an eely colossus (which turned into a
slimy black log when it broke the surface), was an
unpleasant piece of water. I would not be surprised if
Taipo Creek had originally been dug as a ditch to drain
the low-lying farms, as other great ditches, also tenanted
by eels which the farmers sometimes speared with
pitchforks, had been dug across the Ngaere Swamp by
gangs of alarming immigrants, Austrians or Dalmatians.

It was not in the Town Creek's nature to connect
itself with a drain; for, though it ran between grassy
banks without the shingly rapids and sandy beaches of
the other Taranaki rivers, it was a pure and merry water.

More likely, instead of becoming Taipo Creek, it
was the streamlet that joined the Waingongoro a few
miles down from Eltham where Neale Road ended in
the swing-bridge − a perilous contraption which in
childhood we delighted to set swinging above the current − and where George Batchelor, that wonderful
fisherman, cast fly or minnow with rare skill far under
the green arches of the willows.

Where you met the Town Creek in town it was
engaged in crossing Bridge Street, prudently avoiding
the traffic under a stone causeway. There were old
wooden railings, grey with wisdom and warm with sunlight, on which you could lean and ponder.

Tom Stanners, a tall, straight-backed pioneer whom
I interviewed for the Eltham *Argus* when they pulled
down a weather-beaten smithy that stood − or, rather,
staggered − near by, told me that bullock wagons
splashed across a ford there on their way to town in the
early days ... but it is astonishing how little any of us
ever knew or cared about how there came to be a ford

and a bridge and a town at Eltham, or about who first came there from England, so far across the sea, pushing and chopping their way through the dense green bush and braving the resentment of the Maoris. Only a few miles away, though they never actually seemed to have lived or fought much around Eltham, the Maoris had killed the great guerrilla-fighter Von Tempsky at Te-Ngutu-o-te-Manu ('The Beak of the Bird').

Our own immediate affairs obsessed us. Just above the bridge, for instance, the Borough Council in my time tidied the banks of the Town Creek and made a pretty little park of it.

It was called Bridger Park, after the Mayor: a gentleman with long black hair, which he used to toss back from his forehead with fascinating dexterity. He was named, in what I always thought the most exotic style, Ira J. Bridger, and he kept a bicycle shop and belonged to the Salvation Army.

Once Mr Bridger and one of my FitzGerald uncles, in whose veins the Irish blood ran hot and was always liable to boil, fell out upon the Post Office steps over the Borough Estimates; and came to fisticuffs, and afterwards sued and counter-sued each other in the little local court-house. And that was the kind of thing which, rather than the dim and improbable feats of the pioneers, engaged our most ardent sympathies.

Though Bridger Park was a tranquil and enchanting little spot, and from the railings of the bridge you could see the trout swimming tantalizingly in the tidied water, the Town Creek had at that point a somewhat disreputable reputation: such is the effect, even on the purest of waters, of contact with the metropolis.

Our metropolis had a population of about two thousand; but even there the most surprising things used to happen. A farmer put gelignite into the oven to blow up his relatives; a respectable citizen in the Government service crept round by night and stole ladies' underwear from their clothes-lines; an Assyrian in Bath Street, heated by love, belaboured his rival with a dog-chain; a strange man put a notice on his house, 'Beware of the Lion's Cub'. There were fires, even murders; and, just downstream from Bridger Park, the wildest of wild Irishmen started to dig a tunnel which led under the Bank of New South Wales, where he proposed to blow up the strongroom – a large and mighty venture, so it loomed in our childhood, opening the door to a world of power and desperation beyond anything we had dreamed of.

The attempt failed, so our legend ran, because an accomplice got drunk one night and talked too much to the blacksmith, who told the police. Some years later, when he re-entered society, we used to see the tunneller, huge, gaunt, raw-boned and red, stalking about the streets of the town, so bizarre and terrible and utterly removed from the normal life of a man that we hardly dared to look at him; but of course, from a safe distance, did.

He disappeared again after a little while and we never saw him again.

The other crime done near that same spot, where the creek took a turn round a boulder and vanished under willows, was rather more suitable to the locality. It was performed by two small boys – of whom I was not one, I hasten to say – who speared a ten-pound brown trout and could not refrain, so magnificent was the prize, from boasting about it.

In fact, they had it displayed in the window of the fish-shop for the admiration of the whole town on

the great Saturday night shopping carnival. Constable Townsend also admired it; and those two gallant young poachers found themselves up before the magistrate.

For half a mile or so above these scenes of depravity the Town Creek did something utterly mysterious with itself in waters which, for some reason or other, I never investigated; I daresay it flowed through people's backyards. But at last, when it emerged behind the Presbyterian Church away up on the right bank, passed Fred Vincent's backyard and the Convent high up on the left, and wound its shiny way through the green paddocks to the bridge on the way to Chiselhurst, it became our own Town Creek, a place for adventure and delight.

The sort of things that happened there were that, wagging it from Miss Hooper's private school one day (wonderful Miss Hooper, who had once been a missionary in India and had been chased down a dark street by a black man bent on love) I met the wild gang from the Public School, also playing the wag, sunburnt a brilliant crimson and swimming all the glorious long day in the deep green pool where the diving-board poked out its wooden tongue under the willows. I revered them for their wickedness; and was relieved to find that they did not eat me, for we had a steady feud with them.

And then not long after I first began to fish, one day just upstream from the swimming pool I hooked Ian Wylds, the bank manager's son, in the eyelid – for he was standing behind me when I cast – and, believing he was blinded for life, he refused to be unhooked and ran roaring for home, with me after him with the rod, playing him like the noblest trout I ever had on a line.

Years later, when our fishing had progressed and when Taranaki's tremendous rains had brought the Waiau or the Mangahume up in flood, Fin Maslin and I sometimes retreated to these reaches of the Town Creek to carry on with the day's sport, dropping our worms into the waters that would still run clear, though brimming full, in the small round pools or the runnels under the watercress.

And often, late after work, I walked there with my mother to fish the evening rise while she watched the birds and the water. I seldom caught anything better than a dark and rather slimy one-pounder, but we enjoyed becoming expert at finding the nests of skylarks as they shot up suddenly from the long grass at our feet, leaving the cup in the ground and the four brown speckled eggs (containing what skyfuls of song!) still warm from their sheltering breasts.

How we loved that mile or so of rivulet: from the last time I saw the skylarks' nests to days so far back into childhood that seeking to recapture them now is like looking into another world, like peering at algae through a microscope, like watching some speck of life in one of the stream's own hastening bubbles!

Dimly I see in that bubble a tiny splash. It was the day my sister's girlfriend fell into the pool under the grey boulder and, so we thought, was drowning.

How we rescued her, I know not; but I do indelibly remember that we had with us that day a billycart, or it may even have been a perambulator, and afterwards, all the way home down Mountain Road, that heroic and adorable little girl had her small blue bloomers drying on the back of it … and was walking, without them, in heaven knows what pink twinkling. I should be distressed to think that memory was merely rude: in the tiny bubble of that day I had seen for the first time, stark in the crystal depths, the two great mysteries of our existence, Death and Love.

That was, too, one of the days when, besides playing in the Town Creek, we peered into the third and all-encompassing mystery, Nature herself, where she lurked in 'the Caves'; for we never failed, on visits to the stream, to pause and wonder at those two most romantic cavities in the clay bank … a hundred yards or so up from the creek, on the hillside known as Crabtree's Dip, because Mr Crabtree, the publican, had once hurled his car through the wooden fence on Mountain Road there.

I think the Caves, in the years before we knew them, must have been quarries of some kind; perhaps someone had dug them out for clay. But why? There was clay everywhere, the yellow volcanic ash from prehistoric eruptions of Mount Egmont, blanketing the whole province a foot or so under the rich black soil of leaf-mould from the forests cut down by the pioneers.

Why dig two caves in a bank beside a swampy hollow, away down the slope from the road, where you could have all the clay you wanted on the hilltop?

There was no gold or coal in the neighbourhood to dig for; no stone suitable for building; and all the road-metal anyone could require came from the shingle in the Waingongoro, where the Maslins had their crusher.

Perhaps someone dug the caves to clear and imprison the tiny spring that, dripping in notes of cold and crystalline music from the green ferns in the gloom, still filled one of them with its dark water: a drinking supply for cattle or for some settler's hut long since rotted into the earth.

But why do that, when the creek was only a hundred yards away?

And there was no sign whatever of a hut, not even the chimney of clay or stone or brick that usually lives on after bushfire or decay to mark the hearth of the settler.

Sometimes we thought they were Maori caves; but the Maoris had never lived at Eltham, so far as we knew; and seldom lived in caves, anyhow.

These puzzles pleased and haunted us; and so, most of all, did the strange stone head, rounded and slimy, with water trickling over its forehead and dripping from its nose, that, embedded in the clay of the far bank, out of reach across the pool, stared at us with mossy eyes through the ferns.

Was it a Maori carving? So we told ourselves; and never quite believed what we said. Was it a skull? We hoped so. Was it just a stone? Probably; but that was unthinkable. It was the Earth itself looking at us; and we looked back.

And that certainly was true. Children who have the supreme good fortune to grow up in country towns, as we did, live with the earth like one of its own creatures: squelching through the rusty mud of the swamp at the Rifle Range, watching the pukekos and the swamprails; burrowing through the thorny tunnels of the barberry at Jossie Mills's, where blackbirds and thrushes nested; fishing for butcher bees, with a straw which we poked down their holes in the clay banks, on a sunny Saturday morning …

There was one shining, transcendent day at the Town Creek when, long before I began to fish, I first truly made acquaintance with earth in its purest element of water. I had for a long time promised myself to walk that lovely stream, from the pool where the diving-board stood, the whole way to the bridge on the road to Chiselhurst, not tamely on the banks where anyone could walk, but in the water all the time, never once setting foot on dry land; and at last I did it.

How can one recapture in words the prolonged and sparkling bliss of such a day?

The sun shone on the snowy peak and massive blue slopes of Mount Egmont on the horizon. The sky was filled with skylarks, fluttering their little wings and showering their melody for miles over the green countryside. The paddocks were lit by the golden constellations of dandelions. A hare ran with ears flattened, doing its best to look invisible, through the purple clover of the hayfield. And on through tussocks and rushes, past a stray patch of blackberry in a gully, on towards the toi-tois waving their silver plumes in the clump by the bridge, the stream flowed clear and shallow and small, with its mats of watercress, its beach of hoof-marked mud where the cows crossed, its midges and crimson dragonflies, its runnels, its pools, and its little bubbling music.

Somehow all these things must have blended to make ecstasy; but what memory has most clearly preserved is the single, miraculous impression of trampling all day through the water, like walking in liquid song;

and that, as quite unexpected treasures, I found a lot of freshwater mussels in one long shallow run where a kind of rivergrass grew under the glittering surface.

As it happened I did not, after all, learn to fish for trout in the Town Creek, where in all other respects my aquatic life began. But it was in the Town Creek that something of the first, of the most vital importance, happened, not long after Fred Vincent had shown me on the Waingongoro how to tie a cast and bait a worm or creeper on the hook and somehow, without too much confusion, swing it out over the water.

Just upstream from the swimming-pool and near the reach where the mussels lived, I dropped my worm into a nice wide pool; and, behold, incredibly, a very small brown trout, yellowish as he turned, swam breathtakingly, superbly towards it … and he was going to take it! And swam towards it, and swam towards it, and swam towards it – and then heart-rendingly darted away from it. And after him, curiously, swam an eel, about three feet long. Maybe the eel frightened him; maybe, with some convulsive jerk of the worm in the irresistible impulse to strike too soon, I did.

That was the end of him, and I had to fish for two whole seasons before anything so exciting happened again. But what matter? A trout had looked at my worm. I was not merely an admirer of fishermen. I was a fisherman myself.

5

THE PLEASURES OF POACHING

THE EXCELLENT thing about New Plymouth
Boys' High School in my day – for I do not think
anyone can really become a fisherman without having
been a poacher in his youth: you must rove the earth till
it grows up through your shinbones; you must baptize
yourself by total immersion in the ditches – was that it
was still possible, however firmly we were supposed to
be incarcerated behind the grey walls on the hill above
the town, to live, as schoolboys should, like rabbits and
weasels and tomcats.

We heard with amazement of the lives led by boys
at other, more elegant, colleges such as Wanganui, where
the English model was followed and wild creatures such
as ourselves, who should have been shooting starlings at
the slop-barrel with an air-gun, or raiding the China-
man's garden for the cucumbers that tasted so delicious
with sugar, or sneaking through the hole in the hedge

to snatch small tight-lipped kisses from the girls of Miss Bedford's Friday-night dancing-class as one gallantly 'saw them home', spent the interminable months between holiday and holiday wholly imprisoned in the school-grounds – or at most let out for an ignoble walk in a 'crocodile' – with nothing but organized sport to satisfy their thwarted animal instincts.

New Plymouth took its character, and I trust it has not altogether lost it over the years, from that tremendous headmaster, Bill Moyes. Bill Moyes – what a man he was!

Never in my life have I seen a spectacle quite so awe-inspiring as those mornings when some malefactor caught in the worst of crimes, smoking or writing notes to the pupils of the Girls' High School that stood chaste and inevitably mysterious across the river, was hauled up on the stage in the big Assembly Hall for, after prayers, a public whacking. Other masters whacked us from time to time, and we thought nothing of it. The cardboard back of a writing-pad slipped down the seat of the trousers provided, if it didn't give the show away by making too much noise, a considerable mitigation; it was also possible, when gathering the rod from the clump of bamboos that grew too conveniently between the dormitories and the school, to make a neat, invisible little incision in it that made it burst apart after the first two or three strokes, when it became as harmless as a straw broom. But I don't think anybody dared to play those tricks on Bill Moyes.

All the bristles on his black bullet-head stood on end. His dark-brown eyes flashed fire. His bulldog jaw jutted out more formidably than ever. His voice cracked out like a stockwhip. 'You, Murgatroyd! Smoking in your dug-out again! Come up here!' And up shuffled

Murgatroyd to the stage where the masters stood against the wall like a row of vultures in their black gowns, abandoning for once the little scratchings and key-jinglings we all watched with such malicious intentness; and down went Murgatroyd touching his toes, the cynosure of a thousand awed and delighted eyes; and swish went back the headmaster's gown from his square shoulders and his embonpoint, and whack, whack, whack, usually six of the best, fell the long green bamboo, beating the dust from Murgatroyd's trousers and the vice of smoking from his soul.

'And now, all of you!' the rasping, staccato voice would crack out, while he glared at us like a wild black bull from the stage. 'These dug-outs! Nothing but filthy dens where you hide yourselves away to smoke ciga-rettes. Why don't you be a man and smoke a pipe if you want to smoke! There'll be no more smoking, see! And no more dug-outs. Dismiss!'

There was, too, that soul-shattering night when, awaiting a renewed pillow-fighting assault from the neighbouring dormitory, with which we had been in uproarious conflict for half an hour, we caught Bill Moyes in a booby-trap we had prepared for the invaders; and when down on that hard head, as he burst in rage and majesty like Olympian Jove himself through the door, amidst a scramble and a tumble and a flying of small boys as we fled right and left for the innocence of our beds, clattered boots and shoes and clothes-brushes and hair-brushes and, if an enchanted memory can be trusted, a bucketful of water. There was a mighty cuffing of heads that night and some sterner reproof — for we had disturbed the headmaster in his after-dinner repose in his own adjoining house — on the seats of pyjama-trousers ... which form altogether too frail a buffer.

We stood in great awe of Bill, but never in fear. For the public whackings were, after all, a rare spectacle, and one in which everyone delighted; a kind of necessary boiling-over when the school became, at intervals, the volcano which always lay underneath it − how could you have any encamping of five hundred human beings without volcanic pressures developing? − and when the headmaster demonstrated superbly that he, the one man amongst us all, junior masters and boys alike, was in command of the volcano. But there was humour, more often than lightning, in those flashing dark eyes; there was always a grin, wide and brilliantly white, waiting to pucker those majestic features into humanity; above all (I do not speak of his scholastic and managerial attain-ments − how he made that school − for we knew nothing of them) there was the pervading sense of his manliness. He smoked a pipe. He went shooting, and kept at the school a red setter and a black retriever which invariably rushed under the beds in the dormi-tory when we had rifle-practice. He fished for trout.

Had he not practically given us permission to smoke a pipe ourselves? (I pass over with a shudder, as too appallingly ridiculous to contemplate, the spectacle of a very small boy, thin and undersized, embedded in a huge winter overcoat, puffing manfully at his pipe as he strolled back to school from the town one drizzly dusk; shoving the implement in haste into his pocket when he caught sight of Mr Blundell, the drawing-master, also out for a stroll; and thereupon bursting into flames ...)

As to the dug-outs, I don't believe that Bill Moyes meant a word of what he said; and I don't think we believed him then. No attempt, except by vandals in our own community, was ever made to stamp them out. In my first year at school these dank and clayey caverns, the

centre of our whole animal existence, persisted even in
the gully straight below the school, inhabited by
resplendent, tall, hairy heroes who burst out roaring into
the night when one investigated them, thrillingly, by
torchlight; and if later, like other creatures of the wild
retreating before civilization, we had to go as far as the
school farm or even over to the banks of the Te Henui
to dig our burrows, neither Bill nor any of the other
masters came there to disturb us.

I should like to be able to say that it was in our dug-out
under the wattles opposite the school farmhouse (where
lived a farmer who milked a herd of cows for us, while
over his green acres roamed the agricultural students on
their lordly legitimate business, and the rest of us bent
on crime) that our own particular gang of outlaws com-
prising, with myself, Des Carter, Cully MacDiarmid,
Cally Callaghan and, always a little disapprovingly,
Cardo Evans, cooked the magnificent four-pound
brown trout I poached from one of New Plymouth's
public parks; for that was the sort of thing one did in
dug-outs and, cooked there, the fish would have made
the two supreme events of my schooldays both wholly
disreputable. But the fact is that under Bill Moyes's
twinkling dark eyes, fishing was a perfectly legitimate
course of study at New Plymouth; nor, though of course
I lied as to how I caught the monster, can I think he
would genuinely have frowned on a bit of poaching.

There was, indeed, a whiff of illegality in the practice in which he encouraged me on days when,
gloriously escaping from school together, he would
himself take me out fishing: I would go out early in the
morning and, with my air-gun, shoot cicadas for him for
bait – a feat of marksmanship in which I now take an

altogether astonished pride. A smaller insect than the Australian, and making a quieter clacking, the cicadas lurked high up on the trunks and branches of the wattles down the gully from the slop-barrel and, with only an air-gun pellet in them, could be brought to earth almost undamaged. For that matter it seems thoroughly illegal for a headmaster and his pupil – and once, I remember, my English master, Jaz Leggatt: but surely that must have been a holiday – to sneak out of school and go fishing.

I never caught any trout while out with Bill – it was only my second season of fishing – but I was proud enough to have a fine trout come out from behind a stone and *look* at my cicada one day when, wading some stream up around The Meeting of the Waters, I got splendidly sunburned, fishing without my shirt, while Bill, who had struck them all on the feed, caught half a dozen beauties which I netted for him.

And, as a result of having enough fish come and look at my bait from time to time, one never-to-be-forgotten day, chancing upon them in a semi-comatose condition in a stream running through some parkland, where doubtless they had been fed on bread and never associated the shadow of man or boy with anything so barbarous as a fish-hook, I caught not merely my first trout, but my first two trout; and that same miraculous day I crawled out on a log and dropped a worm into the mouth of a fine perch, losing it only because I had not the sense to play it with my rod but tried to haul it straight out on to the log with the thin gut cast.

The two trout – unhappy creatures! – both about a pound in weight, were for some obscure reason lolling about on top of the slightly flooded stream, gently sucking at leaves as they floated down the current, and they gently sucked in the enormous worm I dropped at them without the slightest misgivings; and, still trustingly as it were, came in to the gaff with hardly a protesting flap … which was just as well for my inexperience.

But now I knew that I could catch trout. And when those two deluded innocents had been duly exhibited to the headmaster, and cooked by the school cook and served to my own 'section' at our end of one of the long tables in the dining-room – to be eaten with what infinite pride and relish! – and when, a week or two later, returning to those same waters of triumph (nobody ever seemed to patrol that creek to haul one off to prison for poaching what were surely the municipality's trout) I saw, wavering in the clear water beside a rock, the most prodigious trout in the world, I never had any doubt but that I should have him.

I tried him with the worm. He ignored it. I tried him with a 'creeper'. He ignored it. I tried him with the Coachman, which was about the only dry fly I had heard of in those days. He ignored it. I tried him with a monstrous grey-winged yellow-bellied imitation of the stone-fly, which was one of those lures sold in tackle-shops to catch fishermen and which never took a fish in its life. Rightly, my great fish ignored it. And there he still lay in the shallow sunny water by his rock, a pale silvery yellow in hue through some freak of light or diet, bulging and immovable. I tried him with my Wisden minnow, a beautiful little spotted lure much in favour in Taranaki. I swung this deadly bait, bristling with its triple hooks at fin and tail, wide over the current, dropped it with the inevitable plop and pulled it across his nose, ever nearer with each cast.

No trout can ignore the minnow. If it will not take the lure it will at least butt it out of the way, or at the

worst skitter away from the plop. But the monster never
stirred for it. Then I realized that, basking in the sun, my
fish was sound asleep – I do not know if this is possible
in ichthyology, but it was so. I never saw anything so
sound asleep as that fat trout was. I tried, full of wickedness, for now I was poaching indeed, to jag him with the
hooks of the minnow, but the hooks would not catch;
and, as for the prickle on his side, he seemed positively
to enjoy it, wriggling a little in his slumbers.

No doubt he would have been a perfect subject for
'tickling', had I understood that excellent art. But I got
him in the end more simply still, by wading quietly out
and hooking him with my gaff – whereupon he leapt to
life and, gaff and all, plunged away from me downstream, and I plunged after, and found him again by the
bobbing gaff-handle in deep water, and had him out
safely and superbly at last, flapping like Leviathan on the
grass; and so, in the evening, back to school to weigh,
display, and devour the four-pounder I had taken 'on the
Coachman'.

If these three trout – my total bag for the season – being
practically legitimate captures, could be cooked and
eaten in enviable publicity, there were other oddments
of game that had to be dealt with in no less delectable
privacy. The wild pigeon, for instance, a strictly protected bird, which I shot on a pig-hunting weekend, I
prudently offered to George Bertrand, the mathematics
master, with whom, though he was the most fierce dis-
ciplinarian, with a bristling black moustache and a
fearsome rasping voice, I became friendly during my
inglorious military career as quartermaster-sergeant,
when we hobnobbed over rifles and ammunition while
the school was at drill. George took it home and ate it.

Similarly, when, prowling the school farm, I had the triumph of shooting a cock quail in a boxthorn hedge
with my air-gun, I found it advisable to pack the bird in
my boot-box and take it home to Eltham in the weekend; where, to add to the pleasure of displaying it, I
found Dick Knuckey, a most notable sportsman with
equally notable whiskers, dining with my father on wild
duck.

As for the wild duck which we ourselves – Des
Carter, Cully MacDiarmid, Cally Callaghan and I; I
really must exempt Cardo Evans from this awful deed –
bagged on the ornamental pond in Pukekura Park, a feat
even more glorious than the gaffing of the four-pound
trout and indeed the topmost peak of all my scholastic
achievements, that had to be eaten in a privacy from
which even the most broad-minded of masters, parents,
or sportsmen were excluded. We thought we could be
expelled for it.

By that time we had moved from our dug-out
under the wattles. Such is the nature of man that he
finds all secret societies, whether of another religion or
another race or nation, whether of writers immersed in
their art or merely of five small boys lurking in a dug-
out, intolerable: the enemy there may be plotting his
downfall; worse, they may be thinking superior
thoughts; worse still, they may secretly be enjoying
themselves: and so down upon our dug-out, with clods
and buckets of water down the chimney, with the
clumping of hooves upon the clay-covered corrugated-
iron roof, thundered the Goth, the Vandal and the Hun,
in the shape of schoolboys often unpleasantly large. It is
the law of life; some build dug-outs and some destroy
them; and it was well to have learned so useful a lesson
early.

But I do not recall that our forced retreat from the ruins of that dank burrow in the clay, dear as it was to us, the work of our own hands and the one spot in the whole of our regimented existence where life made sense, caused us any profound regret. True, we had had lyrical times there, smoking Muratti's Russian Blend cigarettes which a dayboy procured for us, cooking sausages stolen from the school meatsafe (raiding which, by means of the loose screen at the back, Cully MacDiarmid scored a tremendous clip on the ear from Bill Moyes one black wet Saturday night): but the collapse of one pattern of life is merely, for ardent spirits, the beginning of another. It occurred to us that an even more desirable residence would be a hut on the banks of the Te Henui at the back of the farm, far from the reach of the vandal, tucked away in thick, tangled bush; and if the New Plymouth Borough Council still retains any curiosity as to the fate of the old grey palings which fenced in its gravel-yard, that is where they went.

There were indeed weeks of happy scrounging when five small boys, loaded like ants, might have been seen – but never were – dragging over hills and gullies their treasures of council-palings, rusty corrugated iron from the cowshed, old bags and boards and bricks and drainpipes from wherever they could be found. It was a noble edifice when completed, wobbly and dilapidated like some palatial pigsty, and we were inordinately proud of it. Nobody else, so far as we knew, had ever built a hut at school.

We were never raided. At ease we swam in the small glittering pools of the Te Henui; at ease we boiled in a kerosene tin the eels we caught from the stream, invariably very thin and black with silver bellies, tasting deliciously; at ease we roved the bush and the neighbouring farmlands, stealing green lemons or eating *ki-kis* (pronounced giggys) which are the fleshy centre of some parasitical growth on native trees, reputed to have been enjoyed by the Maoris; and at ease in that leafy privacy we cooked and ate the great duck from Pukekura Park.

I forget who first suggested that piece of villainy. Probably, since we passed through the Park regularly on our way home from compulsory church on Sundays, the Devil prompted us all simultaneously.

There was always, near the kiosk, a crowd feeding the ducks; and, the tamest of birds but still by definition 'wild', the grey duck of New Zealand that is called the black duck in Australia, the same romantic birds of swamp and river and lake that, with their associations of remote waters and gunshots in the misty dawn, used to hang by pairs in the kitchen at Eltham until Dick Knuckey and my father judged they were ripe enough to eat – there scores of these noble creatures dabbled and jostled, whispered and quacked and skittered across the lake … temptations to both the flesh and the spirit such as no right-minded schoolboy could resist.

Across the water from the kiosk, hard by a rustic bridge, there was a little bay where visitors seldom congregated. It seemed possible that if you stole a slice or two of bread from breakfast, carefully preserving them through the long but sometimes unexpectedly amusing hours of 'Teddy' Strong's sermon, and threw them into that little bay, you might be able to lure the ducks away from the watching crowd; and then if you were a good enough shot with a stone – and Des Carter at any rate had an unerring eye …

Alas, it was indeed possible. I pass over the scene on that bright Sunday morning as quickly as possible: the

crowd by the kiosk, the deluded ducks swimming to the
bread in the little bay, the moment of awe-stricken triumph when one of them fell to our onslaught, the
hysterical mingling of joy and terror when that duck
began to come to life again as Cully MacDiarmid strug-
gled to tuck it under his overcoat while visitors began
to stroll towards us ... I hastily transport myself to the
hut by the Te Henui where, high in a nearby tree, the
bird in a stolen pillowcase (to keep it from the flies)
hung for a week until we, and it, were ready for the banquet.

It is a wonder anyone ever lives through his boyhood. The night we ate that duck – we roasted it in a
kerosene tin – I was so shaking and sweating and freezing with influenza that I could hardly endure either the
heat of our fire or the draughts that whistled in through
the cracks of our ramshackle palace. Yet never did a bird
taste more glorious; never in all our schooldays was
there so wonderful and wicked a deed.

True, a little deeper into Pukekura Park, in a
secluded ornamental pond where he swam alone like a
king, there was a magnificent white swan ... but there
our hearts failed us. Even Bill Moyes, we felt with profound conviction, would not have stood for that one.

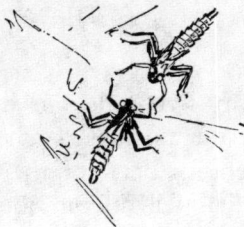

6

THE AWAKINO

EIGHTY miles north of Eltham, hidden over mountains, locked in deep gorges, far across flowery
paddocks, lost in the end or the beginning in the wild
dark untrodden bush, rippled the waters of the Awakino.
Nobody knew about it. Nobody except those masters of
the Eltham fishing, Caleb Maslin, Sam Pepperill, and
Bert Thomas from the garage. Their camp was away up
the side road that turned into the hills from the store at
Mahoenui, where the river was stony and delicate. They
fished it in secret with crickets. And they caught —
enormous trout.

And the trout were — rainbows! a word that to fishermen acquainted only with the sluggish and slippery
brown trout of the streams around Eltham glittered as
silvery in the mind as the flash of sunlight on a rapid, as
the side of the great fish itself when it leapt from the
water.

How remote and wild and adventurous seemed the
road to the Awakino when we followed hot-foot or
hot-cylinder after Maslin and Pepperill and Bert
Thomas. True, eighty miles is no great distance to
anyone accustomed to the straight roads of Australia and
to modern fast cars; but New Zealand roads were
narrow and twisty, and as for the cars we had then — one
night when we were roaring home from the Awakino

at twenty-five miles an hour in Fin Maslin's ancient
three-seater tin-lizzie such poisonous fumes poured out
of the engine between the cracks of the floorboards that
both of us fell unconscious. There is a stretch of four
miles of road somewhere near Inglewood, with a narrow
bridge in the midst of it, that to this day wavers in my
mind like a nightmare, for it was cut clean out of that
night's journey. I suppose it was in some kind of night-
mare that I drove it. I can remember, earlier, putting my
head out the side of the car and beating my face to keep
awake; but I cannot remember those four miles and the
bridge.

But the road, when we were not perishing of
carbon monoxide poisoning, was enchanting. Once, by-
passing New Plymouth, you had left Lepperton and
Waitara behind and were really on the road to the north
with nothing but scattered farmhouses and country
schools and stores to remind you that anyone lived in
New Zealand, you were out in the country of adventure. Through the ragged swampy farmlands of Uruti
and Urenui, between the hills and the invisible sea, the
road ran past famous places where we had fished for
snapper; and on into the Mimi Valley, where the brown
river washed round the roots of gigantic poplars, green
for the summer fishing, golden for the autumn; and up
into the bush on Mount Messenger, where the road near
the summit ran through a curious tunnel shaped like the
arch of a cathedral and where the tuis rang their clear
bells in the treetops; and down the far side of Mount
Messenger into the country that, cut off by that great
green wall, now seemed far indeed, too distant for one-
day excursions from Eltham, sacred to summer camps:
the green Tongaporutu River, where in spring tides
snapper were said to come right up to the reaches along

the roadside, ten miles from the mouth; Rapanui, the creek where the Carters from Eltham camped and where once, accommodation being crowded in their tent, I slept on the kitchen table; the shining small Mohakatina River, the wide and tranquil Mokau.

When, ten miles north from Mokau along the plateau above the sea, you came to the mouth of the Awakino it hardly seemed a river you could associate with trout fishing. From the high headland the coastline stretched for miles, the blue waters breaking white on the long flat beaches of grey and black iron sand, until they were lost in the blue distance towards Kawhia. It was a place for saltwater fishing.

But the road turned inland, and ran like a rock-ledge above the gorge where, in deep blue almost inaccessible pools, sometimes a trout would rise − a rainbow! And from the cliff above the river, nearer to Mahoenui, we saw once the most enormous trout moving below us, a real monster, a fish that could have been ten pounds or more. And, where the bridge crossed the river by the store and the tiny school that constituted the entire city of Mahoenui, there were wide and very fishable reaches, rippling over pebbles between the flat green paddocks, whose secrets we had yet to learn. And so, up the side road into the hills, where Caleb Maslin, Sam Pepperill, and Bert Thomas had said we must go; away from the main road and all traffic; away from the river for a while but back to it at the point where, after its long semicircle across the plains, it reappeared in that pool of blue and crystal under the ridge where Caleb Maslin had said he had never failed to get a fish; and on and up into the hills now ragged with scrub or, in the clearings, scarred where the wild pigs had been rooting; on and up the narrow rocky road beside the ever-narrowing stream half-hidden in the bush and the undergrowth, until at last you came to Thoresen's white weatherboard farm-house, and the road ended. And there, besides the haystack, in the last clear paddock against the wilderness of ridges all covered with dark-green bush where the Awakino had its source, we camped. I said to George Palmer, who was my companion that first trip, what about trying out the water while I went on fixing up the camp: an act of self-sacrifice which amazes me to this day. In ten minutes George was back, triumphant, with a rainbow of a pound and a half. So that was what it was going to be like on the Awakino!

But it didn't turn out like that at all. Something went strangely wrong with the river that trip. There was no doubt it was the most beautiful country, the half-cleared paddocks full of bracken and fire-blackened stumps and lawyer-vine bushes running up to the dense bush on the ranges where the rimus stood out tall and bronze from the dark-green forest around them. Sky-larks sang in the cleared country, tuis in the bush. It was so remote that one sunny afternoon, fishing high up towards the ranges, we saw a mob of wild pigs rooting in a paddock; and, being young and bloodthirsty, we stalked them on our bellies through the bracken and, when we were close enough, leapt out upon them. To our amazement we caught one. It was an extremely small piglet and did not look very well. We decided not to eat it.

In that wild country I was fascinated, too, by the Thoresens, who sometimes took us in and kindly gave us dinner at night, roast lamb and new potatoes and green peas and swede-turnips, the fine rich food of the land. There were mushrooms, too. Mr Thoresen was short and spare and sturdy; he held the mountains on his square shoulders. Mrs Thoresen, dark and comfortably plump, kept in that far place the most spotless kitchen I have ever seen. You could have eaten your dinner off the shiny green linoleum; the wooden sink and the table were worn white with countless scrubbings; the old wood-burning stove shone like a black mirror. It was thus, I suppose, that in the last house on the road, cease-lessly polishing and scrubbing, she kept the wilderness at bay.

And there was no doubt, either, that the Awakino itself up there was as beautiful as the country through which it ran; more beautiful than it could ever hope to be when it grew broader and quieter and deeper in the flat country down below. It was rough going to fish it. Downstream towards Caleb Maslin's famous big blue pool you clambered over rocks through tutu-scrub. Upstream, through Thoresen's paddocks and the bush, it grew so small (though still five yards or so wide), or the undergrowth of lawyer and supplejack and tree-ferns grew so thick, that sometimes, if you cut across country for a while to avoid treading on George Palmer's heels, you couldn't find it again. Right up in the bush it was the loveliest little sunlit stream bubbling down under the arching tree-ferns. It was so quiet up there that one day a fantail perched on my fishing rod.

But we caught no fish in it!

Or, rather, we did. I caught one afternoon the best fish I ever caught in the Awakino and one of the best I ever caught anywhere. He was a six-pounder; and so simply caught, too! In the wide shallow pool full of sun-light, I saw a reasonable fish rise over the sandbank on the far side. Fishing with a locust for bait, I cast it across to him. There was a commotion in the water; and the next instant the superb six-pounder was hooked and, in all his gleaming splendour, leaping half-clear on the surface. He must have raced the smaller trout for the titbit. Either because his weight made him sluggish or else because the shallow pool gave him no scope to extend himself, he was so easy to land and made so little commotion that I was able to cast out again for the smaller fish and got that one, too; about a pound and a half.

Yes, there were the great moments. And there were a few other fish, nothing of any size, for breakfast and for the Thoresens.

But where were the hordes, the shoals of trout guaranteed by Caleb Maslin, Sam Pepperill, and Bert Thomas? Where were the fish in Caleb Maslin's blue pool, where we could never fail to catch one; and did, monotonously, fail? Was it because we were not using crickets? I never really liked using crickets for bait – because, though they don't, they looked as if they would sting you with their long sharp ovipositors. But surely locusts, which swarmed there at that season and sang their small buzzing song on every tree-trunk, were equally good natural bait? Was it because, to cope with all those colossal rainbows we were going to catch, we were using thick 2X casts? But Maslin and Thomas and Pepperill also fished with 2X casts, and it was on their advice we used such cumbersome paraphernalia. Was it the time of the year? Was it because the stream was exceptionally clear and bright, so that the heavy casts looked like a ship's mooring-ropes across the water? Was that the reason that even the small gold spinner called a fly-spoon, afterwards to prove infallible lower down, was scorned?

Were there, simply, no trout there that season? I stood waist-deep in a little pool of that river just below the camp one evening, fishing in the dusk and on into the night, flicking my useless locust on the 2X cast upon the fast-running darkening water, and the trout rose all round me by the dozen ... and not one fish, naturally, would take my bait.

One thing was certain: we did not know how to fish the Awakino. In fact, if we could use a locust in the evening rise, when moths, mayflies, lacewings, all the innumerable busy littleness that drops upon the water at dusk were what the trout demanded, we did not know how to fish at all.

But we learned.

Now when I look back at those times when we were serving our apprenticeship to the Awakino, driving so far from Eltham, camping in strange places and dashing so eagerly into the waters of the fabulous rainbows, they seem to me the epitome of the splendour – and the squalor! – of adolescence. The food we ate! The mess we let our tents get into! The ardour with which we plunged into the water with our spinners, in the dark light before dawn when the mists were still rising from its cold surface; the miles we walked! And the trout we caught!

There must have been times when we ate well. We certainly had plenty of trout and I remember still with doubt and curiosity the relish with which Fin Maslin ate the skins, which he said were the best part of them. If a tin of pineapple was not substantial lunch we used to find it an ingenious way of supplying both food and drink without any bother, and its lightness made all the more satisfying that reviver of beer and fruit-cake which we fell upon, starving and exhausted, when we got back to the camp at dusk. There was, too, that excellent ham (our breakfast) which we used to bring from home and, after one or two grim lessons, hung high in the trees beside the camp to preserve it from the water-rats. I don't know how much use that really was, since we hung our trout there too and often woke in the morning to find only the heads left dangling from the branch; but I daresay it preserved, in a somewhat gnawed condition, the bulk of it. But memory, naturally a connoisseur of what is truly memorable, cherishes most notably a stew I made for my brother Neil, on the solitary occasion he camped with me on the Awakino, with frightful consequences. That, and that appalling wet Easter when, with nothing to do but lie on our camp-beds and watch the river grow larger and wetter and muddier, Fin Maslin and I camped under the veranda at the store at Mahoenui and, all the shops having been sold out of edible provisions when we drove up, lived for four days on duck-eggs and sausage-rolls. When at last, having caught one solitary trout with a spinner in the high yellow flood, we left for home, with what ferocious joy did we hurl the remainder of those dank and chap-fallen rolls and those horrible big green eggs at the offending sky!

That was the most dismal of all our camps; but there was one which, though in a far prettier situation, outdid it in squalor. It doesn't seem to me now a good idea to attempt to wash greasy breakfast dishes simply by leaving them in a little side-stream all day in the hope that the running water and the eels (which used to swarm interestingly up that little stream for the scraps) will lick them clean for the evening meal; still less does it seem advisable simply to leave them lying unwashed around the tent all day, littered with ham-fat or the carcasses of fried rainbow trout, perhaps in the hope that the water-rats will clean them. But that, one way or another, was the way we did the dishes that camp. It still seems a good idea when a weta gets into the tent to get out of it yourself with all possible speed. A weta is a large nasty-looking insect a bit like an enormous dark-brown grasshopper and a bit like a scorpion. It turns its head and looks at you. It hops suddenly and disconcert-ingly, straight at you, either because it does not know where it is going or because it is determined to knock you down. I don't really think it bites at all; but it always looks as if it is going to. But it does seem rather tidier, if you have kicked over a bottle of beer and a tin of runny honey when fleeing for your life from a weta, afterwards to clean up the mess.

But that trip Fin Maslin and I were having a silent dispute. We did not quarrel; we never quarrelled. We were on the high shining peaks of adolescence. We fished all day from dawn to dark and came home and fortified ourselves with beer and fruit-cake, ate trout with more beer and, in the cool night by the sweetly-flowing river, shouted out bawdy songs at the stars. We lay on our camp-beds and talked, in complete lyrical harmony, about beer and girls and trout. But it seemed to me that Fin was not doing his share of work about the camp; and it seemed to Fin that I wasn't doing my share; and anyhow we were both so knocked-up at the end of the day and so eager to start fishing in the morning that we really had no time for cleaning up. So neither of us did anything. The dishes lay about the tent unwashed, grue-some with fishbones; the beds lay unmade and rumpled, objects of great interest to the blowflies, which one day laid their eggs in the blankets; the honey, which really was rather sticky to walk in, lay in a pool in the centre of the floor, visited by thousands of ants; the spilt beer and the empty bottles stank; and I recall all this with shame and a peculiar sense of the injustice of the universe because when some friends of my father's dropped in while we were away fishing and carried far and wide the story of the sordor of our tent, that very day the cows also dropped in and ate a pound of tea and spilt the remains of it in the honey and also left on the floor, beside the honey, a mess which we really had to clean up.

That was our camp just upstream from the main road bridge; and, no doubt because of its proximity to civilization, it seemed to be our fate there to receive visitors. At our other favourite camp, in a green paddock about a mile further upstream, the only intruders we ever saw were some fishermen from Eltham's neighbouring village of Stratford; one of whom, George Carter, taught me a great lesson about trout fishing: which was that you really don't need to walk miles and miles all day after your fish but will do just as well, or almost as well, if you stay at the one good pool. George, while fishing some other stream, had been inexplicably kicked on the leg by a horse. He was walking across a paddock and it just came up and kicked him. He was too lame to walk. So, while we tramped away up stream, he sat down on the stones at the head of a rapid outside his tent and simply kept floating his fly down the current; and he caught, did George, five very nice rainbows. And the next day, having taught us this invaluable lesson, which I have always been too busy walking to put into practice, he and his friends departed.

But down by the bridge, somebody or something, a weta, a bull, or a passing motorist, was continually dropping in. It was a lively place, at intervals, Mahoenui. You couldn't say nothing ever happened there; though very little, on the surface, appeared to. Quite often Fin Maslin and I were visited by a tall, dark, pale-faced young man, very slow-spoken, who used to come down to the bank of shingle below our tent, and skip stones. He was the best stone-skipper I ever saw. Lesser men can easily enough make a stone skim two or three times across a wide pool before it dives under and drowns itself; but this young man, selecting his flat pebble with the eye of a connoisseur, could bounce one up and off the water more times than man could believe. He would have been in the Olympic class, if there was, as there should be, an Olympic competition in stone-skipping. He must have had a lot of practice in Mahoenui; where, I must admit, there usually wasn't much else to do.

But then there was also the Boy. The boy brought quite a dramatic element into that circle of rustic life which moved, all but imperceptibly, around the store and the school and the distant farmhouses. He was a fat, rather stupid-looking boy of about sixteen years of age; and like the Fat Boy in Dickens and still more like Grandfather Piper in Norman Lindsay's *Redheap*, he was generally to be found standing, just standing, in a more or less somnolent condition. We would be tramping across the paddocks; and there, behind a hillock, we would find him, standing. We would come round a bend of the stream; and there, apparently lost in con-templation of the water, he would manifest himself once more – standing. We would look up to the bridge from our camp and there he stood. We were catching so many trout at that time, and such big ones – I am not boasting; this was the Awakino – that we could not carry them with us; so all day while we fished we used to leave them in little pools at the side of the river, shielded from the sun with a thatch of green tea-tree. Sometimes, when we came to pick them up in the evening, they had vanished. The water-rats, we thought. But then, as fish after fish disappeared, it occurred to us that the fat boy had been doing a good deal of standing in the places where we had concealed our trout. We grew exceedingly suspicious of that boy, but it was no use accusing him when we had no evidence; and besides, he was speechless. Standing, not talking, was his accomplishment. So we gave him some trout, just to demonstrate that he had no need to steal them. He was very grateful, so far as we could judge from the momentary gleam in his watery grey eyes; and the next day when we came home from fishing we found that our suitcases had been rifled and our small store of money stolen. Obviously he had been doing a little standing in the tent. This was too much; it was bad enough to have wetas spilling the honey and cows eating the tea, and water-rats eating the ham and the trout, without this downright robbery. We complained to the farmer who employed him. We said that if the money were not returned, we should put the police onto him. The fat boy, in what was for him a torrent of volubility, said he never done it; but next day, when once more we came home from fishing, the money was back in our suitcases. And wherever that fat boy got to after that, we came upon him no more standing, just standing, speechless and innocent, beside a pool where we happened to have left a trout.

And the trout there were to leave for him! If we caught most of our fish in the Awakino on that and other expeditions with the spinner, I should not like to convey the impression that that was the only method we used. There were other equally uncouth devices, which also served us well. In the run below the camp, where the rapid turned at right angles and ran into the long pool under the bridge, lived a mighty trout which, one hot afternoon, repeatedly dashed out at my spinner from his lair between a rock and the high mossy bank and just as repeatedly scorned it. Fin Maslin, who never liked to let a fish defeat him, and who had a liking for weird baits, caught a large black-and-white striped bumble-bee (an insect which can give you a most fearsome sting) in the paddock behind us, and with that caught the trout. It was a three-pound rainbow.

Then there were the cockabullies. These big-headed fishlets, looking like miniature cod, lived under the flat round stones in the river bed, and one speared them, barbarously, with a table fork. It was with a cock-abully that I caught one of the best fish I ever got at Mahoenui. He was in one of the huge long pools down-stream from the bridge among the flowering hayfields, waters which we did not fish very often because they were too wide and deep and still for very profitable results; and he lay, as we had learned all the best fish did when they were feeding in the early morning, right at the head of a pool where the moving water ran in. He was memorable not so much for his size, though he was a four-pounder, as for the difficulty I had in landing him and the surprising distance he travelled before I man-aged to do it. It is a wonder we caught any fish at all with our primitive equipment on those trips. I was using a huge wooden reel, meant for sea-fishing, which had no device for increasing or decreasing the tension, except that you could push a brass knob on it and set it run-ning completely freely. If you didn't push the knob it ran at its full obstinate tension and, being so hard to move, was likely to break the cast when a fish was tugging it. I decided to use it in the free-running position. Right at the head of the pool I hooked that four-pounder, the biggest and strongest fish in the best feeding position, and full-tilt down the pool he raced. With the free-running reel I could do very little to check him, except follow him as best I could along the bank. Down the rapid at the far end of the pool and into the next pool he raced, and I after him. The bank grew steep and high. Scrub grew out of it, making it impossible to clamber along. I took to the water. Waist-deep down the next rapid we went. The water got deeper and deeper. I was in it up to my neck. It was very wet; and, in the dawn, cold. And still the fish raced on and still, so to speak, I swam after him. I have never, before or since, known a fish to travel so fast and so far. If we had not met more or less by accident when we were both trying to get down the fourth rapid into the fifth enormous pool, we might have been travelling yet. But I must have swum ahead of him by that time, for I found him coming down upon me in the rapid and netted him as he went by.

Then, too, there were the inangas. (You pronounce it ee-nonga, with the accent on the ee.) The inanga is a fascinating bait. It is a slim, slippery translucent little fish about three inches long. We believed, whether rightly or wrongly I know not, that they were the adult form of the whitebait which, in season, shoal in teeming millions at the mouths of New Zealand rivers. They were just about as hard as a trout to catch, or harder, but we trapped them in a side-creek by our camp. There is always local knowledge to be acquired in fishing; and the locals at Mahoenui had a special way of tying the inangas, curved on a piece of wire, I think, so that they stretched full out in the water and wobbled like a living fish. But we found it perfectly satisfactory just to put a hook through them as if they were a worm (or a bumble-bee) and drop them into the current; in fact, so avid for them were the rainbow of the Awakino that they would snatch up even broken pieces. Half an inanga, any fragment of an inanga, would do … as well I learned in the run, the wonderful run of swift water, at the head of the pool about half a mile upstream from our camp at the bridge.

That run! It was the most astonishing piece of water I have ever fished. Clear and swift, but not too swift, deep enough to hold the biggest fish but not too deep to be fishable, it broadened from the rapid into the big emerald pool downstream where once, wading out chest-deep through the still water, I surprised a three-pounder who lurked in the green and gold hollow beside a sunken rock; and, early in the morning it held perhaps all the big fish from the pool. It was this run that first showed me what the Awakino could really do. It became, like Caleb Maslin's pool away down the side road, 'my' pool. If I never once managed to hook a fish in Caleb's pool – perhaps he had some secret method of fishing it; perhaps it was the crickets – I never failed to get fish in that run of my own. The first time I fished it I dropped a spinner into the current and six big fish – a sight such as I have never seen anywhere – raced simultaneously to snatch at it, like kahawai chasing herrings in the sea. I caught five trout, none under three pounds, that morning; and next day, with an inanga and with the broken scraps of inanga, caught three more. And thereafter, though I took care not to fish it too often, I got at least one good fish every time I visited it.

And after the inanga, the spinner, and the cockabully, there was, in the end, the dry fly.

For a long time we believed that it would be impossible to hold the big fighting rainbows of the

Awakino with the frail 3X cast necessary for dry-fly fishing. But then one day away up the side road, somewhere in the rocky gorge, we came upon a man standing silent and motionless in the scrub. His name was Mr Kneebone; and he was a plumber, or was it an electrician?, from Stratford. In the clear round pool below him, their great shapes manifesting themselves as they turned in the filtered sunlight over the gravel, swam four huge trout. 'Watch!' said Mr Kneebone. He was fishing with yards and yards of the finest gut imaginable, a cast which he made up for himself; and it was frailer than 3X even, it was 4X, as light and fragile and intangible as a strand of spider web. His fly was the Royal Coachman. 'Watch!' he said, flicking the Coachman straight above his head among the bushes to float down through the air and land lightly as a water-fly precisely a foot upstream from his chosen rainbow. And the fish rose and took it! The cast, alas, instantly snapped. Mr Kneebone did not convert us to 4X gut. But how like a fisherman he looked, standing there lean and brown and smiling in his chest-high canvas waders and, from the shelter of the green scrub, casting his fly so adroitly to the visible fish! We felt ashamed of our heavy gear and our crude, if effective methods. Tramping the river all day, casting blindly with the spinner, with very little chance of losing your fish once you have hooked him, didn't seem fishing at all compared with this delicate artistry.

The next season, fishing with the dry fly, I learned one very curious thing; and that was that the eels in the Awakino rose with the trout in the dusk to feed on insects on the surface. I had never known them to do it anywhere else, and, though it would seem natural enough, I should have thought they would be too sluggish a tribe to snap at flies. But in the big still pools downstream from the bridge, near rocks or against the high clay banks, you would hear a sound of *choff choff*. That was the eels eating moths. It imparted a strange, sinister quality to the dusk. We could hardly believe it was happening, but one night Fin Maslin caught one on a fly, and proved it.

Then there was the trout that taught me how shallow a piece of water can hold a large fish, how nearly on dry land a fish will feed. It was in the late afternoon, on the bank of shingle below the camp, and a fish rose in about four inches of water, about five or six inches from the shore. I thought he was a tiddler and cast a fly to him more for practice than with any intention of hooking him; I wanted to see if I could cast straight along the edge of the water without landing the fly on the stones. I managed to do it; the fish snapped up the fly, manifested himself as a two-pounder leaping in the rapid, and, with great promptitude, snapped the cast and was off.

And then there was the trout, not far upstream from my favourite run, in the country where the stream curved about the farmlands occupied by the Maoris, which taught me how short must be a fish's memory. He lay in a little whirlpool across the current at the head of a rapid, a private and isolated spot. I cast for him once, and missed him; cast again, hooked him, and, for quite a time, ten minutes or more, held him as he raced up and down the rapid or leapt clean out of the water. Then he broke free. Of course there was no chance of his taking a fly again immediately; normally, you would think you would have to come back next day, or two or three days later, if you wanted to have another go at him. But I fished upstream for half an hour and then came back to

him; the same difficult cast across the rapid into the same
whirlpool, and the same fish again took the fly, and I had
him. He was a big fellow, too.

How beautiful a day that was! The trout were feeding everywhere, because the little green beetles, which
we called ladybirds, were swarming in the tea-tree
bushes and dropping into the water. The fly we were
using was the Peveril of the Peak which, despite its
black-and-white wings, has a green metallic body like a
Coch-y-bondhu, and the fish readily accepted it as a
beetle; much more readily, in fact, than they took to the
actual imitation of the ladybird, which also we tried out.
But I forget how many trout we caught. It did not really
matter. It was the fishing itself that was so beautiful; and
the river, and the warm sunny weather, and the solitude.
It was a day that brimmed full not so much with fish as
with the richness of New Zealand summer.

> *On russet floors by waters idle*
> *The pine lets fall her cone;*
> *The cuckoo shouts all day at nothing*
> *In leafy dells alone,*

said Housman. It was that sort of day; a day of skylarks
and warm-smelling hayfields; of ragwort and purple
clover and golden dandelions flowering on the grassy
banks visited by bumble-bees and the black-and-white
spotted butterflies; of dragonflies flashing on the stones
and locusts buzzing in the trees: of bird-music and
insect-music and water-music by the long green pools
and the sparkling rapids. Somewhere upstream near one
of the distant farmhouses an apple-tree must have been
hanging over the river, and all day long as we waded the
cool water under the willows, the ripe fruit came float-

ing down to us like the beetles floating to the trout.
Slowly revolving in the current, the apples looked queer
and planetary as they swam past us, like pale moons and
rosy suns in the green sky of the pools; it gave you a
curiously exotic feeling to take and eat them, dripping
with river-water and their own sweet juice. We had the
whole Awakino to ourselves, from the bridge right
round the two great curves through the Maoris' farmlands and on up to Caleb Maslin's pool in the gorge if
we cared to go so far; we had the whole shining countryside; and, fishing leisurely with the dry fly as we
waded among the apples and the green beetles, we had
the whole long summer day to taste it in.

But after all it was the spinner that, most seasons we
were there, really made the fishing on the Awakino for
us. And, though all right-minded men, myself included,
infinitely prefer the fly, there remains a lot to be said for
this scorned device.

The fact that the kind of spinner we used was
called the fly-spoon made it sound better for a start.
Sometimes it was copper-coloured; sometimes copper
and red, sometimes silver. We did best with the copper.
It varied in size from about an inch in length – about
the size of a teaspoon – to the half-inch size and down
to infinitesimal flakes of metal like fish-scales. The tiniest ones were hard to make spin, and we did better with
the inch-long spoon and best of all with the half-inch.
It floated through the air gently and, with only a single
hook, did not constantly catch bushes and the fisherman
as did the many-hooked artificial minnow which we
used on the streams around Eltham. It was so light and
so cunningly shaped that it began to turn of its own
accord the minute you dropped it into the stream; and,

pulled slowly across the pool, it would spin readily in the stillest waters. It was really quite a delicate little weapon, and to use it successfully required a satisfactory degree of expertise.

I don't know that you had necessarily to drop it quietly in the pools, though we tried to, for once I dropped a fly-spoon with a mighty accidental splash right on top of a trout I could see in clear water and instantly, annoyed with these small metal fish splashing from the sky, he turned and seized it. I don't know, either, that its use obliged you to conceal yourself from the fish's observation so cautiously as the fly seems to necessitate; for once, in that same stretch of water, I watched a trout, so avid was he to eat the metal lure, chase it right past my legs as I stood in midstream. And certainly the strong traces that we used were practically impossible for the fish to break: and once, yet again in that same memorable reach, when a four-pounder wrapped himself round a sunken branch I was able to reach down and unwrap him, by flipping him back over the branch with my hand, without the tackle breaking. Yet we practised care and concealment as in fly-fishing, and there was certainly a fine art in casting a spoon, which one learned to do with a backward flick of the wrist directly from the surface at one's feet out into the current again, to keep it almost continuously in the water and to avoid a back-cast into the scrub on the bank. You had to be accurate, too, for if you hit a stone in the water or a rock on the far bank, the point of the hook nearly always broke off. You could fish the spoon, too, simply by letting it float down a rapid with the current and then winding it in again – the trout would take it either on the downward journey or on the return – but that had certain disadvantages. When a fish took it downstream from you he would instantly dash up the rapid towards you, winning slack line from which he could shake himself free: I see Fin Maslin, short, stocky, dark-haired, dressed in an old black-and-white striped football jersey, perpetually dashing backwards at full speed over the stones so that his fish would not get slack line, and, naturally, falling headlong at regular intervals on the shingle or in the river. It was a heroic implement, the fly-spoon.

That was a most unexpectedly rewarding piece of water, that stretch of the Awakino where the trout chased the fly-spoon past my legs and where I unwrapped the other rainbow from the sunken branch. It teemed with fish. Far up past the huts of the Maoris, away round the second of the river's great curves near the beginning of the gorge, it was a long straight shallow reach of water, about four feet deep all over, between high banks of pasture and scrub. It was always mid-afternoon by the time we reached it, casting and re-casting all the way round the great curve and briefly pausing to lunch on our tin of pineapple, and, pretty though it looked with the sunlight striking through the gently-rippling current to lie in patches of gold on the sand and shingle at the bottom, it seemed of no interest at all for fishing. But the trout lay all along it – you could see them, big fellows wavering in the current or turning a silver side as they pushed the small stones about in search of the larvae of caddis-fly and stone-fly. We never failed to catch three or four good fish up there; and sometimes on the way home we would give a few to the Maoris whom we met in their kumara-fields.

The fly-spoon is 'not done', but I cannot be sorry that we did it – for the miles we walked with it, and for the wonderful fish we caught with it.

It gave me, once, the worst day's fishing I ever had in my life. That was the day Fin Maslin caught sixteen fish while I, winning at least in statistics, lost seventeen. I don't know *what* went wrong. With the fly, you can usually say pretty accurately why you are failing to catch fish. They are 'rising short', not really feeding but just coming up to have a look at your fly; or you are using the wrong fly; or they are not rising at all, the wind, the weather or the time of year is wrong; or, if they take it and you miss them, you are striking too soon or too late – and what agony it is trying to decide which of the two mistakes you are making! But with the fly-spoon you do not really have to use any skill in striking; the fish simply takes it with a rush, and either he is there, or he isn't. This day he certainly wasn't. There was no question of them rising short as, in a sense, they will sometimes do with the spinner, when, not hungry but resenting inter-lopers in their territory, they just knock the intruder aside with their noses. They were not, as once in Aus-tralia, in the Duckmaloi, I saw them, scorning the fly-spoon and, most curiously, trying to swallow the brass swivels on the trace. Dashing backwards over the stones or plunging down the rapids after them, Fin was catching them, one after another, all day; and so, momentarily, was I. They would seize it, they would leap, and they were gone. *What* could have been going wrong? Had I broken the point of the hook on a rock? Was the barb missing? No, for I checked it a hundred times. Was the hook out of shape somehow? No, it was not! Was I using a fly-spoon of the wrong colour? No; it was the same as Fin's; and anyhow they were taking it. Was there some imperceptible fault in the construction of the spoon, so that the leaf of metal got in the road of the hook? I suspected it. But when I changed to another spoon I lost my fish just the same. Had I forgotten how to fish? Had I lost the art? Was I simply no good at fishing? Most grievously I suspected it. All the long beautiful sunny water, round the first great curve and round the second up to the never-failing shallow, and Fin with sixteen great shining three-pound and four-pound rainbows bulging his bag to the brim, hanging in bunches from the buckles of it and parked in shady shallows to be picked up on the way home, and myself with not one fish. Ichabod! There was no good reason for it. It was inexplicable. It happens.

But then it happened one other time in reverse; when, setting out with George Palmer up the pool in the limestone rocks and on to the far country, I caught fifteen fine fat fish while poor George lost I forget how many – eleven, I think – and caught none. And that, though I wished George could have had his proper share of it, was the greatest day's trout fishing I ever had. I could do nothing wrong. Throw in the fly-spoon anywhere, anyhow, and instantly it was snatched up; every time, without faltering or failure, the fish finished up shining in the net. In one of the pools I even caught George Palmer: we were crossing waist-deep through a rapid over a bottom of slippery blue clay and George, having slipped, came floating tranquilly by me towards the deep pool below, his waders rapidly filling to the point where they would drag him under. Considering the sort of day he had been having, I didn't think he was particularly grateful to me for stretching out a hand to him. But George was a true sportsman. I was so confident of catching a fish anywhere that day that on the way home I dropped the fly-spoon into a completely unfishable piece of water in a tangle of logs at the head of a pool and said, 'I'll get a fish out of there, George.' I did, instantly; a very large one which dived down to the bottom and tangled itself around the logs. George had given up fishing by that time; but without hesitation, without even being asked, he plunged head-first into that forest of sunken timber and disappeared underwater. Bubbles and strange convulsions of the logs marked his progress. He was heaving the timber about to disentangle my line; and did, too; and that fish, too, I landed.

Once, from that same camp up the side road, on the grassy slope by the pool where George Carter had hooked his five fish without moving, we caught so many trout that we decided, instead of sharing them with rats, fat boys, the Maoris, and the neighbouring farmers, to smoke them and so carry them home in triumph to Eltham. The Maslins had brought back boxes of the most delectable smoked trout one time after they had been to Taupo; and we would do likewise. But the Maslins had had bags of sawdust, which you must have to make a steady and voluminous supply of smoke. The Maslins had had the use of a hut with a large open fireplace, in the chimney of which was a proper rack on which the fish could repose. The Maslins had had – at least I hope so – wire mesh or muslin to make a screen to keep the blowflies away when, before smoking, the trout were drying in the sun. We had none of these things; and if anything ever epitomized the splendour and squalor of adolescence, it was the smoking of those trout. The splendour was in the trout, dozens of them; the squalor was in the blowflies, millions of them. We split open those trout, rubbed salt into them, and spread them to dry in the sun. The blowflies, naturally enough, thought we had spread them out for the blowflies. They came buzzing down from Thoresen's and the Maori flats, buzzing up from the store, buzzing over the road from the cowsheds; they swarmed all over our trout, and we fought them off with switches of tea-tree. Some we slew; many we discomforted; a few slipped past our defences. At the end of the day's drying we carefully scraped off from the trout any evidence of the invaders. The next morning we scraped off some more; the evidence was a bit livelier by that time.

We cut a fireplace and a sort of channel for a chimney in a clay bank behind the tent. We hammered into it a rack made out of sticks. We cut ourselves great stacks of green tea-tree and dipped it in the river to make it burn more slowly and more smokily. It burned all right. It leaped up in a blaze from time to time and scorched the trout and cooked the clay in which we had pegged the rack. The clay crumbled, the rack and all the trout fell into the fire. Never mind. We rescued the trout, we doused the fire, we rebuilt the rack, we re-lit the fire, and smoking recommenced. All day long in the summer heat, blinded by smoke, roasted by the flames, piling green tea-tree onto the furnace, we watched and tended those trout. So did the blowflies. They must have been salamanders, those blowflies; or they were desperate with the fervor of creation. They flew into the smoke and the flame like firemen saving lives in a burning building, and we took it in turns to sit on top of the chimney and beat them away with branches. We must have been just about as smoked ourselves as the trout were by the end of the day; but in the end it was done. Proudly, having removed the latest immature evidence of the blowflies, we packed those trout in a box with bracken and fragrant mint. Proudly we drove them over Mount Messenger and through the Mimi valley, past Waitara and Lepperton, Inglewood and Stratford, to

Eltham. Proudly, having sneaked them into the wash-house to remove the last of the considerably more mature evidence, we displayed them to our families; and proudly, at last, relating to the company only so much of their history as was proper for them to hear, we ate them. With parsley sauce. They were superb. They were three-pound and four-pound rainbow trout. Their colour was bronze; their flesh was flaky and delicate. They tasted of salt, smoke, tea-tree, and the waters of the Awakino.

7

NORTH TO KAWHIA

ANYONE'S career in sea-fishing should properly begin with tiddlers in rock-pools, and I don't think Seymour Haden and I should really have caught those monsters off the jetty at Opunake. But we did; and even if we were only rather ingloriously holding our fathers' lines while these gentlemen snoozed or yarned at ease on that rickety platform through the interstices of which you could see the green waves blundering like whales against the piles, catch them we did, and it was one of the great triumphs of boyhood.

My father wouldn't even believe me when I said there was something on his line. Small boys always have something on the line. But here was this fish pulling out in the sea like a horse; and a tremendous fish it was, too, when my father eventually stirred himself to listen to my pleas and ('By Jove, he *has* got a fish!') hauled it in for me. It was a great big blue thing, like a blue snapper, ten or twelve pounds in weight, and a rare thing, too, a moki, a kind of fish which perhaps grows only in New Zealand, and which I have never seen since. And then Seymour got his rosy, shining big snapper; and so, leaving our sires to do a bit of fishing themselves from the jetty, which they now began to do with some eagerness, home we went in glory to our cottages with the moki and the snapper trailing half-way down our backs.

But we began, all the same, in the rock-pools; in waters appropriate to our size and with fish no less appropriate. With a tiny herring-hook we fished for cockabullies which dashed at the piece of limpet or periwinkle we used for bait and worried it with absurd ferocity, like infinitesimal bulldogs. We caught with our hands inch-long translucent shrimps and carried them home no less triumphantly than the moki to be boiled on the stove in the cottage until they turned pink and provided their exotic morsel of nourishment. We speared the green crabs that lurked with folded purple nippers in every crevice. With a recklessness that still sends a shudder down my spine we ran full tilt leaping from rock to rock along the tumbled mass of boulders on the left of the bay to fish for paikere in the enormous rock-pool around the point where, in the clear green water full of brown seaweed and darting shoals of small-fry, we always hoped that really big fish, snapper or trevalli, might have been stranded; and where, so legend ran, a pair of lovers, seeking privacy on the pebbly beach against the cliff, had been trapped by the tide and drowned. You could not linger long at the rock-pool or you would have been cut off; but sometimes we raced on past it, right round the headlands to the mouth of the Waiau, where the Maoris fished for kahawai with a white feather tied to the naked hook – quite a sufficient lure for these voracious fish – and so, after catching a herring or two ourselves, came safely home over the clifftops by paths of sand through the lupins.

The usual place for herring, though, was the Tail Race. This was a most curious piece of water. It was a small artificial river created by the electricity people who had diverted it from the Waiau to make power and light when it fell down the cliff to the powerhouse in the bay; and when it had done its duty they let it free again to well out from a concrete culvert and race out to sea in a channel they had made for it against the line of the rocks. It was made for ever memorable to me not so much for the herring we caught, though these bony little fish were at least better to eat than the tasteless paikere, as for the spectacle of Mr Haden, sitting there day after day with his billy of ground-bait on the concrete platform where the Tail Race met the tide.

Mr Haden was one of those figures who, to the eye of youth, loom gigantic and mysterious. He was a big man, with a bushy gingery moustache. He was a slow and methodical man and, being the manager of the Bank of New South Wales at Eltham, used every afternoon at the same hour to emerge from his bank and, seriously, slowly, and methodically, take his red Irish setter for a walk around the block. He was a gentlemanly, impressive man, who always wore good English tweeds and had distinguished connections abroad, for he was related, or his wife was, to Rajah Brooke of Sarawak, and he had some sort of County relatives in England. But what chiefly impressed me about him at Opunake was the infinite methodical care with which, mixing pollard and bread and mincemeat and I know not what other mystic ingredients, he prepared each day his billy of ground-bait; and the patience with which, having prepared it and made his stately progress to the Tail Race, he sat down and fished. It looked so scientific an approach to the art of fishing; it promised such spectacular results. The idea was that with the ground-bait you would catch herring; with herring, in the same tumbling waters of the Tail Race, you would catch a kahawai; and with the kahawai, cutting it up for bait and transporting yourself either to the ricketty old wharf or the still more perilous jetty straddling beside it over the rocks that had been tumbled into the ocean to make a breakwater, you would catch a snapper.

And day after day, methodically amidst the ground-bait which he fed them in delicate spoonsful from his billy, Mr Haden did catch his supply of herring; and day after day, when he put a herring on for bait and threw out into the wilder waters near the Tail Race's mouth, he never did catch his kahawai. Why not, I cannot now imagine. Years later I fished for kahawai from the beach near the mouth of the Tail Race with a trout rod and a fly-spoon, and I hooked, and then lost, because the gear was too light for me to get them in quickly enough, kahawai after kahawai all afternoon. The fish were shoaling all round me, big steel-grey shapes in the waves; you couldn't help catching kahawai. And they must, you would think, have been there in other years at Opunake. Or maybe not. Maybe they preferred the Waiau, and it took them a long time to learn that the Tail Race existed and was worth a visit by a kahawai hungry for a herring. Mr Haden, at any rate, fished for them ...

Opunake, the quiet green bay in its semicircle of tall dark cliffs, twenty-four miles from Eltham round the wooded flanks and towering white cone of Mount Egmont, was the great place for seaside holidays when we were children. From that delectable weatherboard cottage with its serried bunks of sacking which we rented from Mr Arthur, the storekeeper at Ngaere, and under which, fascinatingly, the sea at spring tides came licking with its long white tongues, we saw many wonderful things. In the swamp behind the cottage I saw a sudden spirt of water and, plunging in my hand, brought up, simultaneously, two green frogs. In one of the rocks beside the Tail Race we saw, deeply embedded, a shaft of iron; and we could not imagine how it had been hammered into that hard rock, or who had hammered it, or why.

One day we saw a poor silly drunken man strip himself naked and go swimming in the Tail Race and later, when he was brought ashore drowned, we saw, through a gap in the throng, his strange hairy white leg. 'He's doing fine, boys,' said Mr Graham when we asked was he dead; but that, as we knew at the time, was a kindly lie; and Mr Graham himself, a lean dark-haired man with a brown and purple face that looked like burnt iron, was not long afterwards, back in Eltham, to provide a much larger tragic drama for, detected in some sort of peculation, he cut his throat with a razor ... 'With the carving knife,' so Ian Wylds broke the news to me at choir practice one night, 'I suppose he was just cutting a slice of bread when he up with it and ... ' so, with Mr Graham's ghost pounding behind me, all the way home down Mills Street and dark Meuli Street I fled, and into the house, and through the dining-room and the kitchen, and never stopped until, for some unaccountable reason, I found sanctuary in the furthest corner of the bathroom ...

And we saw, when we went to Middleton's Bay, round the point at the right-hand side of Opunake, past the wharf and the breakwater, a fishing boat, caught broadside on by a wave far out in the open sea, suddenly vanish; and heard, from the empty dazzle of sunlight, slow terrible hoarse cries as the fishermen shouted in unison for help. We saw the boat going bravely out to rescue them, and bringing them back safely through the surf to the black sand. And we saw, not less dramatic in its own way, but much more diverting, Mrs Annie Kegsworth in a bathing costume ... tall, willowy Mrs Kegsworth, who used to sing 'Humpty Dumpty' when the Glee Club met in our drawing-room at Eltham – '*Hoompty Doompty sat on the wall*' – now in a striped neck-to-ankle bathing costume, like a convict's uniform, except that it had a skirt. And we saw the first lady we ever had known to wear the new daring one-piece cotton bathing costume, showing, as she sun-baked on her back in the sand, protuberances that we never had known to exist ...

Yes, many wonderful things; with the blue water far out and the deep green around the cliffs; and the wide stretching freedom of the sands; and the cool water to swim in, always safe except for the day when the big tide dug hollows in the sand and Peachy Haden found himself out of his depth, and Seymour, with two swift purposeful strokes, took off and brought him in again; and the rock-pools with their seaweed and sea-anemones and periwinkles with their green front-doors, called 'catseyes'; and the smell and the sight and the sound and the whole glittering magic of the sea ... But as for fish!

Maybe Mr Haden did once catch a kahawai, but if so I never heard of it. Maybe someone on the wharf or the jetty did sometimes pull up a blue cod, or a crayfish unexpectedly clinging to the bait, but as far as I know that snapper and that moki which two small boys hooked on their fathers' lines one never-to-be-forgotten day were the only respectable fish ever caught at Opunake.

The grim truth was, there was really no good snapper-fishing in our part of Taranaki, the southern fringes of the province. Maybe it was too cold for them. Maybe there weren't the reefs of mussels or the banks of cockles or pipis to bring them close enough inshore.

There were no fish, not really, at Pihama when we drove in, excitingly, over the green paddocks of the dairy farms to that wild rough rocky bay a few miles south of Opunake where, it was rumoured, you could catch snapper. There were no snapper. Just once, memorably, the day a wave washed over him and he took off his wet trousers, Fred Vincent, standing awe-inspiringly on a rock in the midst of the surge with his shirt-tail flying round his hairy legs and unmentionables, brought in a thing called a butterfish.

There were no fish, not really, at New Plymouth, where in five years of fishing when we were let loose from jail, meaning boarding-school, in the weekends, the most notable event was the time I made myself a tanekaha rod and tried it out off the Breakwater … that long concrete esplanade that thrust itself out into the turbulence of the seas smashing against the Sugarloaf behind it; a place you could fish only in fine weather, for in storms the Breakwater itself was under the white foam. I cannot think now what extraordinary inspiration made me embark on so exalted a feat of carpentering as the making of a tanekaha rod. I must have been under the influence of Cully MacDiarmid, who had some capability with his hands. Tanekaha, so we believed, was the toughest wood that grew in the New Zealand bush, the timber from which swordfish rods were made. So, deep into the bush somewhere out Opunake way, we plunged with our headmaster, Bill Moyes, who was also going to make himself a tanekaha rod; and selected our slender tough saplings of tanekaha; and trimmed off the leaves; and brought them back to the school woodwork room, and planed them, and soaked them in linseed oil; and bound them; and hung them up by the tips to straighten and mature; and bathed them again in oil; and put guide-rings on them, and the clamps for the reel; and varnished them; and so, after weeks of devotion, off to the Breakwater with them. And, at the very first cast, mine snapped in half. So much for tanekaha.

And so much, really, for New Plymouth; except for one other foolish occasion when I tied the end of my line round a railway line on the Breakwater and there-upon, when next I threw out, after a train had passed over it, tossed the lot of it into the ocean; and one day of slightly disreputable success when, having been told about oil of aniseed as a lure, I anointed my bait with that deplorable substance and, to our mutual surprise, caught a gurnard with it. How curious and beautiful a fish is the gurnard, as, with rose-pink body, spreading his purple wings like a butterfly, he comes up out of the depths and then, on dry land, begins to walk on his totally unexpected legs. I could have counted him as a very fine capture indeed; but I never could persuade myself that a fish caught with aniseed really counted at all.

There were plenty of fish, in fact teeming millions of fish, at Waitara, ten miles north of New Plymouth, which also we fished from boarding-school; but these I pass over with a shudder. They were herring. Great big fat herring, as big as a trout; up to about a pound in weight. Nasty big oily herring that turned limp and melted when you carried them home in a sugar-bag; herring that even schoolboys couldn't eat more than once in a lifetime unless, as did my friend Ralph Clay-ton, whose parents came from Grimsby in England, you knew how to pickle them. We caught them behind the freezing works where the blood-chute ran out into the awful Waitara River. They were so plentiful that the locals didn't bother to use a rod or line but simply tossed out into the seething mass of them a huge three-pronged jag, made of sharpened fencing wire, and pulled in a herring on each point. 'You boys,' said the clergy-man with the English accent, 'at least you are sportsmen; you fish for them with rods ... ' and turned away from the appalling scene and went off to the wharf and dis-mally caught a kahawai. We would have received his commendation with a better conscience if we had not at that moment been so ardently wishing we had jags, so that we too could have caught those horrible herring three at a time.

Inexplicably, for now we began to go north, and north of Taranaki there was some real fishing in the sea, there were no fish at Mokau; or not in the year we fished it, when we stayed at Mrs Box's boarding-house and when my father, poor fellow, got such an attack of asthma or hay-fever from the lupins in flower all round us that he could hardly do the walk to the river. I think the river was our mistake. It was tempting to fish in; it was much easier than climbing down cliffs and fishing from per-ilous ledges. But you don't catch snapper in a river. Just herring and paikere round the Flowerpot; and the hope, never fulfilled, of a kahawai. One night, and one night only, when we lit a huge bonfire of driftwood, some-thing strange came into the river ... huge mysterious fish that, while shadows and flame flickered over the black water, seized the bait and swam on powerfully and uncontrollably till they broke or cut the lines, so that we never knew what they were ... sharks, most likely.

But, if fish were few, and they were still scarce in
the Mokau when once we made a heroic one-day expedition from Eltham, and ate pickled pork in the rain for
breakfast under the dripping green scrub by the roadside, and Billy Hill, my father's partner in the law, caught
a solitary trevalli – if fish were few, that river had some
notable adventures to offer by way of compensation.

'That's the way we do it up the Mokau!' cried Mr
Christianson. Mr Christianson was not a fisherman; but
he was big and brawny and powerful as a shark, and he
had a coalmine away up the Mokau River and, with our
friends the Carters, who were camping near by at
Rapanui, we were going to inspect it. 'That's the way we
do it up the Mokau,' heartily roared the giant; and, driving his launch, with all our camping gear piled on the
deck, under the overhanging branches of the trees, swept
into the water the box containing all Mrs Carter's cut-
lery, with her best silver teapot on top of it.

So, reduced to one terrible episode, and a phrase
which became a family catchword, Mr Christianson
remains in memory. He was, I think, a grocer at Eltham,
and what he was doing with a coalmine up the Mokau
I don't know. I shouldn't think he could have done very
much with it, for there was no rail transport within a
hundred miles, and the ships, if any, that got into the
Mokau River were few and far between. Perhaps he just
liked having it. And certainly, when he saw it, somehow
having smothered the episode of the teapot in Mr
Christianson's assurance that he would go back some
day and dive for it, for that's the way we did it up the
Mokau, it was a most fascinating coalmine. It was far in
the deep bush, the dark-green wilderness of tree-ferns
and supplejacks where wild pigs and cattle roved; and
when you got to it, tramping up the sleepers of the

tramway through the forest made sweet and rich with the calls of the tuis, there was no ugly great hole in the ground, no sign of industrial devastation, but a little crystalline bush creek tumbled down in waterfalls and runnels over a bed of pure black coal.

So. There is always more to fishing than merely catching fish. And, if Mokau itself gave us no more than that, all around that noble coastline, as beach by beach we made our way north from Taranaki to the fantastic waters of Kawhia, we did indeed catch snapper.

At Pukearuhe, led by an intrepid one-legged henchman of my father's named Charlie Cooper, whose wooden leg was perhaps useful to him as a peg, we lowered ourselves down the white clay cliffs by a rope and waded out to rocks which could be fished only at low tide; and there caught snapper; and, in the making tide, swam and waded back to the beach and, in the dusk, caught small blue sharks which we grilled over a drift-wood bonfire and found very pleasant, a bit strong-tasting, but not too strong, like kahawai or trevalli.

At Urenui we dipped our nets of cheese-cloth into the river-mouth and filled a kerosene tin – or it may only have been the fire-blackened picnic billy – with the shining small translucent whitebait which tasted of so rare a sweet fishiness in fritters, and which the Maoris, when we were very young and that noble race had not yet progressed into civilization, brought round from door to door in their kit-bags of the native flax.

At Uruti, climbing through the fence at the precise spot known to fishermen and walking across the green paddocks full of clover and daisies and dandelions, we crouched on a sloping ledge half-way down the cliff above the sea, and tried, with necessary prudence, to sink ourselves into its bare rocky surface when Fred Vincent cried 'Heads!' and whirled his heavy cord line with its horse-shoe sinker around his head and banged the horse-shoe off against the rocks and bombed us with it; and, in the intervals of the cannonade, heaved our own lines out to the exact position where the snapper fed on the reef of mussels far out and far down in the green water … though never did we learn to throw with quite such beautiful precision as did the one-armed boy who came down at dusk from the farmhouse and, in half an hour, had seven beautiful snapper in his sugar-bag, one of which, to our extreme embarrassment, a member of our party, who had fished all day in vain, sneaked from the bag while the boy was busy with his fishing. It was on that same day at Uruti, when my father lay snoozing on the rock with his line idle in his hand as low tide laid bare the weedy rocks where the snapper fed, and skylarks from the hayfields behind us rose up and sang over the sea, that I sneaked between him and the cliff-edge and gave his line a mighty tug; whereupon my father, never a swearing man, but thinking he had hooked the most enormous snapper in history, said 'Jesus!' …

At Rapanui, camping beside the wild little creek with the Carters, we caught herring at high tide from the door of the tent; we wandered the hot green hills where the karaka berries grew and the shining cuckoo called in the flowering gorse; we caught snapper from the rock and, most excitingly of all, we waded and swam with a net through the swift channel and sudden potholes of the Mohakatina River, and brought the net ashore bulging and flapping with flounder.

And at Kawhia at last – never, anywhere on earth, was there such a place for fish as Kawhia.

It was a place of far and high adventure, for it lay miles to the northward, past all the beaches we had known, nearly two hundred miles, and you could not go there for a day or a weekend or even a week but must pack up and prepare food and bedding and bait and fishing gear for the whole glorious six weeks of a proper summer holiday.

For days beforehand there was the thrill of stretching new lines in the backyard; of catching and salting down eels for bait; of visiting Bill Bracher, the blacksmith, to collect a sugar-bag of horse-shoes for sinkers, helping ourselves from the pile outside the smithy, while, in the cavernous darkness of the interior, the big farm-horses stamped and snorted and the blacksmith in his leather apron drew the golden glowing red-hot shoes out of the fire with his long iron tongs and banged them in showers of sparks on the anvil or plunged them hissing and blackening into his tub of water.

For a whole day before we left my father meticulously packed, from floor to roof, from the wide running-boards to the luggage-carrier at the back, our old open cream-painted Buick with the silver lion on the radiator – the car which we had bought from Mick M'Garry the land agent, and which was a status-symbol of the highest magnitude. Then the whole of the next day we drove; past Waitara and Urenui; through the arched tunnel on Mount Messenger; past Rapanui and the Mohakatina and Mokau; past the Awakino; past Te Kuiti and the Waitomo Caves where once my father made family history by saying, in a loud clear voice just when the guide had told everyone to be quiet or the glow-worms would put their lights out, 'Of course I've been here before, y'know!' (how the young do treasure the lapses of their resplendent elders!); and on, grinding and whining twenty-two miles in second gear through the dark green mountains of Marokopa; until at last, as you crept down the final steep to the sea, shining lay Kawhia before us.

As we drove down to it, to unload all our gear on to old Shultz's launch that would take us across to the headland at Te Maika where our cottage nestled among the sand-dunes and the tea-tree, that mighty gleaming harbour, brimming with the high tide and the yellow light of evening, looked to be full of fish; and so indeed it was. They leapt out of the water to meet us.

And if these lovely big leaping and splashing creatures, white bellied and dark on the back, were merely mullet, a harbour-full of mullet was far from 'mere' to those who, inland at Eltham or fishing the wild ocean from the rocks and rock-ledges of the Taranaki coast, had never seen anything like it. They were fish! Moreover, though we knew they would not take a bait in the normal way, possibly they could be caught. They haunted and tantalized us. Sometimes we netted them for bait; and ate them, too, and relished their strong oily flavour; but that, however pleasant it was to drag a net through the long shallows of the mudflats, was not quite fishing. Maurice FitzGerald, who often joined us on these Kawhia expeditions, and brought us salted trout for snapper bait, speculated as to whether or not, since they leapt like trout, they would take a small white trout fly, a Coachman. They would not. I myself speculated, being at a barbarous age, whether one could shoot them on the wing, as it were, while they leapt. One could not. They never leapt when or where you expected them to. We did not really do very well with the mullet. For some reason which I cannot now understand, for surely we had heard about it, it never occurred to us to try out the one simple method by which they might have been caught: to fish for them with a float and a bait of dough or the soft inside of a loaf of bread – mixed, for preference, to hold it on the hook, with a little cotton-wool. Every fishing place has its own local customs; and fishing for mullet with dough was not one of the customs of Kawhia.

The presence of mullet, of course, proved nothing. All quiet enclosed waters are likely to be teeming with mullet. But Kawhia more than fulfilled the promise they seemed to make. It teemed with all kinds of fish, in all directions. It even, in the soak behind the cottage from which we drew some of our water-supply, teemed with frogs; and these, if hardly prey for fishermen, provided endless entertainment for a diminutive Scotch terrier named Judy who accompanied my almost equally diminutive aunt Eileen FitzGerald, Maurice's and my mother's sister, on occasions when she joined the party. All night long with shrill cries of excitement Judy pursued them, while the frogs, even more shrilly, protested. But all night long, too, the sea beyond the sandhills uttered in a continual low roaring its promise of fish.

There were the herrings, small fry indeed, but exciting enough to hook with a light trout rod, which we caught for bait on the harbourside beach by the jetty. They were not considered very good bait for snapper, though we found that, perhaps because the eyes made it more visible and enticing, the head of a herring would sometimes do the trick; but they were the natural and ideal bait for kahawai, those lean swift fighting-mackerel-like fish that sometimes swarmed into the harbour to feast on them; and so there were the kahawai, too, to fish for. They were either there by the thousand or they

were not there at all; but my father, a patient man, seated
on the rocks round the corner from the jetty, with a rod
and a floating herring for bait, at the spot where my
mother had once caught a twelve-pound snapper and
where you could cast into the swift tide-race running
out to the open sea, fished for them all day in the sun
whether they were there or not; and sometimes, with
immense excitement, caught one. A fine fish it would
be, too, four pounds or more, and excellent bait for
snapper, though we liked to eat them, too. Fresh from
the sea and fried crisp brown and white, the kahawai
was no more to be despised than the mullet.

Maybe the finest for eating of all the fish we caught
at Kawhia were the flounder; and very pleasant and
eerie and romantic it was to go spearing them by night
over the wide shallow mudflats by the light of a carbide
bicycle-lamp, peering into the grey and golden water
until at last you saw that flat, sandy-grey shape on the
bottom which looked so like a flounder and, while you
were pondering this extraordinary resemblance, suddenly was a flounder and, unless you woke up in time to
spear it, skittered away from you into the surrounding
darkness. It always seemed an uncanny form of fishing.
There was the chance, though I never knew it happen,
of treading on a stingaree. There seemed to be a possibility, when you had waded so far out that the shoreline
was lost and there was nothing around you but night
and water and stars, that you would wade on in the
wrong direction and find yourself swimming across the
harbour to nowhere. There was always, much more
probably, the chance that you would spear your own
bare foot, an accident which was known to happen, for,
flat and finny in the unsteady light of the bike-lamp,
your foot kept manifesting itself like a flounder just

ahead of you, so that you could hardly resist having a prod at it.

But the fish that we really wanted, whether for eating or for fishing, when we went to Kawhia, was the snapper: the horny-headed, the gleaming-scaled, the red-gold glowing, the flapping imperial snapper, power-ful in the sea and resplendent as King Neptune himself when you hauled him up the Beacon rock! And just as it teemed with the mullet and the herring and the flounder and the kahawai when they were there, so Kawhia teemed with snapper.

Once there I saw an eighteen-pounder, a great grey ugly sandy-coloured harbour-dwelling monster that somebody caught with a night-line off the jetty. Once, away round the coast where the sea-eagles had their nest on top of a big flat rock, I saw fifteen mighty snapper, none less than ten or twelve pounds in weight, pass by me in rosy procession in a narrow green channel between a rock and the weedy shoreline. I could almost have caught them with my hands; and didn't have a line to throw to them ... Once we went out in old Shultz's launch – I forget for what purpose; maybe to go over to Kawhia township and see where the canoe in which the Maoris first landed from Polynesia lay buried among the tea-tree – and got ourselves stuck on a sandbank, and, just because we were stuck, threw out a line, and instantly caught a snapper, and another, and another, and filled the boat up with them. Once, when dawn lit the waters like a field of daffodils, I went out with Shultz and my father to shoot the godwits as they came in to forage on the harbour sandbanks at low tide; and, when Shultz's boy had rowed us to a sandbank and gone back to the launch with the dinghy we dug ourselves shallow hiding places among the wet cockles, and lay down in them; and, though nobody except Shultz got a godwit, saw a superb great snapper, fins erect and wide tail slowly waving, ruffling among the shellfish beside us. There was a dogfish, too, nosing about us that day, and though the dogfish is a relatively small and benevolent kind of shark, suddenly Schultz's launch began to seem very far away from us; while the shark, as the tide rose, seemed close.

Kawhia was, in fact, sometimes an unexpectedly dangerous place. 'Row, row, row the boat,' sang Maurice FitzGerald in his fleabag in his tent at night:

> *Row, row, row the boat*
> *Gently down the stream,*
> *Merrily, merrily, merrily, merrily,*
> *Life is but a dream …*

And row, row, row the boat he did indeed, with Pierce de Launay, the plumber, one day when we were going to take a dinghy round and fish off the Beacon at slack water. Kawhia, in a purely watery sense, was a very busy harbour. It had an extremely narrow mouth. And when the tide was not pouring into that narrow mouth, it was pouring out again; with great enthusiasm and velocity. Far out at sea, past the headland on which stood the Beacon, but not so far that you could not see the waves standing up and crashing on it, lay the bar. No boat could pass the bar at low water. Naturally, then, when one rowed round from the beautifully calm waters of the harbour to fish the outlet at the Beacon, one went only at dead low tide. If you went when the tide was racing in, it would sweep you back up the harbour, which perhaps wouldn't matter very much; if you went when the tide happened to be racing out, it would sweep you out to the bar, which would matter a great deal.

Somebody must have blundered that day. Somebody's watch was just about half an hour wrong. Down to the Beacon we rowed, not particularly aware of the help we were receiving from the tide; calmly, nice and close to the Beacon, we threw out the anchor. And moved. A little out to sea. And moved more rapidly; quite a lot further out to sea. We could see our friends and relatives fishing on the Beacon, on that secure, sublime solid rock. They receded from us. The Beacon receded. The bar, so to speak, approached us. Or we approached the bar. The waves towered up green on it and crashed down white. And still that damned anchor wouldn't hold. The shore, the Beacon, looked impossibly far away from us now. I restrained an impulse to jump overboard, but took off my shoes with the idea that that would make swimming more successful. 'Ease her to the side a bit, Pierce,' said Maurice calmly; 'we'll ease round into the bay and come back when the tide stops running.' So, at the last moment before we reached the bar, or, say, five minutes before we reached it, we did just that; and in the bay, caught a snapper or two; and so, when it was possible, back to the Beacon, where we caught more. Maurice, always a soldierly looking person with his crisp English military voice and his crisp ginger military moustache, had fought in the Boer War and in World War I. Perhaps that was why, years afterwards when I asked him if he remembered that day at the Beacon, he had forgotten all about it. It hadn't impressed him at all. It impressed me considerably.

Sometimes we fished this most perilous spot more sensibly in Shultz's launch, which had a nice large anchor that would hold against the tide, and an engine to get you out of bother if it didn't. Sometimes, with Shultz in command, at high tide when the waves no longer broke on the bar but reared up on it in towering green walls over which you climbed for a few minutes of the most wonderful alarm, we went right out to sea through the heads and far along the wild uninhabited coast and there, at some point in the ocean which only Schultz and the snapper could recognize, had tremendous fishing. I remember one day there with peculiar affection, for it instilled in me a lifelong reverence for beer: one glass of it, gulped down in desperation, put an end to a very nasty malaise that, what with the rolling of the boat in the broad blue swells, and what with the sickly sweet musty smell of the sharks we had been catching, had been most horribly creeping upon me. When desperate, take beer ... And the fish we caught that day! If we were not hauling in gigantic snapper, we were trying to haul in four-foot and five-foot sharks which pulled like demons and swept along the side of the boat and tangled up everybody's lines, and came up over the side plunging and biting and wrapped round with yards and yards of cord. In the launch they bit lines and feet; in the water they bit our snapper in halves. One, which we disembowelled because we were going to use it for bait, had swallowed the entire head and bony carcass of a kahawai which somebody had tossed overboard. In the end so many of them swarmed around us, biting the snapper off our lines as we hooked them, that we had to abandon the fishing ground to them; but came home nevertheless, over the green turbulence of the bar, with a boatload of fish to be scaled as we chugged through the quiet evening to the jetty.

What on earth did we do with so many snapper? We could always give a few to other campers, if there

were any. We could give a couple to Mrs Gibbons, the
Maori princess who owned the cottage we rented and
who, on ceremonial occasions, could be persuaded to
sing old Maori songs to us in her peculiar high cracked
voice. But mostly we just ate them. I see us all somehow
strewn about that tiny cottage – my father, genial and at
ease as he always was at the beach, my brother Neil, my
sisters Jean and Helen and Shirley, with Maurice and
Eileen FitzGerald and any stray friends who happened
to be staying with us – while, like a goddess half-way
between heaven and hell, moving from roaring red stove
to hissing primus, with a huge frying pan sizzling on
each of them, my tall laughing blue-eyed mother fed us
incessantly with fish. She must sometimes have had a
moment or two away from the stove, for she swam, and
I remember her one day catching two snapper at once
off the point where my father caught kahawai; and one
year at least we brought with us, to help her, our strange
stoop-shouldered housemaid Molly Templeton, who
had a phenomenal catarrhal snort and who afterward
married a cross-eyed greengrocer; but when one thinks
back on the load my mother carried so gaily, cooking
for all those people … I am abashed. I hope that at least,
and I think we did, we dried the dishes. Certainly we
did gather the driftwood for the stove; and a very pleasant excursion that used to be, over the sandhills to the
ocean beach round the headland from the Beacon, and
back to the cottage with armfuls of the beautiful white
wave-worn timber, sometimes riddled with the tiny
holes of seaworms or frilled with barnacles' frail white
shells.

Going out with old Schultz in his launch was the way
to get vast quantities of snapper. Boat-fishing is always

the best, anywhere. But it is too easy. Anybody can catch
fish from a boat.

The finest thing of all to do at Kawhia was simply
to stroll over and fish from the Beacon at dead low
water. The Beacon was a superb place to fish from. In
the first place, for we gave the name to the headland
rather than to the signal pole that stood on its crest, it
was in itself a noble piece of rock. Time and the
weather and the waves had eaten the green spur, where
it met the ocean at the mouth of the harbour, down to
its innermost core; and so, under the soft hills that rolled
away down the coast there lay, we learned, red volcanic
lava; and the hump of red stone, knobbly and full of
holes like burst bubbles, pushed out indomitably to
meet the sea, rooted in a platform of some older, still
harder rock that lay all round its base and sloped at
gentle angle into the water.

From that flat platform we fished. Limpets and
rock-barnacles crusted its sides. Lower, where there was
a narrow shelf at the sea's brim, crabs with green backs
and purple claws came out upon their business. Lower
still, where the mussels and periwinkles clung, red seaweed moved in the tide. No wave, at low water when
we fished, ever drove in menace against the Beacon or
burst in spray over the platform. The ocean wasted its
fury on the bar and came in gently, gently. Northward,
sparkling with white surf, lay the long beaches of black
and grey iron sand, the flat grey tea-tree country stretching behind them uninhabited for a hundred miles.
Southward, where the white cliffs of Pukearuhe glimmered like sails in the distance, lay the rocks where the
seabirds had their nest, and the green spurs where one
day, walking alone for miles along the cliffs, I saw a cock
pheasant, resplendent in crimson and gold, spring into

the air out of the bracken and light up the whole lonely countryside like a meteor. Behind us the harbour glimmered in the sunshine; and out to sea, away past the white thunder of the bar, a haze of rock called Gannet Island lay mysterious in the blue distance. No boat, unless old Schultz was fishing, ever marred the solitude of the harbour. No ships passed by at sea. When you fished from the Beacon you had the whole coast to yourself.

And if the fishing was safe – and to stand on that flat platform with its point jutting out to sea was like fishing from the deck of a battleship – nevertheless it was satisfactorily difficult. You needed a pleasing amount of local knowledge. There was a secret about the Beacon. There was a reef of mussels where the snapper came to feed.

It lay a long way out from the rock and it was completely submerged at low tide as at high, far down in the water but nevertheless known to be there; discovered, I suppose, by old Schultz when he anchored there in his launch, if not by the Maoris before him in their canoes. It needed a long throw from the Beacon with the cord handline and the horse-shoe sinker – my index finger got so cut one year with heaving out the line and hauling in snapper that I had to wear a finger-stall. And, to get just the right spot, at a certain angle from the very point of the platform, you had to throw accurately. You could not fish it at high tide, because the sea washed over the platform; it was no use trying while the tide was flowing or ebbing, because your sinker would not hold in the rush of the water through the heads. You fished just at dead low tide, and half an hour before and after it.

And in that brief hour of glory – to be repeated

twelve hours later when the tide dropped to low again – what fishing! I told George Palmer, who came to stay with us and who, from the cliff at Waverley, had been used to the same sort of grim Taranaki fishing that I had, that he would catch six snapper before breakfast on his first morning at Kawhia; and that is just what George did catch: six big snapper, glistening red and gold from the sea, ten- and twelve- and fourteen-pounders; such fish as had never before been seen, with a kahawai thrown in for good measure.

The day of all days was when the biggest of all the herring shoals came in in a solid mass from the sea, churning up the green waters of the harbour as if it was being lashed in the bright sunshine by hailstones; and, while the gannets plunged down from the sky like spears of snow to feed on the mass of them, and sharks with their black fins showing cruised in and out of the turmoil, after them, hardly less numerous than the her- rings, hunting them like packs of wolves, swarmed the ferocious kahawai. Forgetting breakfast, ignoring lunch, careless of the tide as it swelled up to the platform and washed about my legs, I stood on the Beacon that day and, one after another, using a trout rod and a small copper spoon, caught sixty kahawai – no less!

The best of them all (alas) was hooked by Eileen FitzGerald, to whom I had lent my rod for a spell; but the fish was too heavy for Eileen to play and at least she lent me my rod again to cope with it as, lolling in the run of the tide, it swept far out towards the bar; and so, just as Maurice had done with the dinghy, I eased the big fish to the side of the current and so, inch by inch, back to the bay-side of the rock. It was a six-pounder which, on a light trout rod in the tug of that rushing tide, was no mean fish.

But while this was going on, while the snowy birds were diving, and the sharks patrolling, and the kahawai milling after the herrings, the snapper too began to feed as never before; and not in their usual haunts, away out on the sunken reef, but close inshore, anywhere, feasting perhaps on the broken fragments of herring dropping from the banquet of the kahawai. Everyone was catching them. My mother, throwing her own line out just off the edge of the platform, was bringing in monsters. My brother, my sisters, Maurice, everyone was catching snapper. The whole Beacon glittered with fish. I see my father, clinging firmly to his belief that a floating bait was the best, but probably hoping to catch a kahawai rather than a snapper, dangling his rod, with a strip of freshly caught kahawai on it, hopefully into the calm waters beside the Beacon and the most enormous snapper, plainly visible to us all, nibbling at it … I wonder, now, if he caught it.

8

THE COUNTRY OF
THE WILD PIGS

IN the winter when we couldn't go fishing we went
pig-hunting. It was a barbarous occupation; but if it
needed any justification apart from the fact that we were
young, at least we hunted the pigs at quite a considerable risk to ourselves.

I don't mean that there was any particular danger
of being eaten by the animals, though that was always a
possibility. The dogs got ripped sometimes, and Del
Rose out at Whangamomona had a very uneasy half-
hour perched on top of a fence post while a boar tried
to climb the fence to knock him off it. One of the
MacWilliamses at Mangamingi did get ripped; a boar
charged him on a narrow track between two precipices
along the top of a ridge, and, in panic, not being able to
jump anywhere to safety, he fell over in front of the pig
and dropped his rifle. And if the worst thing that ever
happened to me personally was to be dragged through
a lawyer-bush by a pig while I was holding its tail –
lawyer is a very prickly bush, and this was quite an
extensive patch of it – there was one possibly more

dangerous moment at Whangamomona when Del Rose, who could never be bothered carrying a gun himself, grabbed my Winchester .44 to shoot at a very large boar, whereupon the boar moved rapidly in my direction and, while I dangled in mid-air above him from a useful overhanging tree, paused meditatively beneath me and champed his tusks.

But the roads to the pig-hunting country were really dangerous. They were narrow, twisting, steep, often lost in fog when we drove them, usually with a nice precipice over the edge to drop into, and always harrowingly slippery. In the Whangamomona country, where Del Rose in his old Rugby had two or three times been over the bank, mercifully to be held up by trees and stumps instead of plunging into the gorge below, the road was just a bog of slippery hard clay, and you skidded along it sideways. I remember one night-mare occasion, though that was more my fault than the road's, when I was driving along the precipice above the Tangarakau River on my way out to Rose's and, because I had too much luggage in my small car to get at the hand-brake, which was the only way of checking it round the bends – the foot-brake never worked – I reached for the brake through the spokes of the steering wheel. That would have been all right, except that at that moment I had to take a right-angled corner, and quickly too if I didn't want to drive over the cliff into the river, and I couldn't turn the steering wheel because my own arm was jamming it. For one wild fearful second I had to swing towards the edge of the cliff, and so release my arm. Moral, don't do that again.

There were other odd accidents, or near-accidents, that kept happening: like the time when we were shel-tering from the storm in the old shack on Richards's at

Moeroa, and the wind blew out the back of the corrugated-iron fireplace where we had the billy boiling, and
then blew it in again and knocked the billy of boiling
water all over us.

Then, adding their quota of interest, guns kept
popping off at moments and in directions one didn't
expect them to: as when we were camping in that same
revolting old deserted shack with its unforgettable
aroma of old socks and old shepherds, and my friend Ian
Wylds, unwrapping his packages of .303 bullets and toss-
ing the wrappers into the fire, happened to toss a live
bullet in with one of the wrappers. We never knew
where that bullet went, but the brass case came whizzing
between our legs and dug itself into the wall behind us.
And there was the time when Bob Ward suddenly said
in a moment of whimsy, 'Wouldn't it be funny if there
was a pig on the other side of the gully there,' and,
aiming his rifle which he had been pointing at our backs
for the last half hour while we climbed up the ridge in
front of him, and which of course he thought had its
safety catch on, whimsically pulled the trigger …

And finally, if we didn't get ourselves ripped, and if
we didn't drive our car over a precipice or shoot ourselves in moments of carelessness or excitement, there
was the battle with the country itself; for the ridges running through all that country from Mangamingi to
Moeroa were wild and steep and slippery, and if we
didn't break our necks on them it wasn't for lack of
trying.

The most reckless man in a hundred miles of country was Jim Gregory, that black, squat, hairy-chested,
ape-like neighbour of Del Rose's who had a passion for
building swing-bridges over the gorges. They were dangerous contraptions at any time; but once, to start a

bridge, he stretched a strand of fencing-wire between two stumps on either side of a gorge; and then, to get back to the other side again, put a loop of wire over it and, clinging to this, slid off along his fencing-wire. When he got mid-way across the gorge, the fencing-wire sagged; and there he hung, over the dim creek below, till he dropped …

There was the dog, too, that fell down one of the curious holes like wells, hidden in the bracken in the shell-rock country at Omoana; and climbed out, many days later, with all its nails, where it had been scrabbling at the rock, worn off.

We ourselves seem to have had enough sense not to swing over the gorges on a single strand of fencing-wire, and we didn't fall down any holes; but I did once prudently jump off a horse, because I suspected its intentions, just before it slipped off a narrow track and rolled down the mountainside into the creek – where it picked itself up again quite unconcerned. It used to be exciting, too, to lead your horse down the ridges when it was too steep to ride, and have them come slithering down the clay slopes on top of you. I remember standing with one of my friends, Max Carrie, on foot this time, paralysed with horror on a sheep-track round a precipice, along which the rest of the party, not thinking of the height, had run full tilt after a pig; and I still think with something approaching reverence of the mountainside of bare slippery clay we climbed for a short cut out of the gully one day. It took us three hours to navigate that short cut, when half an hour would have got us to the top by the longer way up the spine of the spur; and the real bother with it was that the scrubby bits of tea-tree and tutu which we had relied on for hand-holds and foot-holds petered out about half-way up, and left us spreadeagled on that almost vertical slope with nothing to help us up, and nothing to stop us slipping, except the inadequate little pits which, flat on our bellies and hanging on by suction, we dug for the next hand-hold with our sheath-knives.

I think the most perilous of all our excursions, at least for the chance of blowing ourselves to pieces with our own guns, and for other things as well, was the time one Easter when half a dozen of us camped with Sam Jenkins in his shack at the foot of the long ridge down from Richards's at Moeroa; beyond which there was one more house – Otto Hahndorf's – and then nothing. Sam was a slow-spoken quiet man with big staring brown eyes who sometimes worked as a drover, and ran a few sheep of his own on this lonely farm in the bush. His shack for some reason was three miles in from that loneliest of roads, right in the middle of nowhere. The track into it followed the windings of a pretty little mountain creek. We loved to stay with Sam for, besides having more pigs than sheep on his property, he kept a

keg of beer in his shack; and beer was very dear to us.
Sam used to put raisins in it 'to give it a kick'.

There were a lot of pigs in the valley where the
shack stood; and all around the valley, except where the
creek ran out to the flat, the ridges stood up in a fan.
Sam had the brilliant idea that he, with the dogs, would
march into the bush and the bracken of the valley and
make a great deal of noise, so that all the pigs would rush
up the ridges to get away; and the six of us, placed at
strategic intervals along the skyline, would shoot them
as they came over. But the point to which neither Sam
nor the rest of us had really given proper consideration
was that if we shot downhill at the pigs we would be
shooting at Sam, and if we shot sideways, as they crossed
the top of the ridge, we would be shooting at each
other. I can still see Sam, brandishing a slain pig over his
shoulder, plunging and shouting in that valley while

bullets whistled all round him; but, by the grace of God, nobody shot anybody. The only real casualties came after dinner that night; when, whether it was too much fresh wild pork, or whether it was that beautiful keg of beer with the raisins in it, there was a scene of agony too dreadful to describe.

Except on that one occasion, when we did have some vague qualms about the probability of shooting Sam Jenkins, I don't think that at the time we regarded pig-hunting as a particularly hazardous occupation; but it was so, and that must have been one of its attractions. We liked the battle with the hills, and we liked, too, everything that we saw there.

It was a queer kind of country. The people spoke quietly, as if hushed by the solitude, or perhaps merely from lack of practice in using the human voice at all. We used to be amazed at the younger members of the Richards family, the two lean quiet boys and the shy girl, in their late teens or early twenties, who, so they told us, had never travelled as far as the sea-coast, fifty miles away, had never seen ocean or cities. Their neighbour, Mrs Hahndorf, was a brisker soul, and maintained, as the wife of the last settler on a backblocks road so often seems to do, a fortress of civilization against the wilderness. She made us pick our socks and trouser-legs free of bid-a-bid burrs before we came into her house, so that we wouldn't introduce that pest into her garden. But Otto, short and heavy and slow-spoken, partook of the nature of the country, and immortalized himself for us by a single phrase, perhaps the only one he ever spoke: 'De peeg vos on de odder side of de goorge.' I don't know why this should have struck us as so funny, nor why it should have lingered so in the memory; but there for ever, by the stove in his spotless kitchen at the end of the road that petered out at his gate and became, so it was said, a cattle-track through bush to the back-blocks of Waverley, a track that no drover now travelled, sits Otto Hahndorf saying in his slow heavy voice, 'De peeg vos on de odder side of de goorge.' It was, I recall, a very beeg peeg.

There was a ghost on that road out to Hahndorf's. It was the remains of a farmer who had gone over the bank, and it lived in the scrub near Flyger's. One black wet night when the mailman was driving along that lonely road it sprang out of the scrub at him and gave him such a fright that he too plunged over into the gorge; but lived to tell the tale. I never saw it myself, but the vague possibility of its jumping out at us, when we were driving home late from pig-hunting, lent a certain amount of additional interest to the road.

There was something even more ghostly, for there was no doubt about its presence, in the noise we heard one bright sunny day when we were walking along a ridge-top at the back of Bob Ward's place. It was a noise like tearing sheets; like somebody, away up in the blue sky, tearing up enormous sheets; a long noise, and a loud noise, and, on that clear calm day, a most queer and alarming noise. Years afterwards I found out what caused it: it is the sound which rifle-shots make when you are a very long distance from where they are being fired. It was only somebody else out pig-shooting. But at the time we thought it was an earthquake coming, or a hurricane; or masses of ice hurtling through the sky; or, possibly, angels passing over.

And it wasn't altogether surprising that queer things should happen in that country, for physically, geo-logically, it was very queer country indeed. It was formed of shell-rock and blue *papa* clay, heaved up so recently out of the sea that, walking on the compressed mud of the sea-floor, you could find whole fossil shells in it, fan-shells and pipis and cockles: most curious things, shellfish turned to stone, to hold in your hand. It was utterly different from the green soft civilized rolling plains of Taranaki that, encompassing the Ngaere swamp, reached eight miles out from Eltham and then abruptly, at the crest of Mangamingi Ridge, gave way to this wilderness of ridges. It was strangely violent country, speaking of old convulsions of the earth and still caught up in the slow turmoil of geological change, for the green cleared hillsides near Mangamingi were scarred with 'slips' where the clay had fallen in landslides into the gullies. The hills were becoming smaller; the gullies, when the grass grew again over the landslides, were broadening into pretty green valleys. The further you went into it the wilder the country got, only half cleared, with scrub and bracken still holding the ridges in their place, and the gorges sharp and narrow; until at the end of the road at Hahndorf's, or over at the back of any farm along the way, you got into bush so thick with supplejack vines that the only way you could get through it was to crawl on hands and knees along the pig-tracks.

But queer and violent as it was, it was beautiful country. We climbed over the high wild ridges with the hawk; we met the blue pukeko on the sunny, shallow little creeks that meandered through each open valley. It was fascinating, crawling those tunnels of the supplejacks, to come across traces of the private life of pigs; the mud on the vines where they had travelled the same track before us, the bristles still clinging to the worn trunks of tree-ferns where they had rubbed themselves;

the muddy wallow under the plumes of the toi-toi bush where a whole pig family had washed itself in the creek. It was fascinating, as once we did, to watch a tribe of pigs calmly sleeping and grunting and rooting up the bracken on a sun-warmed hillside.

The rarest and strangest of sights we saw there was a kiwi which the dogs startled in the bracken one day, that hairy, incredible bird with its fat body and very long beak, heraldic, legendary and wonderful; and another day we stood on a spur for an hour and watched while hundreds, perhaps thousands of quail, in flocks such as we had never seen before, whirred out of the scrub at our feet. Any day, over the hills or in the boxthorn hedges around Ward's homestead, you could see a mob of half a dozen quail; but this day it seemed as if all the quail in New Zealand had gathered in that one far gully. Was it perhaps in the course of some winter migration? One other glorious day, duck-hunting not pig-hunting this time, because Maurice FitzGerald wanted a blue mountain duck for his pond at Eltham, we drove to Omoana and all the long sunny afternoon climbed and waded along some exquisite lost little creek in the bush; and in the end, after we had missed one duck that whizzed past us down the gorge, came upon one suddenly in a pool and, when it dived, caught the strange rare beautiful creature in our trout landing-nets.

The great, the overwhelming fascination of that country was its remoteness; its distances. Going pig-hunting in the winter mornings before daybreak while all the land lay white with frost, we drove up the easy slope of Mangamingi Ridge and suddenly, with their great humped backs and fire-blackened timber jutting out, mile upon mile of the ranges stretched before us, half drowned in a sea of silver mist. Behind us, huge with rock and shadow and sparkling with snow, Mount Egmont reared into the stars; far ahead, half-way across the island, glimmered the white wraith of Ruapehu; and if twenty miles or so behind us the country was tamed and civilized, all ahead was wilderness. And no matter how far into the ridges we penetrated, the distance still stretched ahead until it ended, or really began, in the dark-green mysterious bush that opened its solitary recesses where the road ended at Hahndorf's and the cattle-track was said to begin.

And if we never did really find out if that cattle-track existed, nor follow it round to Waverley as we longed to do, Moewe-awatea, where Del Rose lived, was far enough. It was forty miles out from our neighbouring town of Stratford to Whangamomona; then ten miles around the bluffs of the Tangarakau River to where the metal road ended; then five miles up the clay track to Del Rose's place; and if there was said to be one other family, the O'Deas, living further along the Moewe-awatea Road before it finally lost itself in the ranges, the O'Deas remained permanently invisible. I think, very likely, they were leprechauns.

Del Rose was a phenomenon in the hills. He was educated, he was civilized, he read books; he listened-in with impassioned interest to the debates in Parliament; and he sang. Mightily in his fine baritone he roared out the Toreador Song, as, short, fair, Roman-nosed, and with a chest on him like a bull, he marched us past the cowshed and across the flats to go pig-hunting in the frosty dawns while above him, feathery with light green Prince of Wales fern and dark with bracken, towered his wild country.

He had been to school in Wellington, where he was

born; then to the First World War; then, with his English
bride, home to this remote soldier-settler's farm where
the wool full of bid-a-bid seeds brought fourpence a
pound at the auctions and the most he could make in a
good season was a net income of £400; where the wild
pigs ate his new-born lambs and ploughed up his paddocks and let the bracken, the ragwort, and the foxglove
take hold in place of the grass; where the paddock called
the New Burn, just up to the left at the back of the
house, was such a tangle of black stumps and fallen logs
and ragged second-growth of pungas and saplings and
lawyer that even the pigs kept clear of it; and where, far
across the invisible Tangarakau River, when the last of
the cleared and semi-cleared land gave way to the
untouched forest, glimmered the Maori Clearing.

Yet there, on the slope across the swing-bridge
from the woolshed, Del Rose's house stood neat and
clean as any white-painted weatherboard house in the
country towns; there, by night when we played poker by
the fire for wild pigs' snouts (for which the Government
paid a bounty of a shilling apiece), softly glowed the
ingenious system of petrol lamps which lit the establishment; and there, always beautiful, always calm and
amused, Mrs Rose kept house impeccably as she would
have done in Dorset.

The times I spent there seem to me now the most
curious mixture of low comedy and high adventure; and
both might well be epitomized in Del's great lion-
coloured pig-dog, Mac, whom I see for ever in my
mind's eye crouching outside his kennel by the woolshed over the hindquarters of a very, very dead ram. Mac
and Roy and Rough, the dogs at Rose's, were always
ravenous, except when they gorged themselves on wild
pork and made rude noises and rude odours in front of

us all the way home, and Mac must have stood guard
over that appalling treasure for a month. I don't think he
really tried to eat it; it was far too ripe for that; but it was
food, and it was his, and he stood upon it with his
forepaws and defied the whole universe to take it from
him. Mac was great in heart, not size. He was quite a
small sort of collie mongrel; but he wore a magnificent
ruff of red hair round his face, and no other dog was so
swift to scent and find the pigs, no other so courageous
in attack. He used to dive straight over the boar's head,
straight over the jabbing tusks, and seize his prey by the
neck. He got ripped sometimes; and, in the end, killed.
Then, there was my own dog, Bill. Bill was a son of Mac
by an old blind bitch named Flirt and I acquired him
from Del in the hope that he would be as great a pig-
dog as his father. He was the skinniest dog ever seen
when I brought him home from Whangamomona, with
a tail like a piece of black fencing-wire. He grew fat at
Eltham, and developed some clever habits, such as
rounding-up the fowls, climbing a ladder to rest in the
sun on top of the garage, and waiting conspicuously all
day outside the front door of Casey's hotel when, after a
drink with a client before lunch, my father had long
gone back, out the door at the side, to his office. But
when I took him back to Rose's to hunt pigs, he was no
use at all. In fact he was a menace, for when the other
dogs scented their quarry from the ridge-top and raced
off in their silent pursuit that would explode into barking only when they had come to close quarters with the
pigs, Bill would instantly break into a shrill, excited yap-
ping that meant 'Wait for me! I'm coming! Wait for me!'
and, fat and floundering after the pack, would yap all the
way down the gully, scaring every pig for miles around.
I don't know why I took him with me, except that I

loved him dearly and cherished a faint hope that he would some day come to his senses. My pig-hunting companions, those who travelled by car with me to Whangamomona, loved him less dearly, for the dog had to sit on my friend's lap in the car, and car-travel had grave effects on Bill.

There was, too, Locksley Brown. Locksley Brown was a youth who had a perpetual feud with his own head. He was tall and gangling, and every time he came into the house – he was a jackeroo, staying with Del one shearing-time – he crashed his head on the lamps. When we were in the bush, he was continually hanging himself by the neck on the supplejack vines, or stunning himself with the trees. He used to carry a .303 rifle, which is a nasty, knobbly sort of weapon, and every time he wanted to shift its weight from one shoulder to the other, instead of going over his head he went, so to speak, through it, and gave himself the most frightful bash on the side of his face. The shearers, charmed with his eccentricities, cut a swathe through his long hair from the front to the back with the sheep shears, but even this never seemed to indicate clearly to Locksley where his head was. For years I meditated writing a short story about Locksley: how, driven to fury by the tormenting of the shearers, he took to the wild bush across the road from Rose's and started shooting at the house – I forget how it was to end; but it just shows what liars short story writers are, for Locksley rather liked being shorn by the shearers, and kept on cheerfully bashing his head on every lamp in the house.

Then there was Jim Gregory, continually suspending himself in odd situations from his swing-bridges; and Gregory's enormous black shorthorn bull which used to come bellowing down the road and knock down the

fences and put Del's house cows in calf at the wrong
season, until those same wicked shearers penned him up
one day and tied a kerosene tin to his tail, whereupon
he fled kicking to the high hills and never came back to
bother the house cows again, but roamed with the half-
wild cattle on the hills and put the cows there in calf at
the wrong time.

So isolated, so shut in upon itself for its work, its adventures, and its amusements, with the bush across the road
and the ridges sloping up from the house, Rose's place
was far enough from anywhere for anyone. So close did
the wild pigs venture, that one day we saw a huge red
boar get up with a rush from the fern just on top of the
first ridge behind the house. Going further afield on
other days, we climbed and walked to where the bush
began and saw one morning the skins of twenty-two
new-born lambs lying strewn on the last of the cleared
ridges, with the half-eaten carcass of a ewe beside them;
and, in the bush below, found a mob of seventeen pigs
that had done all the damage – it is a gruesome sort of
refinement in pigs that they skin the lambs as they eat
them. We made many an excursion right into the bush
and once, as a perfect image of its isolation, saw a small
ginger pig quietly trotting along the track through the
trees to meet us … and nobody shot at it, for, because
of its colour, we thought it was Flirt, who sometimes,
blind as she was, gallantly snuffled her way behind us
over the logs and tussocks into the back country to
recapture the pig-hunting delights of her youth.

   Yet, remote as the farm was, there was always
somewhere a little further to go to. We rode three miles
up the road to where Del had a farm on lease, and there
saw the most incredible array of wild pigs that anyone

ever saw. Nobody had been near the place for months, and the pigs were everywhere. We came round a bend of the track and there, right beside the abandoned house, was the most enormous black boar standing at bay with every bristle on end; and behind him, scooting for the safety of the bush, were dozens, scores, hundreds it seemed of pigs. They had rooted up the whole valley for miles. We followed them on up the valley and into the most enchanting glade of the bush, where sunlight filtered down into a creek.

We went, too, once but never again, into the bush that began just across the road from Rose's and rolled on, dark and lonely and forbidding, nobody knew how far.

How black was the New Zealand bush, once you really got inside it! ... those dark massive rimus and totaras and kahikateas that completely shut out the light of the sky; those silent black-boled tree-ferns with their still green wings; those twisting, tangling black supple-jack vines; those shadowy creeks in the gorges; that heavy leaf-mould on which you walked; those solitudes perhaps never trodden by man, not even the Maoris. It was very black indeed in that patch of bush across the road, and it gave us, with some reason, the creeps. One day when Des Carter and I were hunting there, a boar, with all the dogs yelling after it, fell headlong over a cliff into the creek at the bottom of it. We could hear the dogs still barking at it there, but we could not see any-thing, for the cliff was over-hanging. I lay down flat on my stomach on the slope at the edge; and Des lay down and held me by the ankles; and, so held, I poked my head over the gorge. But we were lying on a thin coat-ing of leaf-mould over a surface of hard slippery clay. The leaf-mould began to slip. Des began to slip with it.

It was quite a deep gorge; and, if you did not break your neck, it did not seem pleasant to think of landing head-first on top of an enraged wild boar. When we got out of the mess, which somehow we did, we suddenly realized that we had gone a long way chasing that pig, and night was falling, and we hadn't the faintest idea where we were. We said to the dogs, 'Go home!'; and the dogs, fortunately, did.

Perhaps it was partly because of the blackness of the bush that, of all the far places that tempted us, the Maori Clearing seemed so supremely enchanting. The light shone onto it and into it. It was a clearing. There, far across the gullies and the invisible river, high on a spur it stood, light green in the dark green bush. Who had cut down its trees? Some Maori tribe, we thought, who, defeated in battle, had paddled their canoes up the Tangarakau River and found a refuge on that steep spur above it. How long ago? When and why did they leave it? Nobody knew. What would we find there? Perhaps, though that was not likely, the ruins of their *whares*. Perhaps a weapon or two, a club, a stone axe, or a whale-bone *mere* that they had left behind them. Perhaps just a

clearing, and saplings and tree-ferns; and pigs.

We never got to it. It was just too far for us to manage. But one day, walking along the ridge over at the back of Del Rose's from which we could see the Clearing, we picked up something like a piece of it: an old half-decayed wooden implement, like a kind of spade, which we thought could only have been made by the Maoris. We held it in our hands and, for a moment, touched the far distance.

9

BULLS

ON one bank of the Kapuni there was a roaring
great Jersey bull, tawny as a lion, pawing up the
grass and gouging his horns into the earth; and on the
other bank of the Kapuni there was another roaring
great Jersey bull doing the same thing; and between
these monsters, as they bellowed defiance at each other
across the water, floated, apparently disembodied, a
human head and an arm holding high a fishing rod. Pro-
pelled by some unseen force the head and arm moved
steadily and noiselessly upstream.

It was no more than my companion, Fin Maslin,
taking a ducking in preference to taking on a bull – and
how delicately he trod through that commotion, walking on the slippery boulders as if on eggs! – but it has
always seemed to me the perfect image of the enliven-
ment of our fishing in Taranaki which those Jersey bulls
provided.

It was dairying country, and I suppose the bulls had
every right to be there. Jerseys – the gentle, fawn-
coloured cows, that is; graceful as deer – give the richest
cream. But even cows graceful as deer must have husbands, and every green farm through which we passed

133

was guarded by one at least of these murderous brutes, lord of fifty acres and fifty wives.

Oddly enough, it was a cow – but I think she was a Friesian; and of course she must have had a calf to protect – who first introduced me to the pleasures of the chase.

That was so far back into childhood that most of the details are misty. It was out at Mrs Barr's place, wherever that may have been, and all I remember of Mrs Barr is that she gave us buttermilk to drink, a strange sour substance which I think we enjoyed for its oddity; that she made the most marvellous plump round gingernuts, resembling in miniature the genial rotundities of her own figure, and that she saved my life did Mrs Barr, or truly may have.

For when the black-and-white cow came hurtling after me across the paddock, and I was running from it as I still sometimes run in nightmares, she leapt the fence – could she possibly have done that? – and snatched me up to that comfortable gingernut bosom, and tossed me over the wires to safety or bundled me under them … somehow, at all events, saved me.

It was a cow, too – or so we thought; not caring to take too close a look at it – which gave Fin Maslin and myself a remarkable burst of excitement one night on the Kapuni again.

We first saw the animal, running purposefully towards us, on the plateau above the stream as we were making our way home to the car in the dusk. We hurried down the steep track and paused at the water's edge, thinking that was that. Then we saw the beast, tail out stiff and running like mad, outlined against the skyline on the ridge.

It plunged down the slope and we plunged wildly

across the river; and, wet and breathless, stood on the far bank rocking with uncontrollable laughter. It always seems excessively funny to have been chased by a cow, once you are safe. Then we heard splash–splash–splash across the ford, splash–splash–splash through the darkness. The thing was dashing across the river after us, and we bolted. We didn't even feel safe in the car.

But it was rarely that we were put to the shame of fleeing from mere cows. Whether in boyhood or in manhood, fishing the secret dark waters of Lake Rotokare for eels or wading the streams for trout, it was the bulls that were the menace, and sent us tearing across the paddocks, plunging through the waters, shinning up Taranaki's ubiquitous pine-trees or, on one disgraceful occasion when I was fishing the Awakino at Mahoenui, clambering desperately up a cliff into the tutu-scrub, where I hung from the thin branches above the water like a highwayman from a gibbet.

I confess with shame that it was only a Hereford bull, massive as a mastodon but the sleepiest and gentlest of creatures, that made me, that memorable day, leap instantly into deep water, flounder across the river and, breaking the tip of my rod, fly so absurdly into the tree-tops. True, its colossal red-and-white head manifested itself suddenly and appallingly out of the clear sky over the bank behind me; true, as startled to stumble on a fisherman as I was to be stumbled on by a bull, it *woofed* at me in the most astonishing manner; but, watching with mild surprise my antics in the water, it never moved a foot to follow me, and the only real excuse I can offer for such an exhibition of cowardice was that I had been so conditioned by the Jerseys that no bull could *woof* at me and leave me unmoved.

From the boyhood excursions to Lake Rotokare,

which lurked in its green woods about eight miles out
of Eltham, draining the black waters of the Ngaere
Swamp, memory preserves one supremely ridiculous
picture of two small boys up a dead pine-sapling; a foul
and rumbling monster of a Jersey heaving his shoulder
against the pine to see if he could push it down – which
he possibly could have, for the thing was both slender
and rotten, and why we did not shin up the sound tree
next to it I know not – and Des Carter, with his pale-
blue prominent eyes flashing with determination and
his pocket-knife murderously open, vowing with the
utmost insincerity that he would that very moment
drop from our perch onto the bull's back and ride it
away, stabbing it to death as he went. I don't think I
quite believed him even then; but with that marvellous
capacity which boys have for persuading themselves, in
the interests of drama, that they do believe what they
don't, I took Desmond very seriously indeed and
begged him with feverish anxiety – perched there in
our tree by the roadside, with the bull rumbling and
heaving like a volcano a few feet below us and his bored
cows grazing around him – not to sacrifice his life to
save me.

But Des would; he would; any moment now he
would drop with his deadly pocket-knife ready; he was
going, he was off … until after about an hour of this
magnificently dramatic situation – or it may have been
ten minutes – the bull itself, just in time to save its own
life, moved off.

Was it on a single day, on another of our eeling
excursions to Lake Rotokare, that we enjoyed two vastly
alarming adventures, one with a bull and the other with
a 'coffin'; or has memory telescoped two days in one? It
was surely too much exalted living to have packed into

one day, and yet so it seems to have happened.

There were, with Des Carter and myself that day, two or maybe three of the sturdy, nuggety small sons of Mr Walker the saddler, at whose shop with its wonderful array of saddles and bridles and winkers and ingeniously plaited stockwhips we always lingered long on our way to school. Happily all morning, though perhaps even then a little disconcerted by the size and numbers of our catch, for the dark lake swarmed with the most enormous eels, Des and I and Albert and Sam and (if he was there) young Charlie fished away the hours. But what a sinister place Lake Rotokare was: shut in by its sombre bush, black with the ichor of the swamps, miles away from all habitation, studded and patrolled by strange green floating islands of logs and weed and moss which walked with the wind across the water.

The big, slimy black eels, writhing in their serpen-
tine coils upon the grass, were too much like the
embodied spirit of the place, the demon that lurked in
the bush and under the floating islands, to be hauled
out, however exciting was the fishing, without some
tinge of dismay.

In the afternoon we began to explore the bush; and
there, deep in the dark-green silence where the supplejacks twisted from the branches and the tree-ferns
spread their great wings, we came upon a thing which
to this day puzzles me: though not now with such sinister import. It was a thing in the earth, made of thick
slabs of timber, like a long box, like a coffin, with just the
brown, half-rotten top of it showing through the black
leaf-mould.

A most intriguing object, what could it be for?
What was in it? When, poking with sticks, we contrived
to make an opening in the rotted slab at one end, we
scraped out ashes and bones.

All I can think of today by which to explain it is
that it must have been some kind of Maori oven –
though I never heard of the Maoris covering their
earth-ovens with boards. I don't know what it could
have been. But as soon as we found the ashes and
charred fragments of bone we persuaded ourselves by
the most cogent arguments, frightening our wits out in
the process, that somebody had burnt a body in it. And
at that moment, so it seems, a wind howled through the
trees, thunder-clouds swarmed over us, and rain began
to fall. Hounded by demons we fled, and never stopped
running till we reached the lone farmhand's shack
where the dried carcasses of hawks, very comforting for
some obscure reason, hung with wide-spread wings and
a delicious stink of carrion, along the barbed-wire fence.

Unless the storm was very quickly over, it must after all have been on another day that we met the bull. For it was a fine sunny afternoon when he roared on the grassy lane that led through the hills to the road, barring our way home.

He was really in a rage, that fellow: pawing the earth, gouging it with his horns, his furious bellowing rising to a scream that echoed in the hills around the lake; and when we had crept close enough for him to see us, he came running straight at us with that low, intense, terrifying rumble that betokens murder.

We scattered. Four of us, flying like birds before a gale, found ourselves eventually perched breathless on the ridge-top to the left of the lake; and from there looked down upon the appalling spectacle of Albert Walker, the eldest of his tribe, streaking along the track, back the way we had come, with the bull pounding after him.

Even as we watched, Albert rolled like a pudding under the fence to comparative safety. But our troubles were not yet over, for it was the right-hand fence he had taken and now he was galloping full-tilt downhill towards the wild bush and the lake. There was a strong family feeling among the Walkers. Charlie was sobbing. Sam was moaning, over and over again, 'Me brother Albert! Me brother Albert! Me brother Albert … '

I forget how we retrieved the fugitive and by what devious route over the ridges and far away from the bull we eventually escaped to the road; but years afterwards, so I was told, the Walkers similarly got separated when they were fighting side by side in Crete and ('Me brother Albert! Me brother Albert!') I was glad indeed to learn that the elder brother turned up safe, once again, in the end.

Recalling these hair-raising adventures I really am tempted to forgive myself for breaking my rod-tip on the Awakino and for a certain trepidation that still assails me when anything, while I am out fishing, makes a noise remotely resembling a bull ... though I should not like anyone else to have been present that hot, hot Australian day on the Duckmaloi, round the long lonely bend past Gearon's, when, treading on an imaginary snake at every step to begin with, I heard the most ominous bellowings in the bush on the mountainside across the river.

Naturally I moved on. The bellowing moved on, too. Forgetting about the snakes, I did a quick hundred yards through the scrub, and fished a little more. The bellowing caught up to me. I did another fifty yards to a convenient tree; the bellowing kept pace with me. Another fifty yards to another tree; still the bellowing followed. Another fifty yards, sweating, panting, pursued by the bellowings of hell, all the worse for being invisible.

It was, alas, Mr Gearon droving his cattle home around the mountainside; the most harmless of Black Poll steers.

But the bulls were not, in Taranaki, so harmless. The two most perilous specimens I ever encountered out fishing were a Jersey on the Tangarakau and another Jersey – not that mild old Hereford – on the Awakino. He was a very baffled bull, that brute on the Tangarakau, and he did what I thought no bull would ever do – dived into the river and swam after us like a mad hippopotamus.

Fin Maslin was with me that day, fishing under the willows where the stream, so rich in goodly brown trout, swept curving into a pool between high banks.

There was a six-foot drop into the water on the side where the bull was, and what was annoying the animal, before we wandered along, was that because of the drop, and a barbed-wire fence downstream, he could not get at his fifty wives in the neighbouring paddock.

He couldn't get at us, either – so we thought – because of that six-foot drop, and, fishing safely from the far bank, while he screamed and tore up the ground or ran to and fro, horribly rumbling and seeming to bristle and quiver all over as he sought for some way of crossing the deep pool below him, we thoroughly enjoyed the spectacle of his fury. We were, though, in the midst of our amusement a little awed at a frenzy so majestic, a rage so completely ungovernable.

That was when he surprised us. He leapt clean into the water. It was like an elephant, like a locomotive falling from the skies – such a colossal splash, such a surge of the current, such a steam of sudden spray. It was a thing unheard-of, impossible; it broke all the rules for the behaviour of bulls; it was an explosion. Like fragments from the explosion, we departed. Half an hour later, when with extreme precautions we crept back to retrieve my landing-net which I had dropped in midflight, the bull had also departed: he was downstream fighting with the last fence that held him back from his harem.

No such excuse, the pressure of extreme tenderness, could be offered for the Jersey on the Awakino, for he was in the midst of his wives when he tackled my brother Neil and myself in our tent beside that broad and beautiful stream.

My brother, for reasons with which I am more inclined to sympathize now than I was then, was strangely indifferent to fishing; in fact on this trip to the

Awakino he staggered me, away upstream in ragged wild rocky country, by abandoning the sport altogether one day to go hunting on the cliff for ferns.

But if he was more a botanist than a fisherman, there were at least two episodes on that trip in which Neil took, perforce, the same impassioned interest that I did: the stew and the bull.

The stew – what a concoction it was! Its chief ingredient, born out of vague memories of my mother's making pea soup, was a ham-bone, with large hard cubes of ham for reinforcement. Lacking vegetables to enrich it, we stole a cabbage from a farmer's field nearby, and put that in. We stole some silver beet, and put that in. We stole some turnips, and put them in. Two or three eggs, some mint from the river bank, and a small, rather limp, rainbow trout. When it was more or less cooked it looked too thin and watery; and indeed, with the hard lumps of ham floating about among the cabbage and silver beet like petrified snails in a flooded garden, it failed, somehow, to attract us. It needed thickening. We had one of our mother's delicious Christmas cakes, so we squashed it up and, for the thickening, put that in.

What groanings upon the river-bank, what contortions, what hideous scenes took place later that night I hesitate to describe. But it was, in its way, a remarkably successful stew.

The bull – he was a great success, too. We camped that trip, as so often before and afterwards, on the flat beside the grassy lane that ran down to the river-bank from the side-road; and it was the custom of that bull, a truly gigantic Jersey, to come roaring down the road with his cows every afternoon as they were drifting of their own accord (for we never saw anyone in control of them) to their evening milking. The first time we saw him, bellowing his way down our lane, we simply bolted across the river … a most sensible thing to do.

The next time – we usually got back to our tent for a break between the day's and the evening's fishing just when the bull was due – some fatal spirit of defiance, some indignation at being driven from our own territory, must have taken hold of us. As he entered the lane, trumpeting, we ran up and threw a stone at him. That pleased him very much. He began to lumber towards us. We threw more stones. Overjoyed, he broke into a run. We retreated to a position beside our small tent, and from there cannonaded him again. He gave the most tremendous coughing roar of exultation and charged straight at us.

There must have been time, though he would have been hard at our heels, to make a break for the river; but in our panic we did not think so and with one accord we dived into the tent – instantly to realize, of course, that a tent, a sheet of thin canvas, is no protection whatever.

We lay on the grassy floor, trying to squeeze under our frail camp-stretchers, and quaked with terror while he searched for us.

Where had we disappeared to? That was obviously bothering him; indeed, annoying him. We could hear him searching. We could almost hear him thinking. Were we in that tea-tree bush? In the earth? In that curious white thing perhaps? He dug the ground for us, bellowing. Shaking our frail habitation to its roots, he stumbled over our guy-ropes. Worst of all, he *sniffed* for us. From a distance of about two feet, we could hear him sniffing.

He was at the side of the tent now. If we tried to

escape either from the opening at the front or by pulling
up the canvas at the back and sliding under it, he would
have us before we could reach the river one way or the
trees across the road from the other. If we stayed where
we were, ingloriously under the beds, any second now
he would burst in upon us. By signs and by whispers we
concocted a plan. Clearly, from the lumberings and
groanings and sniffings outside, he was exploring
towards the front of the tent. Very well, then, the instant
he showed in the opening, we would wriggle out the
back and away.

And that is what we did. Only it was then, in that
intolerable suspense as we waited for the monster to
poke his head in our front door, that I began to laugh;
in a whisper, it is true, but still to laugh; and that made
my brother almost as mad as the bull was. It was, I suppose, hysteria on my part; though I have found in other
emergencies that something will rise up in defence of
the dignity of man when things get utterly impossible,
detaching one from the ignominy of terror or disaster,
making them – almost – laughable.

At any rate, I laughed; and my brother silently
groaned; and the bloody great bull poked his head in the
front of the tent; and out the back we slithered and gal-
loped up the lane to the road; and I didn't stop till I was

through the fence and safe beside a climbable macro-carpa-tree; and my brother didn't stop running at all — the last glimpse I had of him he was a mile away up the main road ... hurtling, as I afterwards found out, to protest to the farmer, with all the considerable indignation he had accumulated, at the molestation of two innocent fishermen by his bull.

10

O N C E   A T   T A U P O

WHEN I read the books of the masters, those who have fished the huge swirling pools of the Tongariro where the water races down white and green from the snow, those who have stood in the 'picket-fence' at its entry into the lake and obligingly reeled in their lines while the next man played his ten-pounder, those who have taken their own launch and camped on the cliffs at the far side or trolled in the volcanic deeps for the forty-pounders said to lurk there uncatchable, mythological and immortal, I realize that I have no right to talk about Taupo.

The lake and its rivers, and the other great fishing-places nearby, lay too far off from Eltham. Whichever of the more civilized routes you took, north through Te Kuiti, Hamilton, and Rotorua, or south to Wanganui and up the winding Parapara through the hills of the fallow deer and the wild pigs, it was two hundred miles to go to the Taupo country – which, in the New Zealand of those days, meant a major expedition. There was a direct and much shorter track through the

Tangarakau Gorge, but that was for heroes and explorers. The road was a turmoil of ruts, formed of the stickiest blue *papa* clay, and when it rained, as it usually did in Taranaki, you were stuck there for ever. Besides, with a trout stream running through the middle of the town, and another about half a mile further on, and the rainbows of the Awakino not more than eighty miles away, the fishermen of Eltham had no need to go to Taupo.

Yet the lake, the most famous fishing place in New Zealand, haunted us. What was truly the record trout ever caught there? Was it twenty-nine pounds in weight, or was it only twenty-four? Whichever it was, it was fantastic. And if the average size had decreased a little since the trout had eaten up most of the crayfish that had made the first invaders so fat, anybody could still catch a fifteen-pounder if he was lucky and a ten- or twelve-pounder almost for certain; and that was fishing to dream about. Had not my uncle Maurice FitzGerald, fishing the Ohau channel between Lake Rotorua and Roto-iti, caught a fine nine-pounder? And then there was that story my schoolfellow Spud Cato from Te Kuiti used to tell of how he or one of his party, fishing the Ara-tia-tia Rapids, had caught a small trout about nine inches long; and left it on the line for bait; and with it caught a gigantic twelve-pound brown trout; which, when it was gutted, was found also to have eaten a water-rat ... You could not fish for trout in New Zealand and not, sooner or later, go to Taupo.

And some from Eltham did go there. I refuse to recall the exact details of the expedition made by George Batchelor, that most skilful caster of the minnow in our own small streams. George, with a friend, was the first man to fish some lake near Taupo that had previously been reserved for the Maoris – not, so far as I know, that the Maoris ever took any interest in trout. They preferred their ancestral food of eels; which, presumably because they have some age-old, racial fear of volcanoes, are not to be found in the Taupo area. Maybe the Maoris ate the freshwater crayfish, or maybe they just kept the lake because it was theirs. Anyhow George Batchelor and his friend were the first of white men to fish that lonely disc of blue water in the hills. It was an aquarium. They each broke six or sixteen rods. The trout were all of ten or twenty or two hundred pounds in weight. They caught five thousand of them. Or something like that. It was a dream; it was a nightmare; it was so magnificent that it is not to be spoken of.

But on a gentler, more feasible level, there was the expedition of Caleb and Finlay Maslin. They camped at the mouth of the Tauranga-Taupo river and fished it with frogs – we were all barbarians in those days. The problem they had to solve was that the best fish lay well out into the lake at the river-mouth where no fishermen could reach them; and the solution was to seat the frog on a small piece of pumice and float him out with the current. When he was far enough out, you flipped him off the pumice, and promptly caught a fat fish. Many, many fat fish. They buried them in the sand to protect them from the marauding half-wild pigs of the Maoris; they smoked them with sawdust; and they brought them back to Eltham packed in fruit cases, layer upon layer of smoked rainbow trout from Taupo. I cannot think why I did not instantly bolt for the lake.

I did at least, through a variety of happy chances, know something about the Waikato, the river which flows right through the lake and is called the Tongariro when it comes in and the Waikato when it comes out. I

knew it first at Hamilton, where I used to stay with
Cully MacDiarmid for school holidays. I don't know if
that huge and silent river, lapping the red roots of its
willows as it pours through its green shade to the sea, is
fishable at Hamilton, so many miles from Taupo. Big
rivers are daunting. But we prowled its dark banks and
the rolling countryside around it, rabbit-shooting.
Schoolboys are gruesome creatures! One morning
before dawn we rode our bikes out into the country
and, while the first light broke over the pale flat paddocks, shot twenty-six rabbits. There was nothing
remarkable in that, though I was pleased to get one
white, one black, and one yellow rabbit among them,
whose skins I made into a singularly ugly mat for my
bedroom. But it was a little remarkable that we disembowelled those twenty-six rabbits, and extracted their
fifty-two kidneys, and cooked them in a frying-pan at
the roadside, and ate them. They were very small and
hard, rather like sheep-dung. I don't think we really
enjoyed them, but it was an experience; and at least
we did not die from our breakfast: which now surprises
me.

　　I was rabbit-shooting again, further up the river in
the brown summer paddocks near Cambridge, when I
saw one sunshiny afternoon, a strange, beautiful, horrible and moving sight that has haunted me ever since. It
was a black wild-cat defending her kittens from a hawk.
The cat was lying on her back, right flat on her back,
with her claws out ripping at the air, and the hawk kept
swooping down at her, and every time the bird came
down, a great red monster of a thing with its wings
stretched out and its talons clutching for the tiny black
kittens that were crawling around their mother on the
bare earth, she twisted up on her spine and sprang into

the air to get him. She was almost flying herself. There was something shocking and uncanny in such a concentration of fury. It was like a piece of hell obtruded on the calm sunny hillside, all claws and talons and blackness. The hawk flew off when I came closer to get a shot at it, and the wild-cat and her kittens disappeared into some bushes.

The cruelty of nature, which goes on not only in the sky and on the earth, but under the very ground we walk on! One other day in the countryside of the Waikato, while I was leaning against a fence where one of the posts had rotted and left a kind of peep-hole into the subterranean corridors below, I suddenly saw the terrified glistening brown eye of a rabbit staring up at me, and when it vanished, as instantly it did, I saw the lean, pale-gold body of a stoat that was hunting it. I had not thought before of all the dramas of life and death that must take place in rabbit-burrows; and, so that this one should have a happy ending for the rabbit, shot the stoat.

But that was at Tirau; and Tirau is in the fishing country, only about fifty miles from Rotorua; and Maurice FitzGerald, with his tame wild ducks that he had reared by burning the raupo out of a swamp in his backyard in Eltham and making a pond of it, with his gleaming brass shell cases he had souvenired from the Great War and the even more intriguing bluish bits of shrapnel that he had souvenired from the Boer War and kept secreted in odd spots about his forehead; with his soft-spoken, soft-haired English wife who played the 'cello and who had once, incredibly, been a governess in Russia, and had a passion for the novels of Turgenev – my uncle Maurice with all his impedimenta and his treasures, not forgetting his fishing rods, moved from

Eltham to become County Engineer at Tirau. And drove those corrugated metal roads at sixty miles an hour because he owned them; and took all the time off he wanted to for fishing, or for listening to the rare bell-voiced New Zealand crow in the deep forests of the timber-cutters, because a County Engineer could always be 'inspecting the roads' when he was not to be sighted. We fished … we fished the dawn rise in the Fly Pool at the head of the Ara-tia-tia Rapids.

It was a place of foam and thunder; mile upon mile of rapids broken into mighty separate cascades as the river dropped from one level to the next; and thunderous was its name among trout fishermen. It was there that the Catos had caught the twelve-pounder. The Fly Pool, vast, sinister, slowly and heavily swirling as the masses of profoundly disturbed water swept into it from the main current crashing down the valley, was a backwater, a green whirlpool, at the foot of the first and fiercest of the cascades. All day long, standing on the limestone bluffs above it, you could see huge sunken logs and huge rainbow trout shouldering their way to the surface, and the only difference between them was that the trout would slowly open their great jaws and suck in a beetle or dragonfly or moth before they sank again to the depths. Its dawn rise was famous.

There was no motor road to the Fly Pool on the left bank of the river where you had to go to fish it – the road to the look-out for tourists was on the cliffs on the other side – so we camped two or three miles down-stream; and there, mid-way between the second and the third cascades, had some very peculiar fishing.

It strikes me as faintly criminal now that we wanted the trout for bait. We were going to Kawhia later in the summer, and fillets of trout were considered an excellent bait for snapper. So does familiarity breed, if not contempt, at least disrespect; for even in Taranaki the trout were so plentiful that this awful custom was practised. But if it was improper, it was also a pretty and romantic kind of bait. It was very pleasant to sit on the cliffs at Pukearuhe or on the Beacon rock at Kawhia and cut up the long golden fillets of trout to tempt the snapper: it was like catching two kinds of fish at once.

At any rate that was why we wanted the trout from the Ara-tia-tia Rapids; and it was some excuse, or no excuse at all, for what we did.

Dark green and flashing with afternoon light, the river below our camp when first we went down to explore it, ran fast but fishable. There was a stony beach, and little ridges of limestone, knobbly as a fish's backbone, pushed out into the current, making standpoints from which you could drop in a spoon or wet fly. But on our way down to fish it, Maurice's bright wicked blue eye spotted a little, placid backwater. And in that backwater, sheltered by its low walls of stone, screened with bulrushes at the shore, and golden with the sunlight reflecting from its sandy bottom, there swam, clear below us as we stood on the rocky hillside, a very large trout. There swam two trout. There swam three, four, more; it was a positive shoal of trout, and all of them looked (truly) at least three feet long. Or not much short of it, anyhow. We could see them moving about, sometimes bold, sometimes shadowy, gently fanning their fins as they nosed among the sand. It was like looking into Fairy Springs at Rotorua, where the tame trout fed on bread, and slithered in and out of the keeper's hands; but the difference was that the Fairy Springs trout, however tempting, and people have been known to ponder about them, were not to be fished for; whereas these ... These monsters milling in the backwater!

What to do? If you hooked one, you would certainly disturb all the rest. If you were seen for an instant, you would not catch any of them. We sneaked back up the hillside into the tea-tree. We caught one of the big dark-green New Zealand cicadas that were clacking in the thickets. We put it on Maurice's hook and we sneaked back behind the bulrushes and dropped it down gently in front of the largest trout we could see. Quietly he opened his mouth and swallowed it. Quietly, without the slightest commotion or objection, he allowed Maurice to lead him out of the pool and round the wall that enclosed it, and so to the stony beach where he could be landed. He was an enormous trout all right. He was fully three feet long (if not just a little less) and if he had been fat he would have been a ten-pounder. But he was skinny as the handle of a shovel. He looked more like an eel than a trout. And so did the next we caught, and so did the next and the next. They were ancient, spent fish that had retired from the battle with the rapids to recuperate in the backwater. We caught six of them, one after the other; I don't think there was any limit to the number we might have taken, except that the cicadas were a good deal harder to catch than the trout.

Dusk fell, and trout began to rise in the main river. We put on flies and fished for them far out in the current. What a wild place that was, where the water burned green and crimson between the white thunder of the cataracts! And if the trout had been far too easy to catch in the backwater, they were difficult enough here. Sometimes they took the fly with a snap that broke the cast; sometimes they raced downstream with the whole weight of the river behind them; mostly they came upstream so fast that you could neither reel in fast enough nor run back fast enough over the slippery rocks to keep pace with them, so they won slack line and got off. But, we caught fish.

Night came, and with it the most fascinating fishing of all. Normally night-fishing is impossible. You fall over things. Your cast ties itself in knots. You hook the trees behind you. You cannot see what your fish is doing; you cannot see to land him; and anyhow there usually aren't any fish stirring. Also, by that time, you have usually had enough. But we had not had enough of the fishing in the Ara-tia-tia Rapids. The moon came up so clear and bright that we could clamber more or less safely out on those tongues of rock and drop a fly or spoon into the deep river swirling past us. All night long, splashing in the moonlit water, the trout kept rising. And all night long we fished for them. It was so bright that the brassy spoons we were using still glittered as if in sunlight and we found them more effective than the fly, which would have been the orthodox bait for such a time. I forget how many fish we caught; it was an exultation simply to be there, in that wild lonely place, with the night and the trees and the rocks, fishing the huge silver river.

It was two in the morning before we stopped fishing; and we stopped then because the trout were not rising any more. And so to our tent among the tea-tree; and so, after two hours' sleep, to the track along the cliffs, and the famous dawn rise in the Fly Pool.

The dawn rise is a myth. The trout don't get up so early in the morning. I don't know how many times I have fallen for it, and crawled out of bed at some ungodly hour, and plodded through the river-mist among dripping vegetation, and waited in vain for it to happen. It can never possibly happen, for the trout rise in the evening for insects that have hatched in the heat of the day, and no insects hatch at dawn. Yet I still half believe in it; for it is a very potent myth, greatly honoured among fishermen. It certainly did not happen at the Fly Pool. We were there before sunrise, and not a fish moved in the grey water. We saw the huge whirlpool turn gold with the first light, then blue beside the roaring white fall as the sun climbed higher, and still nothing rose in it except the useless drowned logs. It was a fraud. Trout do rise, huge as the drowned logs, in the Fly Pool, for on other occasions and at other times of the day I have seen them; but not, most certainly not, at dawn.

Myths are very mysterious things. To this day I feel pleased to have fished the dawn rise in the Fly Pool; and believe that on another day we might have been successful. Maurice did catch a very nice trout on the way back to camp by dropping a cicada from a clifftop and leaving it to me – such is the privilege of uncles – to risk my neck and climb down and net it for him; but it was just as well for our snapper fishing, and for the reputation of the Taupo country, that we had found our peculiar backwater and had learned how to fish by moonlight.

On the way home from the Rapids we turned in to the Waikato again to fish the evening rise in the calmer waters lower down; and there the rise duly

occurred, as it always does on fine evenings. There were plenty of trout.

They rose in the shallows at the edge, and whether they were small or large we never knew, for we could not catch one of them. But it was very exciting still to be fishing the majestic Waikato; to clamber perilously round the rough track above the water between the cliff and the shallows, and to cast a dry fly for the trout as they rose for moth and lacewing while, glimmering in the black hollow between dusk and moonrise, the river itself fluttered by with moth-like ripplings and silences.

But that was in the settled, more pastoral reaches of the Waikato, closer to Tirau, and in those waters we usually fished it at Atia-muri.

Atia-muri was a lovely place. The river, still broad and swift but no longer with the turbulence of Ara-tia-tia, flowed through rolling green hills where sheep and cattle grazed. Its banks were low and grassy, bright with golden buttercups and fringed with weeping willows that trailed their long green hair in the water. A pebbly beach ran out to meet the current where we fished. Just there, a little tributary stream joined the main river, and it in itself was a most fascinating piece of water. It was only about a foot deep, and it was warm — most curiously warm. Somewhere not far upstream it must have been fed by one of the hot springs that were liable to bubble out of the earth anywhere in that strange volcanic country. You could take off your clothes and sit in it and have the most delightful bath, half cool, half warm, between the floating banks of watercress. There were trout in it, too; you would see them darting away from you as you went to bathe; quite respectable fish of about a pound; and once, close to its junction with the river, Maurice pulled a four-pounder out of it.

Atia-muri was to provide Maurice – and myself – with one of our favourite fishing stories. I shudder to think of all the long-suffering fishermen, longing to get away and tell one of their own, who have been hooked by this one and played to the bitter end. But at least it is not the story you think it is going to be. Let us get it over quickly. One day Maurice and I were fishing at Atia-muri with spoons, and Maurice hooked a big trout. It snapped his cast, and the fish got away with the spoon. A fortnight later, we were again fishing at the same place with spoons, and I hooked and landed – not the trout, which got away again, but Maurice's spoon.

The real point of the story is not so much the coincidence as the fact that it took place in the Waikato; that even in this gigantic river, wide and swift and deep, with miles of water to roam in, the trout have their regular habitations. We had the same feeling of wonder about a noble five-pounder I caught on another day at Atia-muri. Never moving from the one spot, we had fished all the sunny afternoon with both flies and spoons without getting a single strike. Then I changed my fly – and, instantly, a five-pounder. 'There you are,' said Maurice as I landed it, 'he must have been waiting all afternoon for just that particular fly.' True, or not true? Had he been cruising in the big river, and just returned to the run at the mouth of the creek at the moment when I changed my fly? Had he been asleep, and just woken up for his evening meal? Or was it really the one and only fly he would take? Of such intriguing speculations, never to be finally answered, is the fascination of trout-fishing made.

But – Taupo. That was the place that, sooner or later, however far off it lay, you simply had to fish. Not pastoral Atia-muri; not the Ara-tia-tia Rapids; not even Rotorua which, though so close to Taupo and classified in the same area, is not quite the real thing; not Waikare-moana, that remote and lovely lake on the road to which in my most unregenerate youth I once shot at a trout from a bridge with a .44 Winchester rifle, and, I am sorry to say, missed it ... But, Taupo.

Well, once I did go there.

I must have been about sixteen at the time, and I drove off from Eltham, full of the excitement of being free to explore the universe, in the red two-seater baby Austin with a schoolfriend who had the peculiar but very appropriate name of Wheely Barrow. Wheely was a long, shy, freckled youth, who lived in Waverley.

Braving the Taranaki summer and the chance of being stuck for ever in the mud, Wheely and I picked our way in sparkling sunshine over the ruts of the Tan-garakau Gorge, where tree-fern and rimu leaned their green branches over the road beside the creek and the bush was full of the clear calls and sudden harsh explo-sions of the tuis; and on to Taumaranui, legendary to memory because once with my father and mother I had made a dream-like journey to it by river-steamer from Wanganui; and on to Rotorua, that strange town smelling of rotten eggs and floating on a sea of boiling mud, where, trolling in the lake from a launch with a crude, unbreakable gear better suited to sea-fishing than the royal trout, we caught seven fish before breakfast the first morning with no trouble at all ... and where, exploring the Maori village at Whakarewarewa one other morning before breakfast, we caught the most fabulous monsters I have ever seen in the water – six fat naked Maori ladies wallowing in one of the steaming hot pools among the pumice. We had a very pleasant conversation with them; though an old chief, who had been keeping them company in the bath, stood up and wrapped his towel around him and stalked off with some dignity.

And so, on to Taupo.

Taupo lives in my mind as grey, rainy and desolate; grey mist drifting over the pale wastes of pumice sand and tussock, grey steam rising uncannily among the tea-tree scrub where boiling springs, unregarded and obscure, bubbled at random out of the uncertain earth; grey waves breaking on the huge grey wilderness of the lake. If Tongariro, Ngauruhoe, and Ruapehu, the masters and destroyers of the land, were visible that rainy day I do not recall them; but one sensed their giant presences; and remembered that at least one of the volcanoes, Ngauruhoe, was still always liable to breathe out a warning puff of smoke.

The sandy track in to Tokaanu at the south end of the lake was considerably enlivened by a road-grader, a shapeless mass in the mist, which I thought was moving away from me but which, at the very last moment, proved to be roaring towards me. But, after I had somehow circumnavigated it, all was quiet, grey and desolate again. On the long jetty poking out into the water at Tokaanu a few disconsolate fishermen were trudging hopelessly to and fro, trailing wet flies along the piles. I put on a large dark nondescript sort of fly which I had bought at the store a few minutes earlier, and instantly hooked an enormous trout with it. It ran under the jetty and broke free.

This aroused a certain animation among the fishermen. They gathered around me to examine the wonder-working fly, and asked me its name, which I did not know. A tall, rugged, weather-beaten man in waders and an oilskin overcoat said, 'Well done, young fellow! Have another go.' I did.

And instantly hooked another enormous trout, and, with the reel singing and the greenheart rod bent double, fought feverishly to keep it away from the piles; and watched it dash far out into the lake and leap clear with mighty splashes; and felt the weight of it as it dived deep down; and patiently held it till it moved and ran once more; and, yard by yard, brought it fighting and darting towards the jetty until at last, vast and gleaming in the grey water, it came floating in on its side and the tall kindly man in the oilskins somehow climbed down and netted it for me.

And it glistened on the jetty at Tokaanu. A seven-pound rainbow trout from Taupo!

The tall kindly man, I found out a few minutes later, was the ranger. My weekly licence for fishing in the Rotorua–Taupo area had expired the previous day. We departed.

I thought we should rub a little salt into that trout to preserve it: for one thing was certain, that my seven-pounder from Taupo, dreamed of for so long and at last caught, must be brought home in triumph to Eltham. So we bought a pound of salt at the store, and I rubbed a little along the backbone, inside. Perhaps one should rub a little into the skin on the outside, too? I did. But then, it was going to be a three days' journey back to Eltham, along the Parapara and up through Wanganui and Waverley. Perhaps it needed a bit more salt? And then, on the second day, you really could not expect a trout to travel in a car day after day without rubbing in plenty of salt; and, the bigger the trout, and this was a seven-pounder, obviously the more salt it would need.

I must say it got plenty. In fact it got so much that,

after everyone had admired its splendour, the size of it, the weight of it, the gleaming rosy-striped flanks and the delectable flesh inside so crisp and red from its clean diet of the freshwater crayfish of Taupo; after my mother had baked it and served it with parsley sauce in the way we liked best; after the whole family had gathered expectantly around it where it lay massive on the meat-dish on the table in the dark-panelled dining-room, nobody could eat a mouthful of it.

No. I am wrong. Both my mother and myself, knowing what a fish this was, ate at least two ounces of it before we gave up.

11

THE DUCKMALOI

THERE were good trout in the Duckmaloi and it ran through beautiful country; but I must say the first time I saw the place it gave me the horrors.

The trouble was, I was a newcomer: doubly a newcomer, for I had not been long in Australia, and I had never before stayed at the guesthouse from which we fished. It takes a few years to learn to cherish the more formidable particularities of Australia; and it is a truly terrible experience to arrive for the first time at any guesthouse, even so kindly an abode as was Richards'. You don't know what time the meals are, and where the lavatory is. And all the other guests seem to have known each other for years; and when you arrive they *look* at you. Looking at newcomers was, in fact, a favourite occupation for those who did not ride or fish at Duckmaloi. They used to sit on the veranda all day, on those ancient leather armchairs, and stare at all the guests who came hopefully down the red road in the Richards' car or the mailman's rattling cart. It gave them something to do; and someone to talk about.

Then there was the heat. The valley of the Duckmaloi, a hundred miles from Sydney over the Blue

Mountains and twenty miles out into the ranges from
the bleak flat township of Oberon, lay folded between
the mass of Mount Bindo to the right and the lower
hills rolling away from the Fish River Creek to the left.
The sun hung over it like a white eaglehawk and struck
down mercilessly. There was no escape from it – except
perhaps in one awful retreat under the high-propped
weatherboard house where there were some broken
chairs, a broken iron bedstead, and usually a few fowls
expiring in their dustbaths. Once, when it really was too
impossibly hot to fish, I spent some days under the
house, reading *The Fortunes of Richard Mahony*. I never
really got through that dismal masterpiece; but I did, in
desperation, try … On the veranda, if you preferred sitting and watching for the mailman – he came about
three o'clock every second day – you slowly and steadily
cooked. Out on the long slope down to the river where
a friendly garage-man from Sydney took me the first
day to introduce me to the fishing, a mile over plough-
land, bare grassroots, and fallen timber, it was hot
enough to knock you down.

There were also the flies. Duckmaloi was a great
place for flies. They were those little bush-flies that ride
by millions on your back and leave you with a con-
certed buzz of disappointment the minute you enter a
house. I never thought them as insanitary as house-flies;
and just as well, for if you ever grilled a chop in the
open they swarmed upon it from all directions and, no
matter how vigorously you waved it in the air to make
it at least difficult for them to perch on it while you
snatched a mouthful, you generally ate, on an average, at
least two or three dozen a day. They had a habit of
flying down your throat and choking you if you opened
your mouth to speak and, in a pardonable search for

moisture in that dry country, they loved to nestle in your eyes. The horses thrust their heads into the bushes to escape them and so, often enough, did we. If you wore a fly-veil you could not – or so I have always thought – see the snakes properly.

For Duckmaloi was also a great country for snakes – brown snakes, black snakes, tiger snakes.

We met our first, a nice medium-sized black snake, among the fallen logs on the track down to the river. I daresay there was a snake under every fallen log, and the brushwood fence, over which we clambered warily into that final paddock, was certainly infested with them. The serpent took refuge in a hollow, burnt-out stump; and Horrie, the garage-man, who was also an expert bushman and afterwards taught me many things about the small creatures which inhabited that apparently life-less countryside and empty water, cut a forked stick and neatly pinioned it. Then he proposed to seize it by the tail and crack it against a log. I suggested – sensibly, I still think – that it would probably bite him. Horrie, after some cogitation, agreed that it probably would. So after various futile attempts to get at it with a stick, we left it to bite us another day.

We hadn't been ten minutes at the river before another snake came slithering through the tussocks, and later in the morning there was a really beautiful black snake with a red belly coiled and sleeping peacefully in the long water-grass at the stream's edge. Next day, down near the crossing by Gearon's, forcing our way through the straggling wet undergrowth after a thun-derstorm that had soaked us to the skin and sent a fresh current of life through the baked landscape, we saw, simultaneously, three snakes quietly weaving their way across our track. It was good weather for hunting frogs,

I suppose; but they looked very much as if they were hunting fishermen. To a newcomer from New Zealand, these were quite an appalling sight. The three stray specimens on the first morning were enough to make it almost impossible to walk. And how fish without walking? What is to be done with rod and fly – or I am afraid it might have been rod and worm in those days – when one is standing paralyzed with fear on a tussock heap?

In a sensible stream you could walk the clear shingle at the edge and at least see what you were treading on. Afterwards on the Duckmaloi (the same day that my wife sat on a black snake in a tussock when she was settling down to paint) I did see a tiger snake stretched in full view across a clear grassy patch, drinking from a little pool. But the Duckmaloi had few clear patches of grass, and no shingle at all. In a sensible stream, again, you could avoid the snakes by wading; but the Duckmaloi wasn't wadable.

And in the end it wasn't the heat or the flies or the snakes but the nature of the river itself that so disgusted me that first day. For if you are a fisherman you love water: and what was there to love in that lukewarm brown trickle, sluggish and muddy as a drain, creeping through the ragged grey tea-tree or somnolent in big brown pools? Where was the dance of a rapid? Where, in that hot silence, broken only by the low roar of the flies when you disturbed them from your back, was the music of running water?

And where were the fish?

I don't know how many days Horrie and I tramped that useless, ugly stretch of water between the sandy swimming hole and the bigger hole upstream beyond which, dwindling to a yard in width, the river disappeared in a tangle of willows; how many times we sat at these pools futilely dangling a worm or, dropping an equally hopeless fly, investigated the inch-deep snake-infested rocky runnel between them; how many times we wandered downstream to where, below the ruined old pisé homestead of some early settler, the stream turned wide and shallow and laid its flat waters to sleep amongst quite unfishable bulrushes; how many times, filled with new hope, we slithered down the mountain across the road from the guesthouse to the willowy valley where the Fish River Creek (in which never in my life have I seen a fish) ran green and clean at least, but just as useless as the Duckmaloi, from pool to pool among the tall grasses; how many times, down the clay road in the heat, we trudged the two miles to the foot of the ridge where the Creek met the Duckmaloi and became – with a most resounding falsehood – the Fish River (a most hopeless place to fish, anyhow, because the miners from Lithgow used to camp there at week-ends and, so it was rumoured, slay any fish that *were* there with dynamite); or how many times, to make an end of this catalogue of hot, blank, useless days, we pushed further down the Fish River through the scrub and the briars to the pool below Gearon's farmhouse where the dogs rushed down and bit us and the snakes slithered all round us. The one thing certain is that in all those peregrinations we caught only one trout, a small one of about a pound – and the man who caught that was (I suppose I should have rejoiced; but I do not remember being particularly pleased with his good fortune) Horrie. It is difficult to be sincerely enthusiastic about other people's fish, until you have caught one yourself.

Yet, there were fish enough. The Duckmaloi teemed with them, in fact. There were thousands of them. Down at the junction of the two rivers, where we

usually finished at night because we were fishing from
clear paddocks or from the roadside, and didn't have to
trample on so many snakes, the water, as fishermen say,
simply boiled with trout. After the long hot days, when
the fish were too stupefied to eat, the evening rise was
superb. Everywhere you looked there were hungry trout
gulping down the white moths that swarmed out of the
tea-tree, the big blundering hawk-moths, the lacewings
fluttering past like miniature aeroplanes with their
double wings, the buzzing beetles, the long-horned
caddis-flies, the gnats, flying-ants – the myriad insects
that, waking like the trout in the dusk, stirred that lan-
guid riverside to life. In the shallows flickering with
sunset, small fish leapt clean out of the water. Every yard
or so of the long pool downstream, bigger fish, or fish
that reasonably seemed to be bigger, broke the still surface with their rings of light. In dark places under
overhanging bushes there were mysterious and alluring
splashes. The only problems were what fly to use and
which fish to fish for. It was bewildering and stupen-
dous.

And it was also beautiful. The sunset lay rosy on
the pool, and under it, as the dusk deepened and the
ridges changed from blue to dark blue to black, lay
Mount Bindo's gigantic reflection. Bats wheeled in the
glittering air; and all along the river, with the boomping
of the bullfrogs calling to each other underwater and the
innumerable shrilling of the tiny red and green and
brown and bronze-coloured frogs that lived under every
stone, in the wet grass and under every river-loosened
clump of clay and tussock, began the most remarkable
frog-chorus I have ever heard. The last wild calls of the
kookaburras rang from the ranges; from the tips of
the tallest grey ringbarked trees, gilded with the last of the

light, the magpies sounded their sweet flutes. The infuriating bush-flies went to bed. Whatever had seemed drab and dry and commonplace and nondescript about the river during the day changed utterly with the night. It was deep wild mountain country, the valley full of birds and frogs, the Duckmaloi full of trout.

It would have been better, of course, had we been able to catch those trout. It is possible, being a fisherman, to be so maddened by one's inability to hook a single fish when there are dozens rising all round you, as not even to notice the sunset; and those fish were very hard to catch – impossible, in fact. It may have been that phenomenon which fishermen so often encounter on the most promising and exciting evening, that of all the myriad insects upon the water there is only one species which the fish are taking, and that is one you cannot find in your fly-box; but I rather think that these were nearly all very small fish – too small to take a fly. We used to see them nibbling the feathers of the Coachman or dragging it underwater in a quite futile attempt to swallow it. No fish. No good. What was the use of the country's turning beautiful at dusk if you still couldn't catch a fish?

And then at last, inevitably, for if you keep on fishing you must sooner or later get a fish, triumphantly I caught a trout: about a pound and a half, or let us say two pounds; a little bigger than Horrie's, anyhow. 'I thought you were about due to get one,' said Horrie generously. I thought so too: due and overdue. But there it was: and, flapping on the grassy bank, gleamed in the dusk like the moon.

Extraordinary how one small fish can change the universe!

Even knowing the reasons, I have been puzzled

from that moment to this how I could ever have found
the Duckmaloi – or the prospect of trout fishing in Australia – unattractive. That I should actually have found it
repellent moves me to the most profound apologies.
The valley of the Duckmaloi was the most magnificent
country. Golden and brown and lit with the green of
oats and willows, it lay basking between its mountain
ramparts. The soft blue heat-haze smouldered among
the ironbarks. Eagles patrolled it by day. At night the
plover flew over, uttering their sharp, metallic cries like
the sound of a knife on steel. The gum-trees around the
guesthouse glittered with dew and stars.

I wonder now that I could ever have felt uncom-
fortable in that house – except for one night when I
shared a room with a deaf dentist from Sydney, who
snored so loudly he nearly blew the house down. But it

really was the most hospitable place. The food was excellent; and there was always fresh cream.

If there were a lot of people there, as sometimes there were, and they were not fishermen, which is a disadvantage, that had its compensations, too. You mostly had the river entirely to yourself. Only once, though occasionally I took out amateur fishermen and even girls, who walked ahead of you and scared the fish or stood behind you and got hooked when you were casting, was I ever really bothered by a rival fisherman at Duckmaloi. This was one of the times when Horrie and I had yet another shot at the tiny Fish River Creek – it *should* have had fish in it, that captivating little water with its deep unexpected pools and its clear straight tunnels through the grass. There was even a fisherman's guesthouse on it, Porter's Lodge. Maybe Mr Porter's patrons knew how to fish it. Anyhow we caught no trout in it the day the intruder was there, nor were we likely to. He was a spinner-fisherman – not that I could scorn the spinner-man in those days – whom we had actually brought down from Richards' to spend the day with us: a bristling, bullet-headed man who wore the most enormous boots; and my most abiding impression of him is of these great boots plod-plodding rapidly and determinedly past us while we tried to keep ahead of him. For we, that day, were fishing dry-fly; and a spinner-man, heaving his great hunk of metal into the water and churning up the pools, must keep behind the delicate fly-man, or he will scare all the trout. We tried to keep him behind us; he would not stay. We tried to keep him with us, fishing each pool after we had put our flies across it; he forged ahead. We tried to make him take pool and pool in turn; he raced ahead. So we tried racing through the tussocks to get quarter of a mile

ahead of him; but plod, plod, plod on those vigorous
boots, swinging his beastly spinner, every time, after we
had had about ten minutes' fishing, he caught up and
forged ahead; so once again we had to take to the tussocks and run for it. It was a very athletic afternoon.

Now I come to think of it, one other of the guests
from Richards' whom I remember with the same vividness, must also have been a fisherman; but he was a nice
fellow, this stocky, straw-headed, newly married young
man with his nondescript small bride, and found his
own stretches of water to fish in; and he stays in my
mind for a particularly delightful dream he innocently
related to us one morning at breakfast. I don't know
whether any of us – there were half a dozen men there
at that time, and only the one woman – had really been
eyeing his wife; I shouldn't think so. But he told us he
dreamed that all of us had hooked the one trout, but he
was the one who landed it, because he 'had it by the
tail'. A rude story, if Freud is right; but I liked its innocence. That same young man had his sturdy,
middle-aged father staying with him at the guesthouse,
a farmer or some kind of tradesman, I think, and he
remains memorable, too, because he used to thump
insects. Those were the nights when we all used to join
in a game called 'Up and Down the River', a most
appropriate game for fishermen, which consisted of a
combination of just about every card-game you could
think of, from poker to five-hundred; sitting all together
round the long table in the lounge-room while the
mopokes called across the valley and every kind of insect
imaginable swooped in out of the night to try to
commit suicide in the soft white petrol-lamp in the
centre; and every time a moth or a beetle landed within
range on the table, thump went that old gentleman's

middle finger. I suppose he killed fifty a night: not that that made any appreciable difference to the insect population of Duckmaloi. It may have been a kind of sport, like fishing; but I think he felt, rather, that the insects were impudent. Beetles should be kept in their place.

People are people, even if they are not fishermen. There was a lot of human nature to be observed at that guesthouse; and a lot of merriment, too, as on the night they tied a bell under the bed where a pair of honeymooners were to sleep. To this day I share the misery – and wish I had done something about it – of the spinster from Sydney: thirtyish, dark-haired, pale, obviously longing for her holiday: who arrived one baking hot afternoon, took a swift gulp of the superficial discomfort of the place and, as I might well have done myself on my first arrival, departed next day with the mailman: sitting up so straight in his cart, so proud, so pale, so distressed, so inconceivably embarrassed, as slowly, like a tumbril, the vehicle floated her down the road and out of sight. If only she had stayed two days – one week – to get the feel of the place!

Of all the nights at that pleasant, homely establishment, one stands out supremely. But that was a different matter from 'Up and Down the River'. It was too beautiful to stay indoors; and, very likely, too hot. But the fierce glaring day had gone. The air was soft and warm; and the full moon was up. It was a night so full of enchantment that the whole world refused to go to sleep. There were the frogs, of course, filling the valley with their melodious uproar that, now deep, now shrill, rose at intervals to a scream of batrachian delight. The crickets trilled by millions. But that night, while my wife and I walked along the road through the radiant countryside, the cicadas, too, who ought to be singing only in the sunlight, woke and clamoured in every tree. The kookaburras blew their trumpets on the mountain; and, with notes as sweet and fluid as the moonlight itself, the magpies sang on the bare timber. How magical the day's birds sound by night; and how fantastically beautiful this earth becomes when every cranny of it is filled with soft light, and all its creatures sing!

It was on such a night, on a good many nights of moonlight or starshine – though never another quite like that – that, coming home late over the saddle across the mountain, we used to watch the flying possums, the phalangers, dropping silently through the air into their favourite blossom-tree, a yellow-box, I think it was. Their fur was silver when we turned the torch on them; their eyes, a soft opaline blue if you see them by day, glowed red like rubies. They never showed the slightest fear of us. They seemed to keep the same timetable not only night after night but year after year, coming at the same time in the same season to that one tree out of all the thousands that grew there; for they were always there as we came up through the bush, and we saw them for three or four years in succession. Once, near the guesthouse, the great tabby cat slew one and left it on the roadside; a dreadful crime, yet forgivable because that cat was a mighty hunter and used to come marching proudly back to the house early most mornings with his head high and a rabbit in his mouth. A very proud cat he looked; though it may have been partly the necessity of holding up the rabbit that made him hold his head so high.

There were fireflies, too, along that track to the saddle: not many; not often; but sometimes just two or three, green and ghostly, moving like tiny stars between the trees.

The truth was, of course, that there were miles more of that countryside to explore and to fish than we had investigated in that first disappointing and unadventurous fortnight. It always takes two or three trips for you to get to know a place; and always – for some mysterious reason – for surely you always know how to fish – two or three trips to the same water before you really begin to catch trout. Even in those dull waters we fished the first few days, there were, had we but known it, things besides snakes worth seeing, and fish worth catching.

There were bass. Everyone called them bream. These were a surprising fish. One expects to catch trout in a trout stream, or at least I did, not having been trained to find anything else, except, in New Zealand, eels, which fortunately were usually too slow to take a fly or even a worm if you kept it moving. But here, even in the swimming pool, were these curious bass, up to two pounds in weight, covered with an armour of big golden scales, and looking like a rather ugly snapper. They were good eating, too, with clean white flesh. The locals said that if you caught one you would catch a dozen or twenty, for they moved and fed in schools; and so, perhaps, if you fished in the local technique, lighting a bonfire at night, to the light of which they would be attracted, you would. I never fished for them that way, never having cared for night fishing, but it was very pleasant to dangle a worm for them in the shade of a willow or wattle on days when it really was too hot to move, catching two or three in a morning and sometimes, by a most regrettable accident, picking up a trout at the same time.

For there were trout as well as bass even in that uninteresting stretch of water nearest the guesthouse.

The first I saw in the swimming pool darted up through the water behind a wall of tea-tree and took an enormous Coch-y-bondhu I was trying out in desperation – so startling me that I instantly pulled it out of his mouth. In a little runnel below the pool, flowing sweetly past a grassy bank, I watched a small trout of about a pound snap up a yellow butterfly; and put on some yellow fly myself, and got him. In the next pool upstream there was another trout I remember well, because it required an intricate and really rather pretty bit of fishing to hook him – a backhanded looping cast to put the fly under the tea-tree where he was rising.

Once, in flood, that despised bit of water became captivating, because in every pool from the old pisé house to the swimming pool and on through the willows to the big bend around the foot of the spur, platypus – sometimes two or three to a pool – were swimming; floating among the froth and fallen willow leaves and watching you with their beady black eyes or diving in the brown water with that oily swirl that so often misleads you into thinking that the father of all trout has risen. The floodwaters must have been bringing them a feast of worms and drowned insects to tempt them from their burrows. Nothing is better in fishing than those moments when the river displays its secret life to you; and the platypus, lying flat in the water and watching you, fearless unless you move too abruptly, is the most delightful of all its creatures – though I have enjoyed meeting wombats in odd places and once spent one of the happiest mornings of my life, on the Badja River, near Cooma, watching a pair of yellow-bellied water-rats playing chasings around a half-submerged log: in and out and round about, rippling and gleaming through the sunlit water like an incarnation of its fluid delight.

It was that same flood in the Duckmaloi that gave
me, too, one of the most curious and remarkable day's
fishing I have ever experienced. A couple of days earlier
I had had an amusing morning on the river with a fisherman from Sydney; upstream from the platypus pools,
near where the old fossicker lived alone in his hut.
Under the threat of imminent storm we were fishing
that enormous pool where some scoundrel had a wire-
netting fish trap (which, alas, never had any fish in it when
you pulled it up to take advantage of his scoundrelism).
The Sydney visitor was a very dismal little man with a
large, vigorous wife, leathery and weather-beaten, who
professed – and with reason – the greatest admiration
for him. 'If there's a fish about,' she said, 'my husband will
catch it.' And her husband would have, too. Silent, small,
finicky, inconceivably brilliant in his technique, he was
standing at the foot of a high bank that made normal
casting impossible. A trout rose right across on the far
side of that great green pool.

The fisherman's fly, instead of uselessly banging
against the cliff behind us, as any ordinary mortal's fly
would have done, rose spiralling straight above his head,
up and straight up with every flick of his wrist, until he
had enough line out to reach the fish; then down, delicately down, straightening as they fell, the long delicate
spirals sped across the pool to the trout. For some reason
or other he missed the fish; but it was a wonderful piece
of artistry.

Then five minutes later, accompanied by a mighty
crack of thunder, down came the rain. And it rained and
it rained and it rained and, as we crouched for shelter
against the cliff, the river swelled and turned muddy
before our eyes. 'Oh,' said the Sydney man dismally,
'there'll be no more fishing for a week.' Useless to tell

him that at least you could fish for bass; useless to say
that perhaps it would clear in two or three days. He was
an impassioned pessimist and, true to his convictions,
packed up and departed that night. I hope that, wherever he fled to, it stayed fine.

The Duckmaloi was a bad river in the rain – and
you always get rainstorms at one time or another on any
trip to the mountains. A river that runs high and clear
in flood remains more or less fishable; a river that turns
to mud like the Duckmaloi is useless. The trout go
down to the bottom and stay there. But the Sydney visitor was wrong, all the same. Within two days, though
still full and discoloured, the stream had cleared enough
at least to be worth exploring; and all along the edges,
in a way I have never seen before or since, the trout were
feeding voraciously, lying with their dorsal fins out of
the water and gobbling the drowned insects. All you
had to do to catch them was to drop them any kind of
fly at all. It was most interesting fishing, though, dropping the fly among the froth and fallen leaves, right
against the bank where the current, slower at the edges,
flowed among rushes and tussocks and bushes still half-
submerged by the flood; and it was strange and
intriguing thus to be fishing over what was normally dry
land. The trout, when eventually I cleaned those I had
caught, were full of little water-snails. That is what they
had been eating those two days when the river seemed
unfishable; and so perhaps you could still get fish, even
in the height of the flood, if you used a sinker and something that looked like a water-snail, or a big wet fly, or a
worm …

It was, in fact, on that same stretch of water between the
fish-trap and the platypus pools – and a noble stretch

this was, too, close, rocky and wild, crowded between a high round shaly spur on one side and the mass of Mount Bindo on the other – that my good friend Dr Bruce Hittmann cured me for ever of the worm: an appropriate enough feat for one of his profession.

A little too high up in the world – he was a Macquarie Street specialist – to stay at a guesthouse where you might meet people who weren't fishermen (or who fished with worms) Dr Hittmann took a room at the hotel at Hampton, on the rim of that plateau from which, filled with miles of blue light, opens the superb chasm of the Jamieson Valley. With him came Harry Andreas, who had been a pioneer of both the trout fishing at Taupo in New Zealand and the swordfishing at Russell. Andreas was a fascinating fisherman to watch. He had reached the stage of perfectionism, of meticulous attention to technique, which all good anglers should attain in old age; where the right fly, the right gear, and the right and proper way to fish were infinitely more important than merely catching trout. He carried an iron tripod for boiling the billy in the correct manner. He had his line wound on an elaborate linewinder to let it dry out properly. He had some special gadget for undoing the knots in his cast – both nylon and gut will snap if there is a knot. He wore, as Dr Hittmann did, too, correct riding-breeches and leather leggings to ward off the snakes. He had the most dazzling array of dry flies, something to match every conceivable insect that might be on the water.

The trout were rising when we got to the Fish River – striking across country from Hampton to the big waters downstream from the Duckmaloi country – but by the time poor Andreas had erected the tripod and started the billy boiling, and unwound the line from his line-winder, and greased it, and unravelled the knots in his cast, and selected his fly, and got himself dressed to fish, the rest of us had brought in four trout and the rise was over. It is a mistake to be too finicky. All the same, I don't think any of us would have got any trout that day had it not been for Andreas's expertise; for it was he who suggested, the river being high and discoloured, that something large and bright was indicated – an Alexandra or a Butcher – and both of these flies did the trick. From that day to this, when I have to fish a flooded river, I remember old Andreas and the Alexandra. I have cause to remember Bruce Hittmann with gratitude, too, for he used to tie his own flies and once gave me a large, impossible-looking bit of ginger fluff with which, one glorious sunny day over the saddle from the guesthouse, I caught – wading out deep in the warm summer water and casting far across the big pool to a trout that was rising in an awkward little nook under a grassy bank – a fine three-pound brown.

With these two lords of the angle, the day after our excursion to the Fish River, I fished the Duckmaloi in the stretch between the fish-trap and the platypus pools. It was good fishing, too, though I kept losing fish because I had not then learned to tie the proper knot for a nylon cast – exasperating when you have worked out how to catch a big trout under the willow at the tail of the pool, by casting right across the current and letting the fly wheel round to him, to hook him and have him instantly snap free! But, losing them or not, the fish were there; and the dry flies snaked out prettily over the water. The sun shone; the water ran green and dappled under the willows or sparkled in the shallows. I had made friends that trip with some novice from the guest-house – not a fisherman at all; just a bloke who had

borrowed a rod and thought he'd have a go at the trout
– and, taking pity on his inexperience, I had been
instructing him in the art of the worm. Tom, if that was
his name, was much too modest to fish with Hittmann
and Andreas; in fact I had warned him not to dream of
producing a worm in that majestic company. He just
tagged along with us. But he was there – and so was I;
and both of us wishing that we had dug a hole deep
enough to disappear in for ever – when, coming to a
grassy knoll at the end of the spur and seeing the exca-
vations we had made a day or two earlier, the torn-up
sods lying naked for the whole world to observe, Dr
Hittmann said with ineffable disdain, 'Some fella's been
digging for worms!' Never, never again! Not the
grasshopper, nor the witchetty grub (not that I have ever
been able to find one), nor the freshwater mussel which
I once tried out with no success at all in the Black Hole
over the saddle, nor the cicada which sometimes served
me so well in my misspent youth in New Zealand, nor
the mud-eye, nor the drowned dragonfly (with which
once in the Badja I caught nothing at all), nor the hawk-
moth (which I tried desperately to make stay on the
hook one night in the Duckmaloi below the old pisé
house when the trout were so eager that they leapt into
the tea-tree bushes after the big soft creatures swarming
that night in thousands), nor the frog (which I never
could bear to use anyhow, though deadly deeds were
done with it on Taupo), nor the 'gentle' so beloved of
Izaac Walton but scorned by all anglers of the Antipodes
– never, never again any form of live-bait fishing.

Some fella, some *fella*, had been digging for worms!
That is how dry-fly purists are made. The worst of it
was – or nearly the worst of it, for nothing could surpass
the horror of that accusation and the discomfort of the

air of innocence we had both instantly to assume – was that Tom had been doing pretty well with the worm and had caught two nice trout in the first run he fished the first morning I took him out: while I caught nothing. It is no doubt because he got me into that awful scene with Dr Hittmann that I recall with a slightly malicious amusement the occasion, a few nights later, when Tom got himself lost on the spur going back to the guesthouse from the same reach of water. At least, he thought he was lost. For some inexplicable reason, as we were climbing the spur in the dusk, he decided we must go in totally the opposite direction; down to the river again and across up the other side: which, as I stressed with increasing emphasis, would take us up the side of Bindo and into the wilderness indeed. We had one of those dangerously tense little scenes, on the verge of a quarrel and heaven knows what sort of a mess, that blow up so quickly in a panic, until I persuaded him to climb just a hundred yards or so further to the top of the spur; whereupon, glittering before us like a lighthouse in a storm, shone the distant lamps of the guesthouse – right where they always were. It was just the sort of thing a worm-fisherman would do …

I am glad, all the same, that I had not been cured of the worm on that incredible day, a year or two before Dr Hittmann's visit to Duckmaloi, when Horrie and I caught twenty fish in a morning in one little pool of the Fish River. This was in that most beautiful country which we had learned lay over the saddle that rose from the junction of the Duckmaloi and the Fish River Creek.

Downstream from the junction, the Fish River, as it now began to be called, took a long elbow bend past Gearon's farm and round the base of a spur – ragged country, and not many fish so far as I ever found out: though one day, fishing (alas) with a spinner, I had an exciting five minutes with a two-pound rainbow that dashed round the far side of a little island in midstream.

I also had in that same place an even more exciting five minutes with the most frightful snake I have ever seen – seven feet long it was, so Horrie told me; I was too terrified to think of measuring it. It was a gigantic brown snake, looking exactly like the fallen brown gum-branches it lay among, and when I nearly trod on it it reared up as high as my waist and hissed in horrid defiance. I did not like it at all.

The good fishing and the good water, where the river ran clear and green and deep, with shingle banks and wadable rapids, just as a trout stream ought to be, winding through timbered hills and grassy flats, paralleled all the way by the track of cobblestones where the Chinese fossickers in the early days had built a water-race to aid them in their search for gold, lay five or six miles from Gearon's, a full day's fishing before you got to it. But if you climbed the saddle as we learned to do, sometimes walking, sometimes riding on horseback, and later, when the engineers had made a road of a kind to

construct a pipe-line for the dam at Oberon, perilously
driving over by car, you dropped straight down onto
good fishing … and into that wild country where by
night we saw the flying possums and the fireflies, and by
day the bush was filled with the clear calls of the native
thrush.

A country full of bright water and happy creatures
– of small ticking locusts and louder shrill cicadas, and
honeyeaters that sang along the river all day and dipped
from the wattles to splash their green wings in the pools.
I remember it best in one season of searing drought
when the hills around the guesthouse were teeming
with thousands of rabbits – quite appalling to see; the
whole hillside, eaten down to bare granite sand, would
move in one verminous mass as you came over the skyline – and when all the life of that stricken countryside
had crowded into the river valley to survive. We would
see, vanishing in the scrub along the far bank, the dark
backs of wallabies in flight; or the black snake stretched
out full length on the grass; or, snorting and crashing in
the scrub, a couple of the wombats that had their great
burrows in the sand there; or, most curiously, we would
watch hundreds of exhausted bees crawling about on
the wet sand at the brink of the water, waiting for water
and the cool of evening to revive them. We listened to
the high clear calls of the thrushes and the honeyeaters;
and to the happy singing small locusts and the trilling of
the grey warbler. Bushfires smoked on Bindo; the cattle
stood knee-deep in the stream, chewing great strands of
water-weeds; and the mad old bull, hobbled with a
chain that never seemed to hamper his roving, used to
come blundering and clanking through the bushes and
frighten the life out of us. We grew expert, when it was
too hot to fish, at observing the small life of the stream

that rejoiced in the summer weather: the little bronze
lizards – skinks – which would dive into the water at
our feet and come up triumphantly with a tadpole
gripped in their tiny jaws; and which, so we found,
could be tempted and tamed with a crumb of cake, but
better still with meat. There were mussels living their
dim lives among the water-weeds; and the minute sticks
inhabited by the larvae of the caddis-flies which you
could see fantastically moving about on the sandy
bottom and which, when gently squeezed, would exude
a startled little insect's head; and, most fascinating of all,
there were the ugly small dark grey mud-eyes, larvae of
the dragonfly, that crawled out onto a stone and slowly,
slowly, if you had all morning to watch, wriggled out of
their hard skins, jerked out the soft silk of their wings to
dry in the sunlight and then suddenly, in one dazzling
crystalline flash, took to the air and were dragonflies.

The engineers making the pipe-line had built a
causeway over the river at one place so that their jeeps
could cross and climb, for some mysterious purpose, the
high far hillside; and in this season of low water, the
trout, so we found, could not get through the tunnels
they had left for them. I had always believed – and still
do – that except in winter when they go upstream to
spawn, trout always stay in the one place. It is a fact that,
day after day and year after year, you can always find a
favourite fish, if you can't manage to catch him, in the
spot where you know he lives. But they must, nevertheless, do quite a bit of travelling; for the quite absurd
concentration of trout in the shallow, insignificant,
altogether unimpressive little pool below that causeway could only be explained by the assumption that
migrating fish were blocked there. Perhaps it is the
smaller fish that travel, while the big fish, secure in a

good feeding-spot, stay put. Certainly, none of the trout below the causeway was more than about a pound in weight. But there, anyhow, they were; and all you had to do was to drop in a worm, hook your fish at once, pull it out as quietly as possible, drop in another worm and catch another. So there we sat on the grassy bank in the sun, dangled our worms and, that morning, caught twenty trout between us. When we seemed to have cleaned out the pool Horrie climbed into the branches of the willow-tree that blocked the top end of it near the causeway, and, from a hole amongst a tangle of roots and driftwood, pulled out a nice fat bass. No fish in the Duckmaloi indeed! I think that was the most surprising little pool I ever fished in my life.

But this was disgraceful fishing. And so, too, was that most curious rainy day lower down from the causeway towards the Black Hole when, fishing with a spinner, I found that every pool was alive with big fish, all on the move and all apparently feeding, but the only type of lure which seemed to interest them was the swivels on my trace which, inexplicably, they would follow with intense curiosity through the water and then, not attempting to bite at them, knock them with their noses. The spinner – Devon, Wisden or fly-spoon – never seemed any use at Duckmaloi, though once I did see a local fisherman with an enormous spoon, a rod like a telegraph pole and a five-pound rainbow in his bag ... But it is possible that some smaller lure, the size of a swivel, looking perhaps like some tiny immature fish ... ?

We did, I hasten to say, have great days with the fly, too, at Duckmaloi.

It was in fact on that river that a girl, a mere girl, nondescript and anonymous, one without the slightest

knowledge of fish or flies or insects, a Presbyterian min-
ister's daughter who happened to be staying at the
guesthouse and used to come fishing with me for the
walk – for she was a nice soul, and athletic – made for
me the great discovery of my life, the one piece of
expertise which I can contribute to the art and craft of
angling: Tup's Indispensable.

   We were fishing, the girl and I, at a pool below the
old pisé house in the waters I had thought uninteresting
(the ruined house, too, had its charms, for once I saw a
mother swallow whose fledglings were trapped in one of
the rooms, fly in again through the door out which she
had escaped, and lead her fluttering brood round the
room and along the corridor and through the kitchen to
safety). We were fishing, I say, this noble girl and I, in the
pool below the house and, though trout were rising, I
was not catching them. What were they taking? There
were plenty of insects about but nothing that seemed of
any particular interest. They were taking, said this most
observant and intelligent girl, who had been closely
watching the water while I tried fly after fly in vain, 'a
small grey fly'.

   The only small grey fly I could find in my box –
and I didn't even know its name then – was Tup's Indispensable. I tried it. There were two nice fish rising in
the centre of the pool, near where it curved round the
tea-tree to the tail. They both ignored the fly, prettily
though it floated on the surface right over them. Then,
by chance, it sank. Instantly the first fish took it; and in
a few minutes I had landed the second as well. As simply
as that are made the discoveries which change the
course of history!

   I have caught, I suppose, hundreds of trout since
then on the Tup's. I have taken, or lost, all my biggest fish

on it. It is always the first fly I try in the morning and
the last which, towards dusk, for it seldom seems to
work in the evening rise, I reluctantly change for something darker or whiter. It is not always valid, for
obviously there is no sense in fishing with a blue-grey
Tup's when there is a hatch of white moths or hawk
moths, red ants or black ants, caddis or the black spinner. I am not sure that it works in the very high country
of the Snowy – though that may be because when I
have fished up there it has usually been the grasshopper
season and for that the March Brown or Hardy's
Favourite seem about the most acceptable offerings. But
by and large, any stream and any season, and at any time
of the day except dusk (and even then occasionally) the
Tup's will do the trick.

It is not a very distinguished looking fly. Just small
and grey, as its discoverer said; or rather, small and bluish
grey, with a blue and fawn hackle (no wings) and a
touch of yellow at the thorax, an abdomen of soft pink.
I am not well enough up in entomology to say precisely
what insect it represents; but it is a creature that, if you
watch closely enough, you can see almost every day on
the rivers, small and grey and rising in spirals above the
water, usually in the late (but not too late) afternoon. It
is a kind of 'nymph' – that is, the newly hatched insect
rising through the water to take to the air for the first
time – and for that reason, though sometimes the trout
will take it floating, is best fished wet, six inches or so
below the surface. It usually seems to be tied rather
clumsily and insensitively in Australia – the yellow and
pink too garish – and when I was at the height of my
Tup's Indispensable period, before I shifted my head-
quarters to the Snowy, I used to have them sent over
from New Zealand: from my fishing days in which

country that first astoundingly successful specimen at
Duckmaloi must have been a survivor.

Then, too, there was the discovery we made about the
Black Ant: one day when these excited creatures, dressed
in their shining wings for their brief nuptial flight and
the founding of the new colonies, were swarming in
myriads over one of the big pools across the saddle.

Fish were feasting on them everywhere, ringing the
pool from end to end as if hail were falling in the sunlight. It was a day to catch a great bag of trout. But not
one trout could we catch; and both Horrie and I had
plenty of Black Ants in our fly-boxes. Then, by chance,
we found out what they wanted. It was a Black Ant tied
with a red tag at the tail; that infinitesimal spot of red –
and they say that trout don't see colour! – made all the
difference. I forget how many we caught – half a dozen
or so between us, as quickly as we could pull them in,
until, in the tea-tree or in fish that broke the cast, we lost
the only two red-tied Black Ants we had. Horrie caught
one more fish on a Zulu, which also is a black fly with a
red tag, but the Zulu has a striped body and they weren't
really keen on it. It was one of those discoveries one
stores in the mind for use ever after: when the black ants
are hatching, use a Black Ant with a red tag.

One other fly we discovered at Duckmaloi was the
Olive Green Dun. It was a big winged fly and whizzed
over your head like an aeroplane when you made a cast;
and a pretty fly, too, very appropriate in colour for that
country, over the saddle, of green pools and green honeyeaters. We did very well with it one changeable Easter
season; but it was not as dramatic a discovery as the Tup's
or the Black Ant and what I chiefly remember that time
for was the sudden cold rains, and how Horrie would

light little fires all along the river to warm his hands, and how, drowned at the mouths of their tunnels, we found the enormous golden-brown pupae of the bent-wing Swift Moths that hatch always on a stormy night at Easter. Sometimes we came upon the bodies of the great moths themselves, with stiff translucent wings and brown bodies as big as sparrows. There was, too, one gloriously sunny day that trip when the Captain of Industry who had come to fish with us – an immense man who carried on his back an immense rucksack crammed with fresh lettuces, spare fishing gear, quart-pots and a glove for handling them – charmed us by wading naked all day in the shallows where only the tiniest fish could be. 'I've been having the fun of Cork!' he told us delightedly when we came back at lunchtime from fishing the deeper water downstream; and he had, too – he'd caught twenty little trout in the morning.

Great days, in fine weather or wet! The greatest, in a sense, was the day of the monster: for that was a fish indeed, and if it did not turn the scales at more than four pounds, that is a pretty fair trout; and anyhow I never believed those scales. I first saw him, on my second trip to the Duckmaloi, one sunny morning on my way down to the junction. He was at the head of a pool by the roadside where a little creek ran in; and in the mouth of that creek, in about a foot of clear water, he was chasing water-beetles; round and round the shallow little creek-mouth, a curiously pale, silvery fish, shoul-dering the water aside as he moved, colossal in the sunlight. I was above him on the roadside; in full view of him; I dared not move a step. It seemed impossible to cast a fly downhill over the stones and bushes, landing it, as it must be landed, without a splash or an error of any kind right in that tiny pool where he swam; yet it had to be done; and that, inspired, with just the right length of line out, the fly dropping gently through the air, neither falling short in the tussocks nor reaching a yard too far and hooking the tea-tree on the other side of the pool, I did. The great trout, unimpressed, swam under my fly and continued chasing water-beetles.

He chased them in the same spot for four years, and every year I fished for him.

Once, in the dusk, having sneaked down into the long grass at the edge of the stream, I fished for him in the company of a small snake which rippled across the pool to greet me and disappeared among the grasses at my feet – a slightly disturbing experience. And then, one other night, stealing quietly into that same water-grass and dropping a Tup's Indispensable gently over the brink, I got him. What a commotion in that little pool. What surging and splashing and what a weight on the thin cast as he leapt. What problems with the snag in the creek-mouth. What perils in that grassy island in mid-stream! and what a strange fat silvery monster in the water-grass when at last, bulging out of the landing-net, he was captured. When I gutted him, I found intact inside him a large bullfrog.

It was a night, I suddenly noticed, full of the music of frogs, shrilling or profoundly plonking. It was a night of huge silver stars. The air smelt of cool water and dry grass. There were moths. Ahead of me down the road rose the saddle of the far magical country of the pha-langers and the Olive Green Dun. To the left as I turned for home lay the great dark bulk of Bindo where the eaglehawk towered by day and the white clematis hung its stars among the timber. On the ridge to the right, hanging above the Fish River Creek, the white sally-gums and the black sally-gums moved their glittering leaves in the breeze. And back at the guesthouse, up the long dusty slope of the road, there were, I knew, the most delightful people who would admire, and subsequently eat, my tremendous four-pound trout. The Duckmaloi, you might say, had proved itself.

12

BRINDABELLA

THE AWFUL thing that lean brown Australian bush-man said to me was, 'You can cross it if you're game.' I don't know that I was all that game; it would have been very nice not to have put a car into that fierce fast flooded river. There was a horse and sulky by which we could have crossed in perfect safety.

But one cannot disappoint a lean brown Australian bushman. The car – it was a very small car – entered the Goodradigbee. The Goodradigbee, not to be outdone, entered the car. It did not do our luggage any good, for that was on the floor at the back. It did not do the car any good, for afterwards it cost me fifty pounds to have some sort of stomach-pump put onto it to take the water out of its system. It did not do me any good, for it alarmed me. But possibly it did the lean brown bush-man some good, for it must have been a pretty and even an exciting spectacle to watch from the high seat of a sulky.

It may have been a mercy in a way that the car was instantly enveloped in a cloud of steam and smoke from the drowned exhaust – I believe I should have put a potato in it, or something – so that we could see very little of what was happening. But then it is not particularly encouraging to be drowned in a cloud of steam; and through the swirling mist we could still see, like mountain climbers in a blizzard, frightful glimpses of the scenery. Downstream, where we were driving at considerable speed, aided by the current, there was a rapid. A deep rapid. A rapid rapid. With curling white waves and flashing crests. Upstream, where now we must turn, for that was the way the crossing was supposed to lie (and anyhow it was not advisable, though easier, to drive any further down the deepening rapid) there was a great deal of the Goodradigbee, clear, high and glittering in the sunshine, pouring out of the mountains. It banked up against the side of the car and pushed it. The car began to swim. It also began to tip over. It also, and very understandably, said it had had enough of this, and stalled. It was having some difficulty with a submerged rock. And there, flooded, steaming, swimming a little in a hesitant sort of way as if it wasn't quite sure that it could, tipping a little as if it was quite sure it could do that, it rested. I brought it out in the end, after the gallant stockman had waded in and staggered away with some of the larger boulders in our path, by putting it into low gear and continuously pressing the self-starter button: which again, like water in the engine, is not very good for a car.

So. That was Brindabella in the great old pioneering days before they improved the road and put that wild water decorously running through a concrete culvert. You almost felt that the car was a bullock wagon, except that that really would have been a lot safer.

The road into the valley was appalling; or, if that is

too strong a word, at any rate quite an experience. The trouble was not so much that it ran very steeply indeed down Brindabella mountain; nor that the surface consisted entirely of giant boulders over which naturally you drove with caution and wondered how you would negotiate them on the way up again; nor that these, and an occasional deep rut, sometimes made you wobble nearer to the edge, which was precipitous, than you would have chosen. It was that the camber on all the extremely narrow bends sloped the wrong way, outwards; and that here, for some reason, somebody had usually improved the surface with sticky wet clay, so that you skidded a little; outwards. It looked a long way down through the trees. Once I drove that road with David Campbell when there was about a foot of snow all over it; and really that time I would have liked to get out and walk, but I suppose you had to stay in the car 'if you were game'. When we did get out of the car for a while, just to look at the view, there was a magpie stalking alone through the snowy bush; and green ferns arching out of the whiteness; and very tall strong gum-trees with greenish-coloured boles and branches. The snowflakes were still spinning down amongst them and grey clouds blotted out the mountains. The magpie looked at us and faintly carolled, as if to say summer *might* come again some time, and then flew off. He landed, eventually, in a poem.

When you got down the mountain and into the valley at last, there was no way out of it; only a bridle track through and over the wild ranges at the end of it to Rule's Point and Kiandra. The beautiful green valley, with the trout stream sparkling through it, lay astonishingly between the mountains. You wondered how anybody, in the early days, ever found their way to it.

Were the first men goldseekers following the river down from Wee Jasper? You thought how lonely it would have been for the settlers, probably just one family (was it the Franklins? or the Dowlings?), pushing in there with their stock from God knows where and clearing the green flats under the crowding walls of granite. It must have looked like the end of the world.

It still did; and it was still far enough out of the way to have a character of its own. People lived around it in odd places, and odd habitations, and did odd things. A rabbiter lived alone in a shack by the river, surrounded by piles and racks of dried and drying skins, so many that you could hardly get into the shack for them. He made, so it was said, good money out of them; but he was thin and peaky and shy and suffered from some kind of ailment that made him look rather like a skinned rabbit himself. An old man named Bob lived alone in

another hut a few hundred yards away amidst an unexpected garden of pink gladioli which he preserved in
memory of his dead wife. It was the sort of place where
a novelist could have set some wild, hillbilly story about
the neighbours feuding and shooting each other, or
bushrangers and cattle-thieves hiding out in the old
days. Anything could have happened there.

There were, moreover, two more crossings of the
flooded Goodradigbee to make before you reached
Bluett's homestead. But these, though the car miracu-
lously started again when it emerged dripping from the
river, I thought it as well not to be game about. We left
it wrapped in a white cover to think about all it had
been through, hidden in a grove of sally-gums so that it
would not frighten horses on the track, and rode the
next two crossings in the sulky. Crossing Number Two,
it turned out, was much deeper than Crossing Number
One; and the third was a nasty piece of boulder-
tormented water surmounted by a swing-bridge which
looked even worse to walk across than the river did to
drive.

In the midst of this wilderness Mr W. P. Bluett, who
let a couple of shacks to trout fishermen, maintained a
curious oasis of civilization.

The shacks were called 'chalets', which, such is the
power of words, made one look on them with affection
and respect. The fisherman, as well as the shack, was
ennobled by so romantic a term. And very pretty they
were, too, with their steep shingle roofs green and grey
with lichens among the snowgums, with their useful
stone fireplaces, their walls of slab timber and, where the
walls met the ceilings, the chinks that let in cool mountain air, sunlight and moonlight. Mr Bluett, a small, spare
old man, with a Roman nose and an air to him, used to

bring in with the morning tea each day (where now would you get such attention?), glowing beside the silver teapot and the white cups, a red rose for my wife.

No doubt it was hard to make a living out of a few sheep and a few fishermen among the mountains; and the fare at Bluett's was a little frugal; but interesting. Breakfast was of wheaten porridge, ground by Mr Bluett himself, a strange brown grainy substance that gave you a pleasant and sustaining feeling of living directly off the soil. After the porridge we ate the trout we had caught ourselves, and Mr Bluett's housekeeper was always annoyed when we returned to the river the just-undersized fish with which it teemed and so came home without the next day's breakfast. Lunch, of course, was sandwiches beside the stream. For dinner there was superb asparagus, grown in the garden by the river; and with it, so far as I recall, nothing but a huge bowl of haricot beans. Over this curious repast Mr Bluett, at the head of the table, presided with great splendour, wearing an ancient, faded dinner-jacket. He told us stories about the Admiral, a fisherman who had kept a manservant to pull his boots off. There was another story about someone who had blundered into a cave full of bats, somewhere in the surrounding mountains, and had been frightened out of his wits; and there were Mr Bluett's speculations about the aborigines of old who had climbed into these far places to feast on the bogong moths and had left behind them a few stone axes which Mr Bluett had patiently collected on his walks. After dinner you could examine these relics; or study, always with hope for the next day, a very nice map of Mr Bluett's reach of the Goodradigbee, with every pool shown and named and its most notable catches recorded.

Around the homestead, Mr Bluett's farm, on a high plateau looking out across the river flats and the red road through the rolling country to the mountains, lay green and trim: with neat fences and paddocks and yards, and a haystack in the corner of the clover paddock, and Black Orpingtons scratching around the woodheap, and some sheep, and the house cows, and half a dozen horses and, in an enclosure by itself, a small and rather rude black stallion. The horses and the house cows, eager for the succulent fodder, hung about the edges of the clover paddock all day, snatching mouthfuls under the fence, and one day one of the cows got in and ate till it was 'blown'. It swelled up like a balloon and Mr Bluett tried to ease its discomfort – I forget with what success – by sticking it between the ribs with a knife.

All this was quiet, and rustic, and as civilized as a farm may be. But there was really no subduing the wildness of Brindabella.

The lean stockman brought down a mob of cattle from the snow leases, and all night long they roared and bellowed and groaned around the homestead, speaking of snow and darkness, the granite peaks and the high bush and tussocky uplands where the dogger set his traps for the dingoes. I suppose the cattle were being branded, or the calves were being separated from the cows. They made the most fearful uproar.

In the dining-room at night, thunderstorms came in and rang the telephone. Even in the shack – I beg its pardon; the chalet – even in the chalet on those sunny mornings when silver light came streaming through the chinks in the ceiling and we lay luxuriously in bed drinking Mr Bluett's tea, there used to be, regularly, a display of singular – and oddly beautiful – ferocity. It was given by a little grey bird that flew in and hunted around the undersides of the shingles for moths that had settled there during the night. It would seize on one of these great furry insects, half as big as itself, and, furiously struggling to devour it, batter it to pieces on the dressing-table. Specks of moth-fur, moth-dust, moth-motes, floated up glinting in the silver light.

It was from the shack, too, through the big window that opened onto the great bald slab of granite across the river, that I watched one morning the magpies taking toboggan rides down a gum-tree. It was a day of flying storms and sun-showers. The gum-trees hung great bunches of shining wet leaves in the light. And down these bunches of leaves, from the tree-top almost to the ground, the magpies glissaded one after another in turn, like skiers on a snow-slope or boys on a muddy hillside. Four or five of them, glossy black and glittering white, were rollicking in the game. They filled the whole morning with their delight.

Beyond them towered the mountain. I have never, elsewhere in Australia, felt that impression of the extreme antiquity of the land which so many people have recorded; but here at Brindabella, and particularly when looking at that grey granite bluff across the river from the shack, I did indeed feel the weight of the centuries. It was something to do with the bulk of that great bluff, like the back of an elephant, a mammoth more likely, curving above the tree-tops; and its greyness; its stoniness; its smoothness. It intruded among the trees like a living creature; but a creature of stone, patient, immobile, worn smooth. It was old, old, worn-down country … and, thinking of the rabbiter and old Bob, the lair of old worn-down people.

Wee-loo, *wee-loo*, wailed the black cockatoos, crying

out their ancient aboriginal name as they flew overhead
down the river. They were funereal cockatoos; very
big, quite startlingly so; very black, with yellow feathers
under their wings and tails; and that long-drawn wailing
cry, forlorn and frightening. Everywhere you went there
was wildness. There was the gorge, for instance, at the
top end of Bluett's waters, culminating in a huge round
pool full of eddies and tumbled granite, beyond which
the river stretched on into nowhere; and somewhere in
a dark cleft between rock and tea-tree on the way to the
gorge, a yellow-bellied water-rat, exotic as the wailing
cockatoo, swimming the stream and slipping away to
safety in the undergrowth. He is a very handsome creature, this water-rat; not in the least like the common rats
but as big as a cat or a platypus. His fur, when he comes
shining from the water, is dark reddish on his back and
yellow underneath. And he is rare, too, far less frequently seen than the platypus.

Downstream in the Goodradigbee, where Bluett's
water tumbled down through the hills towards the
sedate green valley, there must have been scores of
wombats. You have to strike the right time to meet a
wombat, at dusk or dawn or maybe in a heavy mist, and
I don't remember seeing any here; but everywhere the
tall netting fence that had been put up to keep the dingoes off the property was tunnelled under and thrust
aside by their burrowings. Apparently wombats object
to fences.

And the snakes! Well, they were not much worse at
Brindabella than anywhere else along the rivers; certainly not swarming in multitudes as on the Badja or as
some friends of mine once encountered them lower
down on the Goodradigbee, near Wee Jasper, where they
were so plentiful and so excitable that my friends got

nervous about walking on them all the time and had to shift camp. But there were snakes; tiger snakes; which – why was it that so many of the wild creatures of Brind-abella chose this dramatic colour? – have yellow bellies, and are dangerous. There were staying with us at Bluett's that time two pleasant fishermen named Mr Henderson and Mr Angus. Mr Angus – a big, burly, florid man, who had some ailment of the leg that would not let him sit down in comfort, so he staunchly stood up for a fortnight – must have been allergic to snakes. He carried slung at his belt a sawn-off 410-bore shot-gun to ward them off; and every now and again, fishing the next pool or climbing round the mountainside to pass him, you could hear him blasting his way through the undergrowth.

I was myself pretty well snake-proof at that time, since I had not then abandoned the New Zealand habit of wearing heavy, chest-high canvas waders, which would really be an admirable garment in Australia if you didn't get so hot in them. But Mr Henderson, who was a novice at trout fishing and had not been many years out from England, wore no protection at all. A very tall man, sensitive and courteous, he clothed himself in shorts and sandals. His long bare legs bothered me when I saw them, and apparently, when a snake was about to bite them, they bothered him too. One day when Mr Angus had disappeared somewhere with his useful shot-gun, I was climbing over the mountain to the pool in the gorge with Mr Henderson; and, under a bush beside the track, we saw the most enormous tiger snake. It raised its head to greet us and flickered its nasty little tongue. Mr Henderson stood petrified. Petrified. No, that is not the right word. Transfixed with horror. He was transfixed with horror when first the snake rustled and rose; he stood, in his long bare legs, his shorts and his sandals, transfixed while I found a stick, while I hit the snake, while I chased it full-tilt down to the river. I think if I had not chased it away, beautifully secure in my waders, he would have been standing there transfixed with horror to this day. Fishermen from England, even if they have been a few years in this country, are not happy with tiger snakes; and I think Mr Henderson paid me the compliment of regarding me as a really tough Australian. I may have marred the impression on a sub-sequent occasion when, after nearly drowning myself wading one of the crossings, I met another tiger snake on the stones at the edge and fell back into the river to be drowned.

The stream itself was a wild little creature, the loveliest and wildest of them all; crystal and silver in the sunlight, dark under the granite in the gorges, green and yellow in the pools with the reflections of the wattles and the ribbony-gums; fierce as a snake in its sharp and frequent floods. In the valley it ran sparkling under willows. Bubbling over rocks and shingle, moving in that ever-enticing progression of rapid and run and pool, rapid and run and pool, sinuous, lithe and musical as it hurried down out of the mountains, it was the very model of a trout stream.

But fish? I stood in the rapid below Bluett's house the evening we arrived and, flooded though the river was, landed, one after another, five small rainbows; and, as they were just under takeable length, returned them, one after another, to the water ... to the subsequent annoyance of the housekeeper. This was promising; but I think Mr Bluett put those fish there for the benefit of his guests; and I daresay everyone caught, and put back, those same five fish. Certainly, there were enough small

fish everywhere to keep one intrigued. Once Mr Angus,
that enormous man, flipped a tiny trout clean out of the
water into my wife's lap while she sat painting a water-
colour by the stream. But I never again caught five
nearly takeable fish in a single rapid, nor did I ever land
one of any size. There seemed to be good fishing downstream, among the tall tea-tree and the wombat
burrows, where the trout in the fast current would take
the fly with a bang and break the cast so that they all felt
like two-pounders; but, though I could always say − I
did − that I had lost a two-pounder, I doubt it.

I doubt if there ever were any respectable fish at
Brindabella. That time I fished there with David Campbell when the snow lay all around on the tops, we
caught no fish at all; in fact, sunny and clear of snow
though the valley itself was, the cold hurrying water,
with never an insect or a rising trout to break the surface of the pools, looked so utterly hopeless that
Campbell went away and sat in a willow-tree and read a
book of poetry − the worst thing I have ever seen anybody do out fishing. The only really interesting thing
we did that trip, apart from driving through the snow,
was to jump into the icy river to help the farmer with
whom we were staying rescue a drowning cow; which,
when at length we had shoved and dragged it to the
bank, promptly, as they say, died on us. The farmer
turned out to be the uncle, by marriage, of the poet
Rosemary Dobson. It is a small world.

There were fish, and good fish too, even mighty
fish, in the Goodradigbee away down at Wee Jasper. I
know, for I have caught them there − that time the rats
drove us out of the old police barracks and we went and
camped with the telegraph linesmen and ate roast rabbit
for breakfast. I have other friends − acquaintances, I

should say – who say they have done well with spinners in the gorge below Brindabella. But with the fly, in the waters from the valley up to Bluett's gorge … I would have to see the fish to believe in them. The map in Bluett's dining-room marked the pools where here a two-pounder had been caught, and there a three-pounder, and that in itself was ominous. Where two- and three-pounders are reasonably common, as in a really good stream they should be, you do not bother to record them. The small, just undersized fish we caught had often had a curiously weazened appearance; dark, shrivelled, old-looking. They were, very likely, fully matured fish; old men of Brindabella who, in that clear swift rocky-bottomed stream, had never had enough tadpoles and yabbies and all the teeming life of quieter waters to fatten them. Just once, away downstream from Bluett's near where the old quince trees grew in the clear paddock, I saw a big fellow. Far across a wide pool and under the screen of a weeping willow, quite out of reach of a cast, he floated in liquid sunlight, showing his rosy side as he swam lazily into the green depths. He was the most superb three-pounder. Two-pounder? Four-pounder? He was the lord of the mountains, the one big fish of Brindabella; and, so well was he protected by the width of the pool and the tangle of willow and tea-tree on the bank under which he cruised, I suppose he is there to this day.

I should like to leave that fish, glowing and elusive as the rainbow from which he takes his name, as the image and epitome of fishing at Brindabella; but that would not be quite true to the tribulations and rewards of this particular expedition: which concluded with the most perilous perambulation across Mr Bluett's atrocious swing-bridge – the wires sloped down towards

the centre, so that you walked the plank high above the
flooded stream with nothing to hang onto; then with
wading the second crossing, in which, while I was
joking with the others on the bank and not looking
where I was going, I let the current nudge me into an
extremely deep rapid and then stepped out to meet the
tiger snake that drove me back in again and finally with
one of the obliging Dowling boys towing the car
through the final crossing and round and round a stony
paddock until, shaken out of its water-logged torpor, its
engine feebly started. We were so late by this time that
we decided that, rather than face the road up the mountain in the dark, we would all camp the night by the
river in our cars. In the bleak and misty dawn, straightening out our cramps, we went fishing to catch our
breakfast. Mr Henderson and Mr Angus were unlucky;
or, at least, they were honest. They put back the undersized ones they had caught. But I bore triumphantly
back to the camp two little rainbow trout each about
five inches long and these, to Mr Angus's intense disap-
proval, but I had learned bad habits by then, we ate.

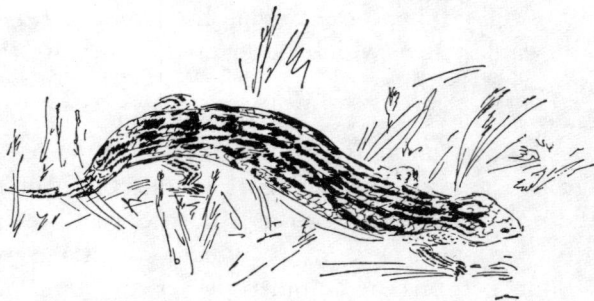

13

THE BADJA

How complex a blending of landscape and rivers and weather, of people and wild creatures and trout, are the attractions of any place where you go fishing.

I used to love the road into Countegany from the turn-off near Cooma, winding twenty-six miles through a tunnel of crowding white sally-gums; with here and there a patch of dead ringbarked timber ghostly with lichens or glimmering with bright green moss; with rocky hillsides to the right where at any moment you might hope to see a kangaroo; and, through the dark she-oaks to the left, glimpses of the lower waters of the Badja gathered in long glimmering pools where you might, and often did, see a trout rising.

The house at Boggy Plains, when at last you reached clear country after the steep climb up from the causeway over the creek by Andy's Flat, was practically invisible. Smothered in tall green broom-bushes, bright with their yellow blossoms, which had multiplied and run wild since some early settler had first planted them as a wind-break, it lay below the level of the road, and all you could see of it was the red corrugated-iron roof, buckled and flattened by years of winter snow.

It was a house full of character. It belonged wholly and perfectly to the hillsides of granite boulders and flowing clean spring waters. It spoke in the one breath of the golden flowering of summer and the white weight of the winter. Its crumbling walls and its dark creaking interior murmured inarticulately of the first settlers, maybe a family from Ireland, who had built it and lived in it for generations. The gunroom, with its ranks of nails driven into the walls for you to rest your rod on overnight without the bother of taking it to pieces, spoke with most pleasant clarity of fishing.

It was a house of white-washed pisé, long and low with a veranda running the full length of the front of it in true colonial style. Whoever long ago had dug a site in the hillside and rammed the clay between boards to make its foot-thick walls, had built it at different levels, so that when you walked out of the kitchen into the sitting-room you fell down three steps: which, after dinner, was likely enough to happen. The bedrooms, which opened onto the veranda, had only one small dark rattly window, so that you left the door open at night for air, snakes, and bats to come in. I never did in fact find a snake in the bedroom, but Molly Snow once killed a copperhead on the veranda. We used to chase the bats out, when they became obstreperous, with a landing-net.

We sometimes had bats in the sitting-room as well as in the bedrooms, but the sitting-room door was usually tight shut to keep out the cold upland winds, and the only animal regularly haunting that room as we sat by the great log fire at night was the household cat, which Molly used to lock up in the ceiling to eat the rats. It thumped and miaowed uncannily above our heads.

In the dining-room, where Jack Snow with his long straight nose and staring black eyes presided nightly at the head of the long table, there burned another great log fire, and I liked the story Jack used to tell about that fireplace. Boggy Plains, or Countegany as the whole district was called (you pronounce it Count-a-guinea) was a wild, hillbilly sort of place in those days, a wilderness of mountains and high tussocky plains farmed by a few scattered settlers living miles off the road in habitations more invisible and inaccessible even than Jack Snow's. The road in to Cooma was difficult at the best of times, often impassable in the winter. There was little entertainment for the adults, except an occasional trip into the saleyards at Cooma or a rare woolshed dance when shearing had cut out. For the shy bush children, who disappeared into the scrub or peered at you with bright eyes from behind their mothers' skirts when you visited one of the farmhouses, there was nothing. It occurred to some fishermen who were staying with Jack Snow one Christmas that they would wake up the plains of Countegany. They would give a great Christmas Eve party at Snow's, and invite the whole neighbourhood. Particularly would they invite the children. They would make the old house resplendent with streamers and balloons. They would feed the kids jellies till they burst. They would have a present for everyone. The chimney above the old white-washed smoke-blackened fireplace in the dining-room was enormous. The largest and most benevolent of the fishermen would dress up as Santa Claus and climb on to the roof and, at the mystic and holy stroke of twelve, slither down the chimney and give the children assembled round the fireplace the surprise of their lives. He did, too. When he came crashing down with his sack and his beard and his flaming red

robe and hood, and a cloud of soot behind him, they
thought he was the devil and screamed and lit out for
the bush. Most of the rest of that night was spent in
looking for them up in the cowshed or down in the
scrub by the river where they had hidden themselves.

The dining-room was notable, too, as it should
have been, not merely for Jack Snow's stories, but for
Molly's dinners. Molly was jolly and plump and rosy-
cheeked, more like a lass from Devonshire than the
traditional lean brown wife of an Australian farmer.
Whether the meal was a chicken from the fowlrun on
the hillside, or one of the red-nosed Muscovy ducks that
used to dabble in the creek behind the cowshed, or lamb
from their own flocks, or pork or beef from the butcher
in Cooma, or a baked trout from the Badja, all her
dinners were magnificent; and they were served, with

truly heroic patience on Molly's part, at whatever hour you chose to come in from fishing. And we came in late enough, too: maybe nine o'clock when we had been fishing the evening rise on the easy waters of the Luncheon Pool downstream, ten or half-past ten when we had done that long climb back through the moonlit sally-gums from the Pockets. There would be just time for two whiskies by the fire, and then it was dinner-time. It is the fisherman's constant problem: how do you fish the evening rise and turn up in time for dinner? Molly had the perfect solution. If there was one disad-vantage in this noble system, it was our fault, not Molly's: and it was her dumplings. Dumplings, some kind of suety construction with jam or stewed apples, were Molly's masterpiece. They were large, they were weighty, they were good; and they would soak up cream like magic. There was always plenty of the most glori-ous thick fresh cream. But however much cream you poured onto those dumplings, they soaked it up and it vanished; so you poured more cream on; and more. Then, exhausted with the long day's fishing, you fell straight into bed … and the dumplings, with their great creamy fists, began to pummel you …

The best place in the house, however pleasant were the fire and the dinner-table, was the veranda. It did have its disadvantages. If it was rarely invaded by snakes, it was made hardly less perilous by a frightful species of green bulldog ants, an inch or more in length, which cease-lessly patrolled it. The ants had a notion that something edible, possibly human, lived on the veranda, and used to send their scouts one by one, like angry emeralds, up the concrete steps to see what it was. If, as was the case with me on one or two trips to Countegany, you were guarding a very small child, you had to pick up these diabolical creatures and toss them back down the steps, whereupon they would shake themselves in a puzzled sort of way, and climb up again …

But straight across from the veranda, magnificent to the eye, the gigantic hump of Mahony's Mountain heaved itself out of the tussocky flats. Who Mahony was I don't know; perhaps he was the first settler, an emigrant from Ireland, who built the old house where we lived. Whoever he was, that is how the mountain was always named, not the conventional Mount Mahony, but Mahony's Mountain. It gave it a curiously personal quality; it was not just a name on a map but always, for all time, Mahony's private property. And, though it was no slow-clad alp, it was a very nice lump of the earth to own. Its great long curving ridge filled the whole sky. Magpies sang their carols at dawn from the silvery timber in its clearings. Eaglehawks patrolled its crest and, when the magpies swooped up to attack them, circled higher and higher above its summit until they lost themselves in blue space. When the afternoon light picked out each individual tree with the bark new-peeled from the trunk, its mighty candlebarks stood out like shafts of gold. The wild chorus of the kookaburras rang out from its gullies at dusk. Black night crowned it with stars. Whenever you looked, wherever you looked from the veranda, there was Mahony's Mountain. One rainy and drizzling day when the weather was too miserable for fishing I climbed the mountain with Jack Snow, and found it, under the huge silent wet trees, lit from bottom to top with wildflowers – buttercups, pale-green mysterious nodding greenhoods, starry gold bulbine lilies, such masses of wild violets, both the blue-and-white and the big plain purple kinds, that if you were going to walk at all you had to walk on violets; and finally, right on top of the mountain, like a wicked little king of the flowers, the yellow double-tail orchid, *diuris maculata*. It was the most wonderful mountain.

A most curious thing to see away up there was the remains of a fence. There were also grass-covered hollows and weedy mullock-heaps of quartz where prospectors had dug for gold. Wherever you go in Australia, no matter how remote the place, you will always find that some optimist has been there before you and fenced or fossicked the wilderness. Whoever it was who dug for gold on Mahony's Mountain had long been forgotten; very likely it was Mahony himself; but the man who built the old fence was Davy Thomas. Davy, who was still a neighbour of Jack Snow's, had been 'struck be lightnin'' in his youth, so he would explain when he came over to help with the dipping. The lightning had knocked him off his horse, and he was never quite the same man afterwards. He still felt the electricity, unexpectedly, 'in me teeth'. So Mrs Thomas, his young wife, had had to help him build the fence for whoever then owned the property; and became a legend of Countegany, bundling her babies into an iron-wheeled pram and pushing them before her up the steep flowery mountain where she swung an axe all day in the heat like a man, and felled the timber and built the fence with Davy. Mrs Thomas, with all those years behind her, used to come over and help Molly Snow with the housework sometimes; and we would see her stalking along the veranda with a broom, very tall, very lean, very dark, secret and black-looking and beautiful like an eagle. She had a peculiarly mysterious air, as if she knew more than anyone else about Countegany.

She was not the only wild creature we saw from that veranda. Sometimes a flock of wood-ducks, those curious birds more like a small goose than a duck, would feed like domestic poultry in Jack Snow's clover paddock. Sometimes a calf would come to drink at the old iron water-trough that stood just outside the fence. Sometimes, to Molly's consternation, Jack would let his newly-dipped sheep in, brown and dripping and clamorous, to 'mow the lawn' for him; and then we would stand guard over Molly's three brave gerberas. Sometimes a fox would come down out of Mahony's Mountain after the rabbits and trot purposefully along through the tussocks. Sometimes, rarely, there would be kangaroos. Often we would watch the strange grey freezing sea-mist, when it had driven us home from fishing, come rolling over the mountain, blotting out the ridge and the trees and the flats until you could not see as far as the front gate, and the whole world was lost and hushed. Though it was inland country, not far from the Snowy Mountains, and the thought of the ocean seemed utterly alien to it, Countegany was in fact quite close to the coast. It was mountain plateau, and at its rim the ridges and rivers fell down to the salt water. Quite regularly, two or three days a week, at about four o'clock in the afternoon, this strange grey breath of the ocean floated over the rim of the plateau and, every moment growing huger, colder, and more dense, rolled over the country like a tidal wave and drowned it. It was quite possible, unless you had the river to guide you home, to get lost in it. The minute the first chill premonition of it reached the river all fishing was finished for that day. The fish went down to the bottom and stayed there. All you could do was pack up and go home – if you could find your way.

When it was not blotted out by the fog, the best thing you could see from the veranda, for after all we went there to fish, was the river itself: the never-to-be-forgotten Badja (so called, it was said, because the first settlers, finding it frequented by wombats, called the wombats 'badgers' and then, changing the word to something that looked more aboriginal, named the river after them); the deep dark tranquil Badja that, flowing almost imperceptibly through this high flat marshy country, gathered itself into long glittering pools, and ran a step or two and paused to dream in another mighty pool, or sometimes, astounding itself, tumbled headlong down a granite gorge, then quietly recovered its breath and once more fell to sleep; the soft slow-running Badja, fringed with blossoming tea-tree and the silver or olive-green stems of its two kinds of sally-gums, ringing with the calls of thrushes, inhabited by enormous trout!

One blinding, baking December day when it was too hot to sit on the veranda and far too hot to think about fishing, and we lay and idled away the hours in the shade of the plum-trees at the side of the house, suddenly we saw the big shining circle of the Sally Hole, a hundred yards or so downstream, dimpled with the rings of rising trout; and when I stood on the veranda to get a better view there were more fish rising in the gleaming reaches towards the Rock Pool, for as far upstream as we could see. When I got to the river it was boiling with fish. It was a marriage feast of the red ants. The air was full of wings, the water was full of trout. Never have I seen so many fish! They rose in that fierce noon when the temperature was somewhere near a hundred; all afternoon when the silver slanting light made the water unbearable to look upon, they rose and they rose and they rose: in the Sheepwash Pool where the yabbie-holes in the grassy bank always looked so much like the lurking-places of snakes; in the shallows by the concrete causeway over the road; in the Dead Hole; in the sandy pool on the corner where the thrush sang in the willow and a big fish lived out of reach in a tiny frothy backwater against the far bank; in the shallow bend at the tail of it where my daughter saw the black snake wriggling across the water-weeds; in the Rock Pool where Jack Snow caught a four-pounder early one morning and thereby proved that his Coch-y-bondhu was just as effective as my indispensable Tup's Indispensable; in the long canal-like straight back towards the Sally Hole where the raft called the S.S. *Boggy Plains* was moored and where by night some monster that was either a platypus or the biggest trout ever heard of used to thump and splash like a crocodile everywhere that searing, sizzling afternoon hundreds of trout were rising for the red ants.

And out of them all I caught … I caught one lean, miserable specimen of a rainbow, less than a pound, from the Dead Hole. On another day it might have been an interesting enough capture, for in that dark deep sinister pool, its waters perhaps tainted by the big trees that had fallen into it, there weren't supposed to be any trout at all. But one lean little rainbow for that afternoon of the red ants! It was disgraceful; and Jack Snow, when I got back, told me so. The simple truth was, I didn't have in my fly-box a decent imitation of the red ant. How can a fisherman be such an imbecile? You must always, as I learned at Duckmaloi, have a Black Ant in the box, ready for the one day in the year or the one day in ten years when you strike the wedding flight of that variety; and you must never, as I learnt with agony at Countegany, fail to carry a supply of the Red.

Straight after that, it snowed. Snow in December

would be surprising anywhere in Australia; here, after the heat-wave, it was incredible. How beautiful it was when we woke in the morning to find the whole valley lying white, and a grey haze over the ribbony-gums loaded with snow on Mahony's Mountain, and the white flakes still spinning and floating down into the dark-green gully between the clover paddock and the road along the ridge. How enchanting it was, when we built a snowman on the lawn before breakfast and decorated it with my father's curved cherrywood pipe. How bleak and curious it was to fish the grey sleety river, as I did for a while, without noticeable results, just to see if the patter of snowflakes would mislead the trout into thinking the winged ants were falling on the water again; and to see, anyhow, how it felt to be fishing in the snow. And how cruel it was. I walked over the white paddocks with Jack Snow − an appropriate name he had, for a farmer on that high plateau! − to see how his sheep were getting on; and, there, over the hillside across the road, were thirty of them lying stark and frozen against the fence. They must have been making for the shelter of the rocky gully where the hillside in the next paddock dipped down into a creek-bed; and, reaching the fence, piled up against it and perished. I admired Jack Snow very much on that occasion. He didn't say one word about the heavy financial loss this meant to him; only, later in the day, got his tractor and dragged the carcasses out of sight.

So, Countegany was memorable for many different things: for the old house and its legends; for the little separate white-washed cottage of the cool-house, where Molly Snow churned the butter; for the water-race in which, for some mysterious purpose, Jack kept captive a three-pound rainbow trout; for the black Polled Angus cattle at rest in the shade of the sallies; for wood-duck in the clover, and black duck flying at dusk; for the blue and crimson lowries in the orchard; for fog and snow and thunder, and strong winds rushing through the valley, and the stars by night and the sun by day that glittered with unparalleled silver intensity out of the steeps of pure mountain air. But the two things for which it was really remarkable were trout, and snakes. I never had such fishing anywhere else in Australia; I never trod on, jumped over, slew, or sneaked horror-stricken away from so many millions of serpents.

Out of the general writhing mass of them, black snakes, brown snakes, tiger snakes and the small vicious copperheads, I recall three with particular vividness: the first for no better reason than I saw it on the first morning of my first visit to Countegany … after, on our arrival on the previous afternoon, we had plodded so innocently through the clover, the long grass, the tea-tree, and the tussocks by the river. It was just a nice, well-meaning, reasonably sized black snake sunning itself in the sparkling morning on the broken granite at the head of the Luncheon Pool (where Jack Snow had caught one of his four-pounders in the backwater and where the trout rose so tantalizingly against the reeds on the far bank) … just a snake. But there is always something peculiarly dampening in your first meeting with a snake in any new fishing spot. You know there must be snakes, because there are always snakes; but you prefer not to see them; then you don't have to think about them. And when you do see the first of them there is always that moment of shock, that curious feeling of betrayal, as if the bright water and sunny rocks have played a singularly dirty trick on you. And the feeling stays with you.

I never saw that snake again after I futilely whanged at it with a stick that first morning; I fished the head of the Luncheon Pool many a day; but I never really liked the place; I always expected it to bite me.

The second snake was the beast which David Campbell and I saw early one morning when we had rashly got out of our comfortable beds to see if the trout, too, were awake in the cold and the dew and the mist. They weren't. But on the tussocky flat just across the river from the house, at the base of Mahony's Mountain, stretched full length across the narrow sheep-track we were following, there was the snake. I cannot really explain why I found this incident so inexpressibly comic. I jumped; and, like one sheep after another, Campbell jumped too. But I jumped clean over the snake, which was the only thing I could do when it was right under my foot; whereas Campbell's great leap, seeing that he was behind me on the track, should by rights have landed him precisely on top of the snake. How he missed it I don't know. But I laugh every time I think of the two of us bounding along that sheep-track in the dawn, and Campbell poised in mid-air with the snake sliding under his boots.

And the third snake – the third snake was the one that lived in the creek behind the cowshed. That holiday, because my wife was busy painting the landscape, I was guardian and entertainer most of the time to a very small child. I tried to make it sleep so that I could go fishing, but it bounced out of bed onto the veranda and played with the green bulldog ants. I took it to the ford below the Sally Hole and we built a small dam and sat in it. I rescued it from the fowlhouse, where it was bailed up by a broody Muscovy duck. I took it over the hill-side across the road, where we gathered the buttercups,

the little pink and white pincushions and the purple
wild violets and threaded them into the quoits on the
veranda to make some weird kind of floral tower. I took
it to the concrete crossing where the road met the
Badja, and we set fire to the tussocks to clear the snakes
away, and built dwarf cottages of the rounded river
stones for the mermaids — it is not generally known that
there were mermaids in the Badja. I took it, bouncing
on the back of Jack Snow's tractor, far across the hills
into the sucker forest where, in a hollow tree-trunk
walled with earth by the white ants, we found the door
of fairyland; which, at the magic words 'Open Sesame!',
opened, or almost opened, to reveal the long corridors
and ballrooms lit with sparkling jewels where the people
with their shining wings danced with each other like
cicadas. And I took it, small and naked as a skinned
rabbit, bathing in the creek behind the cowshed. There
was no possible cover for a snake at that pool. There was
the sandy shore from which we entered, the grassy bank
cropped short by the cows, and the clear water. And, on
the grassy bank, there grew a solitary dock. And while
for a minute I was a few yards down the creek, collecting an old tin to catch tadpoles in, out of that solitary
dock, from under its three or four wide green leaves, a
yard from where the small naked rabbit frolicked in the
water, slowly, with a tiny rustle, there manifested itself
the most monstrous red-bellied black snake I have ever
seen. And it began to glide, with God knows what
intent, whether just to escape or whether to make a
meal of rabbit, straight towards my offspring in the
water. Horror! When we had fled to a safe distance away
on the hillside I stopped to watch; and the snake swam
across the pool where the child had been, then paused
and seemed to nose about on the sand where we had

camped. I don't know if a snake would, in fact, eat a very small child. I doubt it. I never heard of such a thing. But that really did seem to be its intention. I had no regrets whatever when Jack Snow came down from the cowshed and finished that one off with a length of fencing-wire.

It must have been a tribute to the size of the snake or the nastiness of the occasion for Jack to condescend to use such a weapon. Normally, Jack just used to stamp on snakes. It was one of the great sights of the Badja.

Jack was an intrepid fellow in his way. He had served in the Air Force during the war and had had to bail out over Italy. He still did it sometimes. In the middle of the night, when all the old house was silent, you would hear a crash and a thump on his bedroom floor, and that would be Jack, bailing out over Italy. I think he got into the habit of stamping on snakes simply because, when there were so many of them at Countegany, you were practically walking on them all day anyhow. And of course you don't usually carry a wire fence with you when you are walking over the paddocks, and any stick you can find always breaks. So Jack just stood on them. You'd see him across the river or just ahead of you on the track, suddenly start marking time, lifting up his long bony legs and raising his knees above the tussocks, left, right, left, right, like a soldier, and that would be Jack Snow stamping on a snake.

He had a theory that his boots were sufficient protection for him, since snakes always struck downwards at the ankle, and if one did happen to have a go at his leg its fangs would get entangled in the loose cloth of his trousers; and anyhow if you did get bitten and didn't have a knife, all you had to do was to lance the wound with a sharp blade of grass … Everyone, hearing these preposterous ideas or, worse, actually seeing him go left, right, left, right, pounding away in the tussocks, would say, of course, that sooner or later a snake would get him ... and, sooner or later, one didn't. No snake ever bit him, though many would have liked to; he just kept on pounding away, the champion snake-stamper of all time.

As for the fish, they were everywhere. And everywhere along the ten miles or more of the Badja that you could conveniently reach from Jack Snow's we fished for them. We fished at Andy's Flat, away downstream where Jack led us miles over the timber-strewn hillsides, loping unconcernedly over the wilderness of fallen logs as if the country were breeding some kind of human kangaroo; and there, among the green cherry-trees growing around the site where Andy, whoever he was, had had his habitation, we saw the reddest of red foxes; and there we waded waist-deep all day, catching fish, in the delectable straight rippling waters where, on one famous occasion, a fisherman named Lee had caught twenty-two trout in an afternoon, and had put them all back. He fished for fishing, not for fish.

We fished the long mysterious gorge up from Andy's, thought not to be worth fishing but secreting fine large pools. We fished the pool above the gorge where, one wild rainy day when there was no hope of a fish, I did get a trout, and a fine fish too, in the run-in against the high stony bank where grew one solitary specimen of the delicate, lilac-tinted alpine mint-bush. And the curving pool above it where trout lay near the fallen tree, and where the sandy bank was always delicately furrowed by the trail-marks of snakes. On upstream, through the thick tea-tree which it was so tempting to by-pass, we fished the pool against the cliff; and there I learned how right Jack Snow was when he said that, on those clear bright Countegany days, fish would rise only when a cloud-shadow fell across the water; and there I learned, too, when a brief rise to some brown-winged insect that looked like an Egyptian felucca took place one day in a cloud-shadow, that the right fly for that insect was neither the dry Hardy's Favourite nor the wet, but the dry allowed to sink an inch or so below the surface.

We fished, but mostly at evening, the Luncheon Pool, where the long quarter-mile straight of deep water, filled with rosy clouds and golden light in the sunset, would be ringed from end to end with rising trout, dozens of them, scores of them, hundreds of them. That was the pool, too, where there was always one monstrous, uncatchable fish, right in the shallow at the tail, who used to dash upstream out of your way with a bow-wave like a battleship. And it was at that same pool that once I perceived the explanation, or so I think, of that phenomenon which so troubled the naturalist Gilbert White: the subaqueous hibernation of swallows. White sometimes suspected, in common with other naturalists of the eighteenth century, that swallows spent the winter under water; hibernating, like clusters of bats, in caverns beneath the surface of the river. It was a pleasant but dubious legend, and White spent a lot of time arguing with himself about it. Well, I was watching the swallows hunting insects one glittering evening at the Luncheon Pool. They were wheeling everywhere above the water, they gathered in a flock, and suddenly, instantly, there was not a swallow to be seen. They had not flown away, or I should have seen them go; nor was there a tree or a cave anywhere where they might have taken shelter. Had they, then, all dived together under the water to start hibernating? There was one small, ragged tea-tree bush, so insignificant that you would hardly notice it, hanging low over the water's edge; and that was where they had all gone; like a flash; like a dark flash instantly extinguished.

Whether it was wildlife, whether it was fish, whether it was merely water, there was no pool of that lovely river that did not hold something worth remembering. Up from the Luncheon Pool, in the next nondescript piece of water, hardly worth fishing it seemed, a small pool in a small gorge, there was one glorious night when the white moths were pouring like a soft blizzard out of the tea-tree bushes, and I caught three fish one after another with, of all things, the White Moth. It was supposed to be impossible to take a trout with the White Moth at Countegany, even when the real insect was hatching by the million. The imitation they took that night had a small tinge of pink on the body. Maybe that was the explanation. Whoever tied that fly was a genius.

Except occasionally at dusk, when the thing that seemed to be a crocodile, a bunyip, a platypus, or the father of all trout splashed and thundered in it, we didn't fish the Sally Hole too often, for we felt that, since it was visible from the house, Jack rather liked it to be left intact as a proof of just how many fish there were in the Badja. But just across from the Sally Hole there was a nice place of dry land, and there I had some of the most remarkable fishing I ever had at Countegany. It was a benevolent stream, the Badja. When it flooded, it never got dirty. The clear waters simply brimmed over the paddocks, and Jack always swore that you could go fishing anywhere over his farm and catch trout. He said he had caught them from the fence in the potato paddock. So, firmly disbelieving him, one day in the flood I crossed the Badja by means of the S.S. *Boggy Plains*, and strolled round the base of Mahony's Mountain back towards the Sally Hole; and dyspeptically dropped a dry fly among the tussocks in a nasty-looking hollow filled with floodwater; and instantly caught a three-pound brown trout, and instantly lost another. Jack was a truthful man; and if he had said, after that, that he had caught a trout on the roof, during exceptionally heavy rain, I should not have doubted him.

And on and on, mile after mile towards its source in the marshes, we patrolled the fishable Badja: the long stretch and the pools up from the house to the road crossing, the Sheepwash Pool, where the brown snake lay on the bank just where you clambered over the fence; the long gorge beyond it where I saw and did not catch a very big fish in an unreachable backwater and where, one day of tremendous thunder, David Campbell and I crouched beneath a rock at the water's edge while the lightning flamed around us and the floodwaters swelled up to our feet and drove us out into the storm again … and so, by-passing a stretch of river so rough that we never quite got through it, on by the road to Pound Creek, or Pepper's Creek as some men call it for a reason I have never fathomed, where I dropped David Campbell's three-pounder out of my landing-net and where one day when the rolling mist had put an end to fishing we met at the mouth of his burrow on a rocky hillside the most somnolent gingery old wombat who was either so sleepy or so blind that he couldn't be bothered to move until we tickled his back with a rod-tip.

And so, back where Pound Creek met the Badja, to the Cow-paddock; where I still cherish in my mind the spectacle of Jim Ryrie of Michelago up to his waist in the wide water, an immense man with an immense rod trying to cast half a mile of line to reach those unreachable monsters that cruised among the lily-beds; and David Campbell crawling through the steep bush on the far bank to catch, which he did, and then lose, one of those same monsters; and the thunderstorm which, when we had clambered down the gorge at the tail for one very small trout in a rock-pool, came roaring down the river and wet us through and then unkindly turned round and roared back up the gorge and wet us through again … and the morning when, acting as guide to some fishermen new to Countegany, I disgraced myself by sneaking upstream and catching three trout on a Tup's Indispensable while they stayed at the Cow-paddock and caught nothing. I was sure they thought I had got them with a worm, if not with a spinner.

And so, at last, to the reedy little circle of the Sawpit Pool where the waters that had crept invisibly through the upland swamps and soaks suddenly, for the first time, became the Badja River.

We fished everywhere, and everywhere we caught fish. And everywhere, on the road by the Sheepwash, among the rocks at Pound Creek, lurking by the logs in the Cow-paddock, we tripped over or jumped over writhing coils of snakes. And the snakes and the fishing reached, as was fitting, their climax in one place together. The Pockets.

The regular inhabitants of Jack Snow's, besides Jack and Molly and the cat, were a strange tribe of elderly fishermen who walked unceasingly, year after year, the flat and easy stretch of water from the Sally Hole past the house up to the Dead Hole and the road crossing.

Sometimes, greatly adventuring, they fought their way half a mile downstream to the Luncheon Pool. That was why it was called the Luncheon Pool. They fished down towards it all morning; they ate their luncheon under the one big ribbony-gum that stood on its clear banks; and then in the afternoon they fished home again. They were not greedy men; they had no wish to slay vast numbers of fish; moreover, they wanted the fishing to continue. So every time they landed a trout they gently returned it to the water. Year after year, with great good-will, they caught the same fish all over again. They got to know every trout in the river, some of them even by name. The Pockets were just too far for them; we had the fishing there to ourselves: three lonely wild pools, plus Fred's, lost in a fold of the hills between the water-fall that tumbled down from the Cow-paddock and the gorge upstream from the Sheepwash.

There were three ways in to the Pockets, and each of them was a mighty long walk. You could drive in a jeep, as once we did, across the paddocks on the near side of the Sheepwash, and over the hills to the sucker forest where the door of fairyland stood; and then, leaving the jeep there, hike down the clear wide boggy slopes to the Bottom Pocket glittering small and blue in the distance. That had one disadvantage: exactly where in the sucker forest, that wide-stretching, all but impenetrable thicket of thin white sally-gums – exactly where, in the forest and the gathering dusk, did you leave that blessed jeep? We did find it in the end; but not without that nasty feeling of panic you get when you have temporarily mislaid the universe. Then, leaving your transport at an invisible spot marked X along the road, you could take to the hills and the marshy uplands bright with bulbine lilies and a dwarf golden guinea-flower,

and break out through a bushy ridge right onto the Top
Pocket. Or, best of all, because it also gave you Fred's to
fish, and most strenuous of all because the climb down
the mountain from Fred's was a hot long steep way
down and a very long hot steep way back, you could
strike into the paddocks where a fence-line met the
road, cross the Badja by crawling and swinging through
the tea-trees over a cluster of rocky islets, and follow the
river down to Fred's, and on to the water-worn granite
plateau where once I took a trout that rose for a dragonfly while we were having lunch; and so, over the
brink of the world, down to the three Pockets, Top and
Middle and Bottom, shining afar in the scrub.

Fred's was always called just Fred's. Not Fred's Pool,
or Fred's Paddock, and not Fred Anybody's Pool; just
Fred's. And a most noble piece of water it was, the
biggest pool in the whole Badja I should think, the great
wide oval of it lying bright and motionless between the
rough hills across the river and the green cleared paddock from which we fished. There were always fish in
Fred's. They lay in the shallow run-in. They lay off the
lily-bed beside it, where I lost my superb six-pounder.
They lay among the rocks in the centre and grievously
broke your cast. They rose, invariably they rose, all day
over the submerged rocks in the deep hole near the tail,
where you fished for them either by standing against the
high bank and hooking yourself up ten thousand times
on the brier and the tree behind you, or by lying prone
on top of the tall granite boulder that jutted out into the
water and dropping your fly straight down as if fishing
from a wharf. In the great year, the year of the drought
when you could wade far out and really get at those
waters, we fished the tail of Fred's from the far side and
had such fishing among those sunken rocks, then with

their brown tops showing above the water, as has never been heard of before or since.

And, down from Fred's, the Pockets.

I must admit that once at the Pockets I had one of the worst day's fishing I have ever had in my life. There are the great days, the rare days, the days you live for and fish for, which every fisherman knows; the days when nothing goes wrong, when you have exactly the right fly, when you cast and strike with such beautiful, deli- cate precision that really you respect yourself; when you never let a fish wrap itself round a rock or a sunken log, when your cast never breaks and your rod-tip never foolishly drops out of its ferrule, when you never fumble with your landing-net and when, superb in confidence, you catch every fish you see. There are also the dreadful days. This was the dreadfullest of all dreadful days.

God forgive me, I had had slightly too much claret with dinner the night before. It is an unforgivable thing to do on a fishing trip. The sun shone, the water sparkled, and I was not quite comfortable. In fact, I was hot. When I hooked a good one in the run-in at Fred's, I lost it for no reason at all. When I struck another beauty among the rocks in the centre it got under a rock and took my whole cast with it when it departed. The only other cast I had was, as I perceived when I hooked the next one, beside the big rock at the tail, rotten. Well, you can still fish after a fashion with the stronger, thicker remnant of a rotten cast; but what can you do when the river, in one of its high clear floods, is running so full that, after you have climbed down in the baking heat through the horrid dry bush and over the horrid rough rocks to the Pockets, you can't get over the usual cross- ing under the tea-tree bushes? Everybody knows that you have to fish the Pockets from the far side; and here you are, in the heat, with a broken, rotten cast, with snakes probably crawling up your trouser-legs, and with something suspiciously like a hangover, marooned on the wrong side among briers and tea-tree, all vilely in flower, with a nasty high bank of rough speckled rock behind you, making casting totally impossible. Why, in God's name, do we go fishing anyhow?

David Campbell was with me that day. He had already, quite unforgivably, caught three fish in Fred's.

The river was high. The river was deep. The river was swift and dangerous. There was no possible way of crossing it. The crossing, as I have carefully explained, as I explained then to Campbell, was drowned. And any-body who tried to get over the river by leaping from point to point where a series of smooth, rounded, slip-pery granite boulders, six feet or more apart, did suggest a crossing that perhaps a chamois might manage, would certainly be drowned himself. So over the Badja, leaping from boulder to boulder, Campbell went. 'You just keep going,' he said to me in memorable words later.

And, doggedly if not so daringly, I kept going myself. A fish began to rise on my side of the river and, all among the tea-tree and the briers, I fished for it. And not one fly, of a dozen I tried to tempt it with, would it look at. Across the river, fishing from the very rock which in better days had always been regarded as my inviolable property, Campbell hooked a trout – reason-ably small, I was glad to observe – and having no landing-net, played it to a standstill, then leant head-first down the rock, got his fingers through its gills and held it up for me to admire. It was hotter than ever. The rocks blazed with light, the water glared. A bird of some kind began making unpleasant noises in a tree. 'Listen to that thrush!' called Campbell.

I gave up. I dismantled my rod and, deciding that if Campbell was going to be drowned when he jumped back over the boulders there was nothing I could do about it anyway, I climbed the hideous mountainside back to Fred's. 'I got over at the tail,' said the poet when he found me eventually sitting at peace under a black sally in the green paddock, enjoying the pleasures of not fishing. 'I got that one you were fishing for,' he added, as a sort of casual afterthought. And showed it to me …

But that was in another year. And it was in yet another year, at cold silver-glittering Easter, that I stood on the plateau above the Pockets and saw not a single fish stirring in all that magnificent water. Huddled into the hills it seemed then, waiting for the winter snow.

The great year, the year of the drought, was the first year we ever fished the Pockets. Nobody had been near them, nobody had touched them, nobody had disturbed either the fish or the snakes for five years, so Jack Snow told us. And I believed him. As we came out of the bush onto the Top Pocket the first thing we saw was a great heap of driftwood piled up by the winter floods; and, as we approached it to make our way down the stream, three enormous black snakes slithered simultaneously into its horrible interstices: over which, gingerly, we stepped. And gingerly we stepped thereafter, and with reason, for there were many snakes at the Pockets. And many trout.

It was the drought that did it; the drought and the isolation. The high swamps and soaks and springs were dry; the tributary creeks were dry; and all the wildlife of Countegany, whether fox or rabbit, currawong or kangaroo, skink or water-dragon or snake, had concentrated at the life-giving Badja. The river itself was half dry, so that the trout too were concentrated in the pools and could be seen and reached where they sheltered by lily-beds or sunken rocks normally too far out in deep water to approach. And nothing came there to disturb this concentration of life, whether on land or in water; no human footfall, not even cattle to trample the scrub along the banks or wade out and chew the water-grass. There was nothing all day but bird-calls, snakes, and trout.

We had a fly called the Burrinjuck Wonder; at least I think that was its name, for the Burrinjuck Wonder is the nearest equivalent to it I have since been able to find. It was a local fly sold in Yass and Canberra for fish-ermen who frequent the Goodradigbee and the Burrinjuck Dam; a big, orange-bodied thing with a long tail, which may have represented a wasp. Of course we lost our stock of them that season, and the official Bur-rinjuck Wonder has never seemed quite the same thing; but while our supply lasted, whatever the fly's true name may have been, it certainly worked wonders for us.

I forget how many fish we caught with it. Chiefly I remember the delight of wading those remote calm pools all day, with the hot dry bush all round us and the brown water so cool around our waists; and the fascination of seeing those enormous trout, three- and four-pound rainbows, swimming around the rocks or shaking the narrow leaves and little white cups of the water-lilies as they slid and fed beneath them; and the long, lovely walk home, after the day's fishing, through the white sallies silvered with the moonlight.

We caught so many fish that we put back everything under two pounds; and still came home with such a bag of three- and four-pounders that we didn't know what to do with them. We used to put them in the farmers' letter-boxes and then ring up the farmers from Jack Snow's when we got home to tell them to go and pick them up. We ate them fried for breakfast, and soused for lunch, and baked with parsley sauce for dinner. We caught so many trout that one day I said to David Campbell, 'I don't see any point in catching fish after fish like this. I think I shall become one of those old codgers who spend half the day studying the stream and tea-tree bushes and the insects on the water to find out what fly to put on; and get so interested in that that they hardly bother about fishing at all.' Words which, on barren days since then, Campbell has unkindly recalled to me.

One day that royal season I was perching on a rock which jutted out from the bank into the Top Pocket. It was the very rock, incidentally, from which Campbell caught the small fish on my day of despair. I had adopted it as my favourite station, partly because I could always get a fish from it in the lily-bed downstream, and chiefly (I am ashamed to say) because it was away from those scrubby banks, a nice clear rock where the snakes couldn't get at you. Jack Snow, tired of catching trout, was sitting on the bank behind me. There was a huge black snake curling against his back. 'Jack,' I said calmly, very proud of my self-possession, 'stand up quietly and step straight forward into the river.' The snake seemed to be trying to wrap itself round him like a boa-constrictor, or nuzzling against him like a kitten. Perhaps it just wanted to wriggle up his back to have a look at his face. 'Eh?' said Jack. 'Why?' And, seeing the snake, stood up with perfect tranquillity and stamped on it. There was a very nasty commotion for a while, but Jack won. 'Yes,' he said when I was telling the story at dinner that night, 'it must have looked funny all right. There was something funnier, though. I didn't tell you at the time because I didn't want to interrupt your fishing. There was another snake, a copperhead, coiled up in a crack of the rock just behind *you*.'

14

SWORDFISH WATERS

WHAT I liked best at Russell, when my father had retired there and I came back from Australia to visit him, was to drive alone in the station-wagon over Flagstaff Hill, where Hone Heke cut the flagpole down and started the War in the North, and down the road to Tapeka: which, at the foot of that steep winding track, past hillsides of yellow gorse and a gully with cows and a creek, was most gloriously nothing, only a bay and a hill and farmhouse, most gloriously nowhere, a solitary green footprint of the land tramping into the quiet waters of the Bay of Islands in the far north of New Zealand.

What was it about that lonely place which drew me to it day after day whenever there was a gap in the pleasurable uproar of a family reunion? – thousands of my sisters, or at any rate all three of them, with their husbands and hordes of children; and all of us, who had been children together ourselves, now mysteriously changed into parents and uncles and aunts and looking to the young, I suppose, as huge, unpredictable, and extraordinary as my own FitzGerald uncles looked to me when they came home to us at Eltham after the

Great War: giants in khaki uniforms, laughing.

It was the creek you had to cross by the log-bridge before you got to the farmhouse: the pool alive with splashing and honking Muscovy ducks with their red wattles, a superb place for a boy to fish in, if there had been one at the old farmhouse, for herring came up it across the sands at high tide; even snapper sometimes, Mrs Wardell of the farm told me; and there were eels.

It was the weatherboard, weather-worn old farm-house, so spacious and mysterious, with unexpected rooms opening one into another like caves, exotic with sea-shells and staghorns and guns and mouldering leather-bound books, unpruned grapevines running green and wild along its verandas, wild fruit-trees clustering around it. A magistrate lived and died there after he retired from the Bench, and now his housekeeper lived on in it alone. Before he died, she said, this tall, lean, powerful woman, he used to take his chair out into the paddock and watch her grub out the encroaching gorse.

Mrs Wardell was haunted by a hawk: a huge insolent bird that sat on the hillside all day and watched her. I saw it there myself, strutting about amongst the red and black calves not a hundred yards away as if it were one of her domestic poultry. She said I should shoot it for her, but of course when it saw me with her shotgun it sprang into the air and was soon wheeling high out of range over the green ridge and the sea. A week before, she said, that villainous bird had taken a Muscovy duck from the flock on the creek: which indeed was so noble a capture for a hawk that I was glad I couldn't get a shot at it.

But there was more than the creek, the farmhouse, and the hawk to draw a fisherman to Tapeka. There was the famous flat rock, only to be reached at low water, from which, so my father said, and so Mrs Wardell said too, you could catch twenty blue-cod in an hour.

A delectable fish, smoked as we get it in Australia, is the blue-cod; still finer fresh; and a noble fish to catch as it comes up slate-blue and purple, with its fins spreading like a fan and its great mouth gaping, from the kelp where it loves to hide. Even in New Zealand the blue-cod is something of a rarity, for you do not catch him at many places around the coast: mostly at Nelson in the South Island, I think, or away down in the Sounds of fiordland, at the end of the world.

But where exactly was this famous flat rock? I had no precise directions given me.

First I tried around to the left of the green spur that formed the backbone of the Tapeka peninsula; past the mouth of the creek and the three dark-green Norfolk Island pines — not often seen in New Zealand — with their quagmires of ebony shadow where the pigs came rooting for our lunch-basket and the cattle sheltered from the heat; past the white beach where one happy day we swam with our assorted children in the warm shallow water or, sunbaking on the sand, watched the blue islands dreaming in the bay and the smoke of gorse-fires rising over distant Waitangi; past the pohutukawas that would have been a mass of crimson blossom in the spring, hairy with ferns and lichens and clinging to the rocky slope with their strong roots; past the pools of anemones and shrimps, and the tip of the headland broken and washed by the waves into islets of curious shapes; past a gut of the cliff littered with all the shells of the ocean; and so, wading through shallows or scrambling over ribs from the great central backbone now high and steep overhead, to a narrow bay that took

the swirl of the waves racing in from the open sea: and
there, ending in a cleft where the surge burst in spray
against the cliff, was a perilous ledge which, by a considerable stretch of the imagination, might possibly have
been called a flat rock from which you could catch
blue-cod. I caught two small snapper from it, on an
admirable bait-casting rod I had borrowed, and one
infinitesimal red rock-cod.

Though it was satisfactorily cut off by the tide
before I left, and I had to climb the steep flank of the
ridge to make my way home, that was the wrong rock.
I found the right one, eventually, or I think I did, on the
other side of the spur where the open sea came rolling
in fine blue swells into another, broader bay.

The flat rock lay isolated from the mainland across
a strip of sand which would obviously be under water at
high tide. From its sides and seaward end, its level,
limpet-encrusted surface never more than a couple of
feet above the ocean, it fell sharply into deep water, clear
and green and gently heaving with the swells. It was like
fishing in some big calm pond, a fishpond indeed, where
all the tribes of the ocean should have gathered to feed
in peace; and so, no doubt, on its good days they did. It
was surely no idle legend that the blue-cod haunted
those caverns of weed and green water. But all I caught
before the rising tide forced me to splash my way to the
shore was, once again, two small snapper.

But what, after all, are fish?

If it is fishing that takes you to a place, it is the place
itself that keeps you there and draws you back again.
However many fish you may catch elsewhere in the
teeming waters of the Bay of Islands, and however wary
the blue-cod may happen to be the day you go to
Tapeka, it is truly a most pleasant thing to sit all day on

a flat rock in the sun, with the green water at your feet and the blue water rolling in from the horizon, and a grassy ridge with pohutukawa-trees behind you and, while you watch all this with only an occasional stimulating click of the reel to remind you that you are supposed to be fishing, no company at all except that of two red-legged, red-billed herring-gulls which, running ever a little closer across the limpets and then flying back a few paces in alarm at their own temerity, are thinking of stealing your bait.

The whole place was so very like New Zealand! So much what New Zealand should be; so like the lonely, warm, fishy places I had known in boyhood at Pihama and Opunake, Mokau, Rapanui, and Kawhia.

It was almost as good to take the other road out of the township, over the top where the mossy graveyard is, to Long Beach; and there, wading out into the shallows, to fish for kahawai and snapper in the sunset.

True, Long Beach was grossly over-populated. There were at least three, perhaps four or five houses, including one, with narrow, sparkling windows like a chapel, which a woman built with her own hands out of clay, dotted along the green covert between the white sand and the cliff.

Once when we swam there, two or three other people dared to arrive in a motor-car and swam too. And once when my small daughter and I were building houses of driftwood and stone and seaweed for the mermaids, for whom also we provided gardens of marram-grass and some succulent plant of the sandhills, we were actually approached by a woman who wished to speak to us: or so we thought, for she came nearer and nearer over the sand, and when we quietly moved off a hundred yards, and started building again for the

mermaids, she followed; and when we moved again, still
she followed; until in the end we had to climb the
shoulder of a ridge into a far, narrow inlet, most delec-
tably unpopulated by anything except shells, from
which, climbing to the spur again to watch the progress
of the enemy, we took the offensive and, with alas only
sticks for rifles, shot her. Perhaps it is just as well that her
death did not seem noticeably to affect her, for we
learned afterwards that she had not been pursuing us at
all but was gathering tiny shells which she afterwards
would thread into necklaces to sell to visitors.

Altogether, it was reasonably solitary; and round
the headlands at either end, especially at the north
where we boiled the billy and had a family picnic, there
were those miraculous little bays where nobody ever
came; where there was nothing under the sun but the

ridge, the tussocky sandhills, and the little waves wash-
ing on the shingle.

I grew, indeed, positively to like the company of
the one man who came to fish Long Beach with me in
the dusk; who never spoke or even nodded but, obviously a fanatical trout-fisherman far from his proper
habitat, strode tall and severe in his waders along the
beach, flicking out a big wet fly, such as they use on
Taupo, into the wavelets where, clearly outlined against
the last of the light, you could see the kahawai swimming. I was after the kahawai myself one memorable
evening when, standing well out in the water to escape
the sandflies, only to have my bare feet gently nibbled by
the crabs – a rather unsettling experience – I hooked
and landed (not on a fly, of course) a fine rosy snapper;
which I presented to a lady who appeared mysteriously
out of the dusk and said that she had had nothing to eat
in the house but was certain the Lord would provide ...
I thought it prudent not to tell her she was mistaken in
my identity.

But these – a snapper here and an infinitesimal red
rock-cod there – were disgraceful days for a fisherman
at Russell ... where my father and I, trying a little more
seriously, filled the dinghy with snapper in a morning
simply by rowing a hundred yards from the black pebbly
beach of the township; and where if you really wanted
to catch fish you could do as well as – and maybe better
than – anywhere else in the world.

We had one tremendous day, chugging out in my
father's launch with the whole mixed clan aboard to
anchor just clear of the surge of the waves as they beat
back from Red Head, when we saw the snapper shoaling so thick with their backs and dorsal fins out of the
water that you could have walked on them; and when,

though these shoaling fish would not bite, having some dark obligation to get to Cape Brett as quickly as they could, everybody on the launch was kept busy all day long – my wife hauling up a monstrous crayfish to flap on the floor of the boat, my daughter catching a blue-cod (at last!) and a big parrot-fish bright as the bird it takes its name from; my brother-in-law Joe Blakely gravely imperilling one of my father's rods as he bent it double trying to heave up a mass of kelp from the sea-bed under the not unjustifiable impression that it was only a little-larger snapper than usual; and Alec Wilson, the expert, baiting his hook with huge lumps of sword-fish so that he did not need a sinker and, throwing his hand-line sometimes out to the water behind the dinghy, clear of our shadow, sometimes, in search of stragglers, to the shoaling snapper passing in a steady procession near the line of the ruby red cliff, hauling out one red giant after another, snapper of ten and twelve and up to fifteen pounds ...

Was there a moon, or half a moon, already show-ing pale in that rosy sky over the gleaming waters as we came home past the reefs, the islands, the white beach of Tapeka, and round the headland into Russell? I think there must have been, for I began repeating to myself, in ecstasy with their music as it sonorously rose and fell and changed into the very slap and splash of the waters at our bow, those lines from Tennyson:

> *The long day wanes: the slow moon climbs: the deep*
> *Moans round with many voices.*

There is not much of the freshness of nature in Ten-nyson, not that essential roughness which is in the nature-poets I like best – Wordsworth, Clare, Hopkins,

Davies, Edmund Blunden – matching and reproducing the roughness of earth or salt water; but what music there is all the same, what melodious exactitude of language!

So, from rock-cod to snapper to the titan, we came to the supreme excitement which Russell has to offer: swordfishing.

For if it is good to sit on a flat rock in the sun all day and do nothing, so also it is good – and especially for one who, at anchor or drifting in the roll of the waves, is likely to be seasick – to be moving all day, miles out to sea in a launch powerful and luxurious, sitting at ease facing the stern in the special swordfisher's chair and watching the kahawai you are trolling for a lure leap from wavecrest to wavecrest with the pull of the boat or burrow in the dazzling wake; while reefs, rocks, islands, cliffs, headlands, seabirds, shoals of mau-mau, kahawai, snapper and trevalli, and other launches trolling or anchored to some colossal mako or marlin, float past in what seems some quintessential dream of fishing.

And if it is good to fill a boat with snapper off Red Head, it is also very good – surely the supreme experience in fishing – to come home with the mighty swordfish lashed across the stern: even if that most regal capture has fallen to the rod of one's brother-in-law, Joe Blakely … as, alas, happened.

Even the gear for this tremendous gladiatorial combat – for that is what swordfishing is – is exciting. The strange rigging which the launch carries, of high poles over which your line will be slung so that the bait will troll properly on the surface; the two swordfishers' chairs, swivelled and with backs that can be removed when you are heaving your giant fish in to the gaff; the stout rods and giant reels with miles of tough thin cuttyhunk line on them; the harness you must put on to hold your rod when you have a fish, and to hold yourself in the boat.

And everything else about it is exciting.

True, the first day Joe and I were out after sword-fish we caught nothing. But that was the day when the wildness of the sea, high and blue and glittering after a storm the previous day, alone made it a rare adventure; and, because the boatman thought the rough weather would keep the swordfish away from the coast, we did not head for the usual fishing-grounds at Cape Brett, close offshore, but ploughed straight out to Sail Rock, fourteen miles away across the open sea.

There was the eager anticipation as we cruised through the quiet waters of the Bay, the air chill in the early morning and the islands lost in mist; the sun break-ing through to a world of gold and white as we reached the rocks where the kahawai hunt the herring; the trolling for these splendid, strong, green-and-silver fish – an experience that in itself would make a fine day's fish-ing in any other country. Two pounds, four pounds, up to five and six (the two-pounders are the best bait for the swordfish) they struck at the Maori lure of curved wood inlaid with paua-shell, pulled mightily against the drive of the launch and came up flapping and fighting over the stern and into the bait-box.

Then there was the straight plod for Sail Rock, with the big launch dipping and plunging through the rollers. Then more trolling for kahawai round that lonely red fang of rock foaming with angry surf, while the boatman steered his craft so close that when a wave lifted us high and heaved us sideways into turmoil, it seemed impossible that we should not be wrecked. And then that long, long dazzling day as we trolled far out to sea and along in the end to Cape Brett, with the sun burning our arms and faces, the blue swells chasing us from behind and welling up at the stern as if they would engulf us, and at every minute of it the chance – even if it was not fulfilled – of a strike from a swordfish.

That was the day, too, when another brother-in-law, Dr Whittlestone, the scientist, provided one of the most singular displays of fortitude against sea-sickness I have ever encountered.

We are inclined to condemn the scientists these days for using mankind as guinea-pigs for their experiments; indeed, for using even guinea-pigs as guinea-pigs; but we forget that they are at least always willing heroically to experiment on themselves. About half-way over to Sail Rock, when the sun had nicely warmed the ocean, we broached a bottle of beer. Soon the scientist, who had never really been at ease with the rollers, was to be observed kneeling in the cockpit in an attitude of prayer, his arms spreadeagled along the gunwale and his head over the side. When, in about ten minutes, he had finished his devotions, he disappeared into the cabin. Then, pale, but undaunted, clutching the movie-camera with which he was going to film the swordfish we didn't catch, he emerged. 'My word,' said Dr Whittlestone, in a tone of intense scientific interest, 'that beer acted on me as a powerful emetic ...'

The next time we went after swordfish, about a week later, it was sunny and blue and calm; a perfect day on a perfect sea.

We were many times up and down the coast by the Cape, close by the cliffs and out to sea, and round Bird Rock and through the archway where the sea has made a tunnel for itself through the headland, and out to sea again in a cloud of birds and back again to that big rock

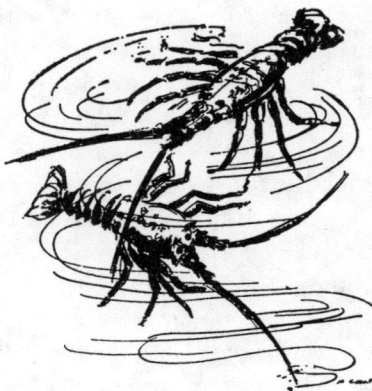

whitened with the birds' droppings, sometimes passing close by another trolling launch, sometimes watching one rocking and drifting far out to sea as some lucky fisherman played his swordfish – when suddenly ... I forget who saw it first, Joe or the boatman; there was a tail or a fin above the water, something was interested in us.

It vanished for a dreadful moment; then there most superbly it was, a great magnificent swordfish, back and dorsal fin clear out of the water, sword cutting a path before it just under the surface, skimming, racing, the incarnation of the sea's power and rapacity, straight in one green and silver rush for Joe's kahawai. And took it!

The curious thing then is, you do nothing. The unchecked reel spins, the line runs silently and swiftly out, the fish vanishes; and, for many minutes, ten minutes perhaps, ages and ages, you do absolutely nothing: only the boatman cautiously fingers the line, trying to make out if the fish is still hooked or not. We thought it was gone. And then, quarter of a mile away, far to the north at an angle which seemed to have no connection with the course our fish had taken, there was a sword-fish leaping full-length out of the ocean, more like an apparition than a fish, flashing, gigantic, and incredible. He was on; he was hooked: strike, brake, hold hard to the rod as the reel sings; slip the back out of the chair and heave, heave, as if the ocean itself is on the other end of the line.

Swordfishing is, perhaps, too much like a gladiato-rial combat to take on too often, unless one's temperament lies that way. It is a bit mechanical, with all the heavy and intricate gear. It is certainly, when the boatmen chat from launch to launch over their radio transceivers, too 'touristy' unless you persuade your man, as we did, to switch the noise off. It is all, even to your tactics in striking, playing and landing the fish, too much under the control of the boatmen. But in spite of all that I have never fished with such intensity as I did for the rest of that day after Joe landed his prize. And once at least on any holiday at Russell, for the glorious day on the sea and the magnificence of the capture, I would assuredly tackle it again.

We caught no more fish that day, though I held to my rod and watched the leaping kahawai till the last moment of daylight as we turned into the Bay for home. The long day waned, the slow moon climbed over Tapeka, the deep moaned round with many voices; and we came round the point into Russell with the flag of triumph flying and, gleaming across the stern of the launch, immense in the pale light, Joe's swordfish.

15

PROSSER'S

HEAVEN knows how long that ramshackle boarding-house which we called 'Prosser's' had stood on
the top of the world at Rule's Point. Maybe it had been
an inn of the coaching days when weary and terror-
stricken travellers, having breasted the mountainside up
from Talbingo, paused for refreshment, as well they
might, before going on to Kiandra. Maybe the heroic
settlers of the Miles Franklin country, having somehow
clambered with their horses out of the lost valley of
Brindabella, poised there for a while, as if in the sky,
before dropping down the other side of the range to
Tumut. Possibly it dated right back to the gold-rush days
at Kiandra and had seen the great tide of the miners
flow up the road and back again; leaving in the end no
more to mark their enterprise than a cluster of grave-
stones on the hillside, the windy great oval of the
Three-Mile Dam and, in the township itself, a few grey

cottages even more dilapidated than Prosser's, and some families with Chinese names.

Prosser's, if it wasn't perhaps quite as old as that, was old enough. And primitive. The bedrooms, each a narrow little box, opened side by side off a veranda running the full length of the front of the house; and contained iron bedsteads of a remarkable height, instability, and lumpiness. One went to bed by candle-light, and, if wakeful, was entertained by groans, snores, and other revolting noises penetrating the thin walls from the sleepers on either side. The cold, clammy bathroom was shared by the community of fishermen and stray tourists, and you had to be quick to get it. The dining-room, by some freak of architecture common in old country hotels, and possibly intended for coolness, was a dank dark cavern excavated between the store-rooms and the kitchen, cool enough indeed, but admitting neither light nor air. The long low weatherboard house always looked as if it were just about to fall down. It was not that the corrugated-iron roof, buckled by winter snow and summer sun so that it channelled most of the rain into the bedrooms, ever actually blew off; it was not that dry-rot or white-ants ever quite ate away the veranda; it was not that the thin old boards with most of their paint long since peeled off by the weather, ever really melted into thin air ... but something like that, because of its age and its crumblingness, always seemed likely, very gradually and gently, to happen.

The Prossers themselves could do nothing, or very little, about its woeful state of disrepair, for it was owned by the Kosciuszko State Park Trust, or some such body; and the body, whose duty it was to repair it, would never do it. They must have decided that, since it was going to fall to pieces however you tried to patch it up, they would let it. And so year by year, very gradually and gently, it did.

And yet, what a good place it was!

It was irradiated by Mrs Prosser's cooking. No matter at what hour you arrived – like the time we drove over Kosciuszko way and the fan-belt broke and, red-hot and boiling, we had to crawl over the hills through the night back to Kiandra where some Snowy River workers, out on the spree, came to the rescue with a new belt; or like that famous night when we stopped at Old Adaminaby for a meal at eight o'clock and the fat boy in the café said simply and finally, 'I'm off!', as if being 'off' at eight o'clock were an unalterable law of nature – no matter at what hour you arrived starving and exhausted at Rule's Point, Mrs Prosser, like other great fishing hostesses before her, could always find you something to eat. No matter at what time you came in from fishing, and sometimes after the drive home from Kelly's Plains we were very late indeed, there was always a hot dinner waiting for you in that dank dark dining-room; and this was served, for Mrs Prosser understood fishermen, after a decent interval for refreshment by the log fire in the little private sitting-room which we used to hire as an 'extra'. And what meals they were! Mrs Prosser was an expert at 'sweets'. There were always at least three delicious pies and steamed puddings and crisp light meringue-concoctions to choose from, and these were so tempting that we generally ate all three, some-times one at a time, sometimes all on the plate together. One of Mrs Prosser's specialities, if you asked for it, was cold trout, soused in vinegar, to take with you for lunch by the river; one of the best of all ways to eat trout.

Only one meal at Prosser's was ever a disaster, and that was our own fault, for we asked for it. However exciting it was, after that day in the Gorge at Kelly's, to come home laden with hats full of mushrooms and bags full of trout, these do not make, for breakfast, a desirable combination. In fact …

How Mrs Prosser cooked her wonderful meals over the old wood stove in her kitchen, and survived, passes understanding. It was a most comfortable place early in the morning, or in the bleak alpine weather of which Rule's Point had plenty, but one summer's day when we were there Colin Prosser's thermometer on the back veranda said 100 degrees Fahrenheit; when he took it out into the sun, for curiosity, he got some astro-nomical reading like 120 or 130 degrees; and in the kitchen, where still Mrs Prosser went on cooking all day, it must have been hellish. She was slight, wiry, and indomitable; and when she was not cooking she was dashing about the bedrooms with a broom.

But if Mrs Prosser was energetic, and stoked up the life of the house with fine and nourishing food, and attacked its decrepitude with her broom, everything else around Rule's Point was full of a profound leisure, as if it had taken a deep drink of sunlight and gone to sleep after it; and that was its special charm. It took its pace, maybe, from the steady crumbling of the old house, or from the long motionless red-gold expanse of Kelly's Plains which, stretching from the veranda to the hori-zon, lay beneath its curious tree-line like the basin of some shallow primeval lake, waiting in timeless patience for the water to fill it again. Nothing ever moved across Kelly's Plains except sometimes, high above it, a crow or a hawk going about its business and once, most memo-rably, a great bellowing mob of red and black cattle taking the softer route over the grass as they made their way down to Tumut.

There were a pair of robins which had built their nest on the axle of a hay-rake which was parked in front of the veranda; and they were the busiest creatures in the whole community; darting off to catch a fly or a grass-hopper for their four gaping-mouthed young and diving back with it through the spokes of the wheel; perching on the rim of the iron seat for the cockbird to display his crimson breast; twittering for a moment together; then off again for more grasshoppers. We used to hope that no one would drive off with the hay-rake and break up these happy small lives; but there was no need to worry. Whoever had parked that hay-rake seemed to have forgotten it; or maybe he had parked it for robins. Nobody at Prosser's was going to dash off in a hurry and make hay.

Sometimes in that leisurely country I myself forgot that I had gone there to do anything so energetic as fish-ing. Once for three whole weeks – so it now seems, though surely I went fishing at intervals – I helped Colin Prosser with his shearing. There was none of the usual dust and uproar of a shearing-shed at Prosser's. In fact, there wasn't even a shearing-shed in the proper sense of the term; but a couple of pens in some nonde-script old building at the back of the house, and a machine at which only one solitary shearer could oper-ate, if it was in working order, which it usually wasn't. Colin didn't have many sheep, anyhow, and those he did have he couldn't usually find. Sometimes he did manage to muster half a dozen of them and pen them in the shed, and then bravely he would start the machine, if it would start, and vigorously shear half a sheep. Then the machine would break down, and he would spend the rest of the day fixing it. The next day it would rain, and everybody knows you can't shear in the rain. Two or three days later, when the sheep had dried out, we would start again. And the machine would break down. Or Colin would have to go and get a load of wood for Mrs Prosser's stove. Or a fisherman would have engine trouble, or break the tip of his rod; and Colin, who was a wizard with both engines and rods, would obligingly stop shearing and, one way or the other, get them mobile again. Then there was the rodeo in Tumut, and nobody could shear sheep when he had to be riding in a rodeo. Dark-haired, blue-eyed, stocky, bounding with youth and confidence, Colin had energy enough to set against the prevailing somnolence of Rule's Point; but I don't think we ever got as far as shearing more than one whole sheep in those industrious three weeks.

I used to talk, too, perhaps when the shearing machine had broken down, to Mr Prosser, senior. I never knew quite what Mr Prosser's role in the household was, except, of course, that he was head of it. He owned, as well as a few acres at Rule's Point, a piece of land down Tumut way; and so, I daresay, was kept busy enough, in an unhurried sort of way, as a farmer. He was a tall, slow, quiet-speaking man, and knew all the lore of the district. He told me once that one winter he had 'tracked a fox', following its footprints in the snow, all round the hillside at the back of the house; and there in seventeen different hollow logs, at which the fox had paused, he found seventeen rabbits which the wise animal had stored against the season of scarcity. Apparently, on the day when he tracked it, the fox was inspecting its larders. He also told me, which I had heard before from others, that when the Three-Mile Dam lay frozen to ice in the winter, and all the slopes around it were buried under the snow, the foxes came down to the hidden shore of the lake and dug there for the yabbies in their holes. Mr Prosser told me, too, that in kinder days of summer he had often seen black snakes wriggling along under-water at the bottom of the streams, or coiled there in a nasty writhing mass. I never knew quite what to make of this story, since it is a common legend of the outback which most naturalists would deny; and certainly a snake would have to come up to breathe. But is it quite impossible that a semi-aquatic creature like a black snake would sometimes forage for its food under-water? Snakes do swim, of course; in fact I was once tempted to hook with my fly a small yellow snake that slid out of the tussocks and looked back at me from midway across the Murrumbidgee not many miles from Prosser's, only it looked at me so appealingly, and anyhow I couldn't imagine how, having landed it, I was ever going to unhook it … Snakes do swim, and do dive. Are they then to be found at the bottom of the stream, the very place where the fisherman thinks he is most secure from them? It is an unnerving thought. Sometimes, when I tread on a nasty-looking slippery stick in the water, I remember Mr Prosser, and shudder. Who are we to question what the countryman says he has seen?

There were days during that hot idle summer when I did at least occasionally investigate a piece of fishable water. Partly because I cling to a belief that the shallowest and most hopeless of tributary creeks shelter a monstrous fish that nobody else has ever thought of fishing for, partly because any piece of water should be investigated for its own sake and for what minute life of tadpole and water-beetle and drinking bird it may contain, I explored with my daughter the creek behind the pigsty at Prosser's. But there were no monsters in that ragged scrap of water twisting down to the

Murrumbidgee through its tea-tree and red-berried briers; only a solitary very small trout, about five inches long, which we failed to catch with our hands; and so, instead of energetically fishing, we spent the laziest of days there building a dam for a small boy named Bill, an appendage of the Prossers, who had somehow got himself attached to us. Bill was a disconcerting small boy. After we had initiated him into the art of picking up a stone from one place and setting it down in another, after we had built quite a noble wall and persuaded the streamlet to bank itself up fully six inches deep behind it, and after we had generously christened it, in his honour, 'Bill's Dam', Bill said he didn't like dams and wanted to go home. Never mind. I like building dams.

　　We explored the same creek again, lower down its course, where we crossed it in order to look for kangaroos on the ski-run cut into the bush across the road from Prosser's, on the mountain rampart of Kelly's Plains, but that was an expedition more idle even than poking about behind the pigsty. There were no kangaroos on the clearing; just bush, with the small orange pea-flowers of bacon-and-eggs in bloom; and there were no trout in the creek; there was hardly any creek in it really. With no Bill's Dam and no briers or blackberries to hold up its waters for a moment, it ran flat and shallow between green banks where the cattle had cropped the grass level as a lawn, and was no more than the tiniest tongue of water, licking a granite boulder as it disappeared round a bend. And how beautiful it was! What is there so fascinating about these infinitesimal creeks in the hills, where there is no more to be seen than the hoof-prints of the cattle in the sand, and little dark black-spinners skidding under the shelter of the banks, and the water-beetles minutely furrowing the shining surface as they chase each other for love? Water is life, I suppose; and besides it makes, as Judith Wright has said, 'Summer's bubble-sound of sweet creek-water'.

We did, too, go fishing … if you could call it fishing to wade knee-deep in the silver sparkle of the Murrumbidgee when you first met it half a mile across the plain from Prosser's; where the track crossed the rickety old wooden bridge, always with so much timber missing from its decking that you thought your car would fall through into the river, and where years ago there were said to have been good trout. I could never really believe, and still don't, that that stretch of the 'Bidgee would not continue to hold good fish. Why not? It was water. It was the Murrumbidgee. It was not too many miles from Kelly's Plains proper, where the fishing was famous. And if, being so near its source somewhere over the plain towards the heights above Brindabella, the river was small and shallow, there were holes about four feet deep where surely a trout could have lurked. I thought everyone despised it merely because it was so close to Prosser's. It was a beautiful stream to fish, glittering and singing over its shingle; it teemed with little trout that kept you interested and hopeful; but it provided after all the laziest and most delightful of all ways of filling in a morning around Prosser's, for not one takeable fish ever showed itself, and in the end you just sat down on the sand and watched the current dance by, or even stripped off, and, in a foot of water, went swimming.

But if life at Prosser's could thus be so pleasantly idle, the real fishing, when we did get round to it, was strenuous and even heroic. This was because I did most of my fishing with David Campbell, who had a singular capacity for turning the most tranquil piece of water into an athletics arena or a battlefield. If the fishing was easy on the side of the river where you were, then the poet was always to be found on the other side. He was continually to be observed perched on inaccessible rocks or crashing through thickets of tea-tree. If there was a crag in sight, he climbed it. If you could fish the water quite sensibly by wading up to your knees, then he would wade up to his neck. If you could fall in, he did. Repeatedly. One of his favourite exercises, when in later years we fished the waters further on from Prosser's and over towards Kosciuszko, was to cross to the far side of the Snowy when the over-flow from the Guthega Dam was likely to come pouring down the gorges, so that he could drown himself in the rapids on the way back. 'I like river where you can wade out and *battle* with it,' he said to me once, as he emerged blue and dripping from the Thredbo, into the slippery granite waterholes of which he had three times plunged full length. And at Prosser's he did considerable battle; and I, perforce, with him.

There was, for instance, the wild black stormy October night when we found ourselves, by some mysterious chance, in the little back upstairs bar of the Royal Hotel in Gundagai, with a shearer and a shearer's cook. We were heading for Tumut and Talbingo. I was at that time interested in old bush songs, Australian folklore which I was collecting for an anthology; and the shearer's cook, who was a plump dark seedy little man, with a squeaky voice, began to sing a folksong which I had never heard before:

And a little bandicoot played a tune upon his flute,
Three native bears came down and formed a ring.
The pelican and the crane flew in from off the plain
And amused the audience with a Highland fling …

'This is marvellous,' I said. 'Would you sing a bit more? Would you mind if I wrote it down?'

'He's a *Bulletin* man,' said Campbell encouragingly to the cook, who was a bit suspicious of me. To be a *Bulletin* man was, in those days, a guarantee that you were interested in the Outback.

'*He's* not a *Bulletin* man,' said the cook, with somewhat unnecessary scorn.

'You wouldn't be having us on, now?' said the shearer, very softly and pleasantly. 'You wouldn't be trying to make a goat of my mate in any way?' He was Irish, this shearer; not a very big man, but lean and hard, with red hair and an exceptionally bright blue eye.

'Have another drink,' said Campbell genially. 'Of course he's a *Bulletin* man. He's collecting songs for a book.'

'Then I'll *sing* you the song,' said the cook; and he did; and a most peculiar song it was:

The goanna and the snake and the adder wide awake
With the alligator danced 'The Soldier's Joy'.
In the spreading silky oak the jackass cracked a joke,
And the magpie sang 'The Wild Colonial Boy'.

'Ah, the little man can sing all right,' said the Irish shearer. 'He's the grand champion cook and he's the grand champion singer of the Monaro. But the trouble with this little man' – and here he gulped down his whisky and placed the glass with exceeding gentleness on the counter – 'is, he won't fight me.'

'*Oh, the little bandicoot played a tune upon his flute,*' sang the cook. He had, it appeared, met this situation before. Singing, not fighting, was his recreation.

'Is there nobody then,' said the shearer, in a gentle appeal to the bar, 'who will give me one little tap in friendship, just for the pleasure of it?'

Somehow, there didn't seem to be anybody available in the bar, not counting the melodious cook, except David Campbell and myself.

'Now you,' said the Irishman, measuring Campbell's six-foot proportions with an appreciative blue eye, 'you can fight like the divvil. I can tell it at a glance by the appearance of you. Now in friendship, like, and neither of us doing the other the slightest hurt in the world, would you fight with me then?'

'Aw, I can't fight,' drawled Campbell who, besides once having won a boxing Blue at Cambridge, suffered from a peculiar sense of humour. 'Here's the fellow who can fight. He got a boxing Blue, at Victoria College, in New Zealand.'

What a lie! It filled the Irishman to the brim with pure and ferocious friendship. He danced a little circle round the bar in his delight. 'Then here's the boy for me,' he said. 'So you're the great fighter, you are! Then would you,' he begged, 'let me give you one little tap on the nose? Just for the simple pleasure of it?'

I forget how I talked myself out of it. But I found, later, that the cook's bush song was quite well known and had long been duly recorded, so there wasn't any need to have collected it at so much peril.

That, surely, was enough heroism, pusillanimity, etc., for one night. But more was to come. It seemed to us, as we drove on through the black pouring rain

to Tumut, that it would be prudent to spend the night
in that town rather than face the drive on to Talbingo.
The road between Tumut and Talbingo ran parallel to
the river, and, in wet weather, was flooded. On the other
hand it seemed prudent to the publican in Tumut, when
we awakened him, not to have any accommodation
available. I don't know if he was just inhospitable, or
sleepy; or if he thought we were interstate criminals or,
possibly, shearers. He said we could easily make Talbingo. So, on through the night and the floods. You
could not tell in the blinding torrents of rain that dashed
on the windscreen which was the river and which was
the road, but it didn't make much difference anyhow, for
by now they were both the same thing, except that the
river, had we turned into it, would have been rather
deeper. By God's grace, when we did run off the road,
which we did three times, we skidded uphill and found
ourselves perched, rather absurdly, among grass and
blackberries on the bank. And so backed down into the

flood again, and plunged on. The things that you suffer for fishing!

And the next day still more heroic adventure, or at any rate high, strange, and heroic country awaited us. We had intended that trip to stay the weekend at Talbingo, without going on to Prosser's, for we had a curiosity about the Tumut River there, partly because we had previously caught fish in it, higher up, partly because on sunny days it always looked so exceptionally attractive, tumbling down through its huge round granite boulders in the reach beside the hotel. But, in the morning light, it was a wild high torrent swirling across the paddock almost up to the hotel door; and the only possible thing to do, we thought, was to drive on up the mountain and try the Three-Mile Dam.

So we did. And, in clear sparkling sunshine after the rain, there lay that noble sheet of water, a white wilderness of ice! All around, on the banks where the wildflowers used to grow, the snow lay thick and soft; it clung to the branches of the grove of black sallies where the bees rejoiced in summer and where, casting, you snapped off so many flies. Fortunately the ice on the great white circle of the lake was mushy at the edges so that we were not able to walk across its thin crust; as, remembering a friend who had skied across it one winter, David Campbell was much tempted to do. Near the outlet, where the creek ran down to Kiandra, we found a clear black hole and fished in it hopefully, then hopelessly, like the Eskimos. And when, without seeing a fish all day, we drove back along Bullock's Head Creek to Kiandra, and back through snowy banks and slopes of heath still crushed flat from the weight they had borne all winter, back past Prosser's and down the mountain to Talbingo, we found that one wise fisherman, instead of driving so many miles to fish a hole in the ice, had sneaked with a worm up the creek at the side of the hotel and, flood or no flood, caught himself a very respectable trout. Point to remember: when the main river is flooded, try the tributary creeks or, as on the Badja, the backwaters.

What a contrast to that expedition was the day when David Campbell, Professor Manning Clark and I drove down from Prosser's to fish the Yarrangobilly – that clear, sparkling little stream, all sunshine and gentleness. We found the nest of a white-throated honeyeater, with three pink eggs in it, hung among rosy-blossomed tea-tree over the water. It was a wonderful example of birds' care and cunning: set among such slender twigs, so perfectly concealed among the green foliage and grey twigs that matched the nest, and the blossoms that matched the eggs, that no robber of nests, hawk or fox or snake, could possibly have got at it. Only a big flood down the gorge of the Yarrangobilly might have reached it; but there weren't going to be any floods, for that was the summer when no rain fell anywhere around Kelly's Plains, and the temperatures were over the hundred, and, in the warm shallow pools of the Murrumbidgee, the trout lay too stupefied to eat. Which was why we went to fish the Yarrangobilly, for, hurrying down its gorge through the limestone caves, that water should have been comparatively cool. Comparatively cool it was, but not cool enough, for there were no fish to be caught there either.

Or, rather, there were two. One was a very small trout which rose downstream where David Campbell and I were fishing and to which, waist-deep on the slippery pebbles in that narrow water where the banks were too steep and too overgrown to let you get anywhere

ashore, we cast fly after fly in vain, rocking with laughter at our imbecility in competing for so ridiculous a
prize; and the other was a slightly larger rainbow which
Manning Clark, who was then new to fishing, triumphantly took upstream with a Coachman. It was a
thoroughly idle day, yet had its own heroic quality in the
splendour of the scenery around us; for, miles down in
the deep forest at the foot of its limestone crags, bubbling with the secret strange springs that well out among
its pebbles, the Yarrangobilly was truly a magnificent
little stream. Its extreme slipperiness, moreover, and the
fact that you could never climb out of it once you were
in, made it very useful indeed if you wanted to wade
neck-deep or fall over. Both of which, frequently, we
did.

We did, at least, since we could not walk along its banks,
fish the Yarrangobilly. At Kelly's Plains we usually did far
more hiking than fishing.

We had one perfectly absurd day over there with an
assortment of David's squatting friends, Gordons and
Osbornes; three carloads of us. The minute his car
stopped on the river-bank Forbes Gordon was off
upstream like a kangaroo on his long lean legs, heading
for the pool where he had caught the four-pounder by
the stone under the overhanging wattle. Mollie Gordon,
his wife, took off manfully after him. Sam Osborne was
racing past Forbes to reach a long straight pool he knew
about, further on. David and I, to circumvent the lot of
them, were haring it across the paddocks. Nobody spoke
a word to anybody. Everybody raced. The whole countryside was filled with fishermen streaking for the
horizon. And there, right at our feet, upstream and
downstream from the cars, lay perfectly fishable water.

It wasn't just the fact that there was rather a crowd of us that caused this ridiculous relay-race; nor was it mere vulgar competition for the best bits of water. It was the belief which all fishermen hold, and none more ardently than did David Campbell and myself, that the fishing is always better Further On. In fact, Further On is the only possible place to fish. It was that belief that had sent us, at the Badja, miles across the mountains and down a waterfall to the Pockets, when we might have caught all the three-pounders we wanted at Jack Snow's front door. It was that, no doubt, as well as the sluggishness of the summer Murrumbidgee, that had sent us down the mountain to slip along the Yarrangobilly.

And further on, at Kelly's Plains, there was the Gorge. It was a long way further on. In those days before the Snowy Mountains Authority so rudely strumpeted the whole countryside it was all but inaccessible; not because of the difficulties of the country, which was all flat going till you actually reached the Gorge; but because of the distance. It could only be reached, really, for a day's fishing, by a long-distance Olympic runner. It was where the plains ended and the mountains began and the river fell away in long unfished pools through the granite slopes to Yaouk (pronounced, for some unknown reason, Yi-ack). It haunted us.

There was, in fact, excellent fishing to be had miles before the Gorge began. There was fishing, for instance, in the bare tree-less country right where you came to the ford and parked your car. There where the stream ran sparkling through the tussocks, fishing one day with a man named Len, who impressed me by going fishing in a Rolls-Royce, I surprised him by catching a three-pounder in a backwater (which he thought an unlikely place) while he surprised me by catching

another three-pounder in water not more than two feet
deep beside a grassy bank, which I thought so unlikely
a place that I walked right past it.

There was fishing, again, in all the country we had
raced over with the Gordons and the Osbornes, where
you turned off the main track at the stockyards, and met
the Murrumbidgee in the hollow beneath the deserted
farmhouse. There was, for instance, that immensely long
pool, the very place where Forbes had caught his four-
pounder, in which a most noble fish took my fly the
very first time I cast into it, from the little marshy point
midway along it; where one day, absurdly, I fished the
whole length of it for my hat, which had blown into the
water and proved, when at last I had hooked it, a fantastically heavy sort of fish to land on a 3X cast; where,
more dramatically, my small daughter as she was then,
standing on a marshy ledge and wholly absorbed in her
fishing, also became absorbed in the bog, and sank
slowly out of sight, or almost, and had to be rescued
with considerably more urgency than my hat; and
where, in the evening, big trout rose with exciting and
maddening inaccessibility among the deep channels
through the weeds and water-lilies at the tail.

There was fishing, or there should have been, in the
deep hole where the river turned at right-angles against
a high stony hillside; and, if I never could manage to pull
a fish out of that most likely looking place, deep and
swirling and frothy, at least there was the pleasure of
looking at that fine sunny hillside, crested with spider
gums floating like shadows against the blue sky and
ribbed and knobbled with broken brown rock covered
with a curious red lichen. There was fishing among
the tussocks, where we saw the small yellow snake in the
water; and very good fishing indeed in the pool further

on where the casting, with your back against the cliff, used to be so difficult and so rewarding and where one memorable day I thought that David Campbell, perched behind me in mid-stream on a flat rock stained with the droppings of the wild ducks who also roosted on it (when it was unoccupied), had caught the biggest trout of all time. There was the most almighty splash behind me, such as only a six-pounder could make. It was, however, only the poet himself; who, for no reason at all, unless from force of habit, had decided to fall headlong into the water.

Yes, there was fishing; I don't think we ever came to Prosser's from Kelly's Plains without trout. And, with snakes, bogs and flat rocks from which to fall in, there should have been adventure enough. But further on, so far further on! lay the Gorge. Where the waters ran down to Yaouk. Where the Murrumbidgee, that shy laughing dancing maiden that she was on Kelly's Plains, began to grow up, and think about becoming the really mature river she would be by the time she got to Cooma. Where the pools lay shining and solitary in the mountains.

So, full of hope, full of the spirit of exploration, full of the most unwarrantable energy, we set off from Prosser's and drove over the long red plains where the groundlarks flew up from the wheel-tracks before us and, whether leading us away from their nests in the kangaroo-grass or merely as athletic as fishermen, raced along ahead of us at thirty miles an hour; past the solitary grove of black sallies where the track crossed the soak, past the hillsides timbered with spider-gums, so light in leaf and limb that they were hardly there at all; down to the right at the stockyard and round beneath the deserted farmhouse and, crashing through bogs and bumping over tussocks, far across the long flat paddocks until in some final bog the car refused to go any further, and we left it; and on, two toiling midgets under the eye of the high circling eagle, miles across the flats in the hot sun until at last the mountains began to close in, the country shaped itself into a funnel, and there, bright among rocks or gathered into long green pools reflecting the white sallies on the ridges, lay the unfished waters of the Gorge.

And there was fishing indeed! I remember David Campbell's elated voice, floating far and faint round the bends from some still more distant place he had got himself to, 'They're rising down here!'; I remember a sunny day of autumn when right at the entrance of the Gorge the whole river was alive with rising trout and we caught seven of them, rainbows, in less than an hour.

But the bother with fishing the Gorge was that, after you had done the long hike, and after you had had these few moments of excitement and splendour, it was time, in almost no time, if you didn't want to be benighted quite so far from anywhere, to set off home again. The Gorge was a thing seen in flashes.

The deserted farmhouse, we were to find one night when we had extracted the car in the dark from whatever bog we had abandoned it in, wasn't so deserted as we had believed. There rose upon the night air from the shadowy, tumbledown old building among the trees on the hillside above us the most terrible, blood-curdling screaming. There are, of course, no such things as ghosts. It was not really likely that any mad station-hand or swaggie was murdering there either his mate or a pig. It was certainly, if that made it any better, that most fascinating creature known as the Murdering Woman Owl. As enthusiastic amateur naturalists we should have

rushed up the dark hillside to investigate it. But somehow we found that we really couldn't keep Mrs Prosser
waiting any longer to serve us our dinner that night; and
so, into the car with more than usual celerity, and rapidly round the hill where the black cattle that always
chose to sleep across the track made navigation somewhat difficult, and through the grove of sallies at the
soak where one night we saw a wombat, and on across
the great open plains where the groundlarks still got up
and raced us in the glare of the headlights, and over the
rickety bridge at last, and safe home to the Prossers.

For excitement, for adventure, for the feeling of
being far away from home among trout by day and horrible noises by night, there was nothing to match the
Gorge. But by far the best of our fishing anywhere
around Prosser's, as distinct from hiking-fishing, was in
the Three-Mile Dam. Sometimes, as we bounced and
bashed over the pot-holes on the way up to Kiandra to
fish it, we used to think that the Eucumbene, which
wriggled like a crystal snake through its bed of green
tussocks in the gully beside the road, would repay further investigation. In fact, we knew that it would. There
was the fabulous story of how Forbes Gordon and Sam
Osborne were fishing one evening in that strange, enticing round billabong you could see from the road; and
how while one of them was playing a seven-pounder
the other hooked in the same pool a trout of eleven and
a half pounds – and both brought their fish home to
prove it. Yes, indeed. Moreover it was from the Eucumbene, even while we were staying at Prosser's, that Mr
Smart, the jeweller from Tumut, brought home one
night the most glorious eight-pounder. But what a nasty
mess of tussocks, crawling with snakes, the Eucumbene
was! It was far from attractive water; and moreover it was

visible from the road. It was neither athletic nor adventurous, even if you had snakes crawling down your neck
the whole time, to fish a river that could be seen from
the road.

Far and high lay the Three-Mile Dam; far and high and
solitary. No fishable water lay higher; none, in those
days, was more remote. The old gold-seekers had made
it, by damming Bullock's Head Creek, and there in its
basin right on top of the mountains it lay, the great
broad circle of it in the rolling landscape, blue and silver
to the sky, shivering in the slightest breeze, rimmed with
low banks where alpine daisies glittered like snowflakes
among the flowering heath, and guinea flowers and bulbine lilies, with minute white orchids among them,
shone gold and yellow like the sun. Sky and water and
flowers! The most enormous trout rose all day in it, leaping clean out of the water for dragonflies.

They rose, it must be confessed, quite out of reach.
Wicked, ingenious men, I have been told, fished for
them with balloons. You tied a child's balloon about six
inches above your fly, and let it float out with the wind,
a most reprehensible device. We didn't try that (perhaps
because at that time we hadn't heard about it) but we
did try everything else we could think of. We trudged
round and round that lake, waist-deep in the very cold
mountain water, casting as fishermen never casted
before. We sneaked up on them where they rose a little
closer in, under the grove of sally-gums, and got ourselves hooked up in the branches. We waded out up to
our necks to perch on an islet of rocks. David Campbell
found a queer unstable kind of raft, like a rocking-horse,
and rode out after the monsters. But the maddening
thing about those trout was that no matter how far out

you waded or rode after them, they still rose just out of reach. They retreated before your advance. I suppose you would have needed a dragonfly, or a fly as large as a dragonfly, to tempt them anyhow. But they were fascinating trout to fish for; they kept you eager, and wading, and wet, all day. And sometimes, under the sally-gums, where they came in for falling beetles, or among the islets of logs and tussocks where the creek flowed in, and best of all at the rocky point where a low ridge thrust far out into the lake and, so to speak, did most of your wading for you, you could catch a trout which, if not the equal of the mighty dragonfly jumpers, was still a fish worth catching.

And then, at dusk, the big fish started to come in. They came in to the shallows to rise for moths and flies. And when it got quite dark, and sometimes even before then, you could catch them. We fished with two people who knew the tricks of the trade around Prosser's far better than we did: John and Peggy Dutton, two more squatting friends of David Campbell's; and John and Peggy Dutton showed us exactly how you caught fish in the Three-Mile Dam at night.

There was a fly called the Styx Special. It was the most enormous dry fly I have ever seen. It was as black as its name would indicate. It was a mass of very stiff black bristles; and it would float superbly. You lit a great bonfire on the banks to attract the moths and maybe also to attract the trout; you turned your car headlights on to the water for the same purpose; you tied on a Styx Special and cast it as far out as you could into the black water, and you left it there floating, and waited … And *splash* went those mighty trout as they took your fly in the night!

I have seen a night at the Three-Mile Dam when

John and Peggy Dutton, David Campbell and myself were each and all of us simultaneously wrestling with a fish in the darkness, and as soon as we had landed one trout, and cast out the invaluable Styx Special again, we would hook another, and another; a two-pounder, a three-pounder, a four-pounder; with the white moths dancing in the beam of the headlights, and the smoke and the sweet smell of burning snowgum wood billowing down from the bonfire, and stars overhead, and, black, mysterious and enchanting all around you, the top of the world and the water. And when something out in the blackness took your fly with a splash like a whale leaping, and streaked out to the horizon and broke you off round a rock or just wasn't there any more, that, no doubt, was one of the monsters that leapt by day for the dragonflies ... never really to be caught and landed, for such things are hardly possible, but always, immense out of the blue water by daylight or invisible by night, to leap in the mind's eye when you think about the fishing at Prosser's.

16

THE SNOWY

THE first time I fished the Snowy I did it more or less by accident. Once in November we were going from Cooma up to Kosciuszko to see the snow; and, at the foot of the long hill into Jindabyne, suddenly the great river flashed into view, broad and blue and glittering as it twisted from the mountains through the green valley. It was the most famous of all Australian trout streams, and I must fish it, that was certain; and on the way back from Kosciuszko I did.

And I saw that day the biggest trout that I ever saw in the Snowy. It was just upstream from Jindabyne, at the point where Wollondibby Creek came in. And there, right where that rather muddy water entered the deep swift current of the river, rising again and again as he gulped down flies in a sheltered pocket, swam that most regal trout. He showed himself each time as he rose, big and dark in the evening water, and he was a four-pounder if ever there was a four-pounder; and it seemed to be likely enough five or even six pounds, a monster. How to land him if you hooked him seemed quite an insoluble problem. There were snags in the pool, and it was much too deep to wade. The tangled mass of

blackberries, seven or eight feet high, growing right to
the water's edge on both banks of the creek made it
impossible to get to the main river and cope with him
from there. The Snowy's bank, anyhow, was equally lost
in blackberries. The likeliest thing was that he would
simply dash out into the river and disappear round the
bend and down the current. But then the unlikeliest
things do happen once you have hooked your fish. It
might have been possible to plunge down the pool,
more or less submerged, or roll yourself over the blackberries. The first step was to hook him.

And, rising as regularly as he was, carelessly and
greedily feeding as he patrolled round and round his
pocket at the brink of the river, that seemed distinctly
possible. It was a most difficult cast. High blackberries
everywhere behind you, blackberries all round the
trout's parade ground. If you cast too far, out into the
main stream, it would be useless; if you cast short or
made any kind of disturbance you would frighten the
fish in his quiet pocket. Flung high behind you over the
tops of the blackberries, whipped forward with immac-
ulate precision, the fly must land, with one long delicate
cast, exactly where the monster was rising. There are
times when one can be inspired. The fly did everything
it should have and floated down, light as the feathers it
was made of, right on his nose. And the mighty fish …
ignored it.

That exasperating trout! Nothing would induce
him to take any fly I offered. He rose all round each one,
eating whatever it was that he was so fond of; and then,
full fed or annoyed with all those artificial flies dropping
on his parade ground, worked his way out into the
Snowy and vanished.

Well, you can't expect to catch the biggest fish in

the Snowy just like that, dropping in like a tourist and flicking a fly about for half an hour. You must earn your fish; you must get to know your waters. And the proper way to fish the Snowy, and all the beautiful streams round about it, was to stay at the famous old fishing lodge, the Creel.

The Creel had begun its life as a hotel and, though it was built of timber instead of the more appropriate stone or pisé, still kept its ancient form: long and low, with rooms looking out onto a wide veranda and beyond it to the grove of imported pines and elms, and beyond them to a glimpse of the Thredbo whose rippling waters murmured into your sleep when it was calm or, in its frequent floods, rushed and roared through the night as the wind rushed through the pine-trees. As more and more guests came over the years the house had expanded in all directions; and all about the grounds, under elms or old red gum-trees, stood a strange collection of out-houses called 'cottages' and 'chalets' where hardy fishermen braved the ancient bed-steads and the thudding of the motor that made the electric power.

There were Black Orpingtons leading their cream and sooty chickens about the yards; and turkey hens sunk in the inveterate misery of their kind, and their melancholy young darting their beaks like snakes to snap up flies from the sunny walls of the implement shed, and resplendent cock birds puffing out their feathers and fans like Chinese emperors. There were cows and a red calf. There was a pretty white she-goat who was usually tethered under the lichen-covered old plum-trees in the orchard and spent her days yearning for fruit and green leaves beyond her reach. How eloquent are a goat's pale yellow eyes when she pleads for food; how daintily, when she is given a plum, she munches it round in her mouth and politely ejects the stone! She was always getting herself so tangled in her chain, that goat, that she had usually more or less hanged herself when you called on her; but often, too, she broke free and instantly made for the garden in front of the veranda where, amidst great commotion from people trying to drive her away, she snatched mouthfuls of gerberas and honeysuckle. There were wild birds, too, among all these domestic creatures. All day long the thrushes called with their sweet voices in the high trees; magpies warbled; the lowries and the rosellas rang their small dainty bells to each other or flew in shrieking flocks, with flashes of green and blue and crimson, to feed on the plums and apples – you would see them, solemn and wicked, a red bird in a thicket of red fruit, taking a bite here and a bite there, always ruining, as is their mischievous way, more fruit than they ate.

Some distance from the house, along the track to the gorge where the Thredbo rushed down in a white cataract, there were three or four ginger Tamworth pigs in a yard of rough-hewn saplings. They too were very partial to plums, but not as polite with them as the goat. It was here, at the pig-yard, so we were told by Billy Stanton, that quiet, slow-speaking, smiling man who managed the Creel, that there had occurred the most horrifying episode with a snake. Billy had had somebody helping him build the yard, a guest or a labourer, who had two dogs with him. One of the dogs put up a big brown snake in a pile of loose rocks near the yard. The snake instantly bit it. The other dog rushed in to join the fight and the snake bit that one, too, and hung on to it. And in the midst of all the yelping and barking and snarling and commotion and confusion, with the dogs trying to kill the snake, and the man trying to drive the dogs away and get at it with a stick – in the midst of all this savagery the snake, mad with rage, struck the man too: twice, on the legs. By good luck he was wearing leggings; so the man recovered of the bite, the dog it was who died. It did, too, poor creature. Both the dogs, when the snake at last had been killed, ran away and lay down in the river. One, after an hour or two, got up and staggered away and was sick for three days before it recovered. The other died in the river. It was a story that considerably increased my respect for snakes; it added a slightly uneasy flavour to the pleasant, pastoral occupation of feeding the pigs.

But it had happened some years before; and if there were probably still a few snakes around the property, particularly near the Garden Pool where the jungle of blackberries seemed to be crawling with them when you fished it after dinner in the dark, nobody was ever eaten by them. It was a pleasant place, the Creel: and, with the notice-board in the old dark dining-room recording all the fish over three pounds which had been taken for years and years past, and occasionally a new name and a new fish being added to the list, with the fishermen coming home at night with their catches to be cooked for breakfast next morning, and with all the talk about fishing, there was certainly a flavour, a feeling, an atmosphere – what is the word? – a *slither* of trout about it. It was haunted by the shades of mighty fishermen of the past, who rode in with pack-horses and camped by far pools of the Snowy when fishing was really fishing; and it was patrolled still by a few survivors of the heroic days and by their direct heirs and descendants, tall, silent, formidable men who trod the veranda in big boots and disappeared early in the morning.

There was one reach of the Snowy not far from the Creel where I had some lovely fishing one year. That was the water just downstream from where the Thredbo flowed into the bigger river, and it was a year when the grasshoppers were swarming. They stripped the farmers' fruit-trees; they ate the paddocks on the hills down to little more than granite sand, with only a few red fronds of sorrel left to nourish the hungry sheep. They clapped their yellow wings and whirred like flocks of fighter planes as you walked through the tall yellow weeds, called snake-flowers, to the river. All day long, taking off on their senseless flights, with no notion of where they would land, they flopped into the river and paddled with an air of surprise to the shore again; and all day long in the shallow run at the meeting of the two rivers, in the rapid downstream and in the long straight pool below it, the trout rose and feasted on them.

I don't know why, when the whole length of the Snowy from Island Bend to Jindabyne was pleasant to fish, as were all the other rivers near by, this particular reach should have seemed so supremely delightful. It was not an adventurous place to get to; it was not famous; it was not conspicuously beautiful; and I never caught any big fish in it. Many small strands of pleasure made the rope that holds it in my memory.

One of them was solitude; for it so happened that year that I always fished there alone, and it is good to be alone in the sun. Then there were the skylarks. There would be half a dozen of them in the air at once, dark specks poised high in the blue on their fluttering wings, and the whole immensity of sky and mountain and river-valley would be ringing with their music. What a torrent of shining melody that tiny bird can pour out! At the base of a dry thistle on the flat between the

Thredbo crossing and the Snowy I found a nest with three brown speckled eggs in it, and every day on my way to the river I used to stop and look into the little grassy cup to see how they were getting on.

Then of course there was the river itself. If it was sedate enough there, nevertheless that was the point at which it came pouring out of the long wild gorge that ran unbroken and hardly touched by man miles and miles through the mountains from the steeps of Kosciuszko; and there was a special, gentle charm in its sedateness. Green forest and distant blue walls of mountain upstream, green paddocks and willows below, it was a nice mid-way point between the wilderness and civilization. And, when finally you got to it, wading the Thredbo at its one crossable point and on through the snake-flowers and thistles and the last hot sandy hollow of its flood channel, aromatic with the fallen leaves of the sally-gums, it was a pretty bit of water with its own small intriguing difficulties. You could try to cast under the overhanging tea-tree on the far bank, or into the swirling backwater across the rapid, from which the current would always snatch your fly away just as you had landed it in that likely-looking spot. It was pleasant to fish up the run and notice how quietly the Thredbo waters came in, brown over the brown pebbles, rippling into the blue and crystalline Snowy; pleasant to wade out into the rapid and as far downstream as you could go into the long deepening pool, green under its white-flowered tea-trees.

Moreover, I made a discovery there; and it is always very satisfactory to discover for yourself something about the art of fishing. It was the fact that, though they all seemed to be taking their grasshoppers from the surface, the trout preferred a wet fly to a dry fly; and

moreover that they were particularly interested in a huge dark-red fly called the Claret and Teal. The one fly they certainly did not want was the official dry-fly imitation of a floating grasshopper. Maybe they eat most of their grasshoppers drowned, or maybe a grasshopper-imitation on the surface doesn't kick enough to look natural. Any large fly would do, for the grasshoppers were all sorts of colours. I even persuaded the fish to take notice of a colossal salmon-fly, spotted yellow and black, that had stayed in my fly-box from days at Taupo in New Zealand, years before. But the Claret and Teal was the one they really fancied. I had great luck with that fly until, with infinite grief, I lost it up a tea-tree bush somewhere below Island Bend.

So, with the aid of that discovery, I did catch fish, even if they weren't very big ones, in that delectable spot. And, not the least of its fascinations, there were always, as there always are, what seemed to be enormous fish rising quite out of reach all the way down the long pool.

Once in that spot, one other year when I was fishing it with my daughter, I saw a most amazing sight. Out of nowhere, out of the green forest, down the long gorge from Kosciuszko, came a small fat New Australian floating in a little yellow washtub. Heaven knows where he had come from! One moment there was just the empty river glittering in the sunshine, and the next moment there was this thing on the water, a little yellow raft with a man in it. He couldn't have been a more surprising apparition if he had been a Martian in a flying saucer. Naked to the waist and wearing green floral bathing trunks, he was fishing dry-fly as he sailed, and he might have solved the problem of how to catch the unreachable fish in the long pool if he had been able to manage his craft a little better. But while he was talking to me he dropped his paddle overboard and then went round and round the pool in circles, paddling with his hands. 'I frighten all the fish!' he said to me with great good cheer. I might have agreed with that, but we had just discovered that the only trout that seemed to be rising that morning, which had been coming up with a mighty swirl under the tea-tree right at our feet, was a platypus. So we left him there, paddling in circles and frightening the platypus, and where he got to I never will know. Maybe he floated out to sea in the end in his little yellow raft, or turned up in some farmer's irrigation paddock a thousand miles away …

A mile or so downstream from the long pool was a famous fishing place known as the Gutters. You could have walked down to it easily enough, but it always seemed too hot for that; and besides, there was a bull that used to sing all day to its cows in the first paddock downstream and seemed disposed to investigate any trespassing fisherman. So it seemed more attractive to drive down the Jindabyne road to the property known as Hiawatha, where sleek black mares and their foals whiled the summer hours away under the shade of the pepper-trees at the gate; and so across the paddocks where the little brown groundlarks, apparently hypno-tized, flew along the wheeltracks in front of the car at twenty miles an hour and never seemed to be able to get of the track and go home. The Snowy at the Gutters, a big river by now, split itself into deep swift channels that ran between reefs of granite, and in that maze of water-ways very big fish were said to lie. One of the mighty men from the Creel used to drive over at dawn, not fish-ing, just for the pleasure of watching them. Somehow I never got around to exploring the Gutters properly myself, and all I ever caught there was a lean, disgrace-ful little brownie of less than a pound; but I was at the Creel when that same watcher of the dawn brought back a four-pound rainbow from those waters. On another occasion he caught something even more remarkable – a Judge of the Supreme Court. The Snowy had a very dangerous habit of silently, without warning, rising into flood when they let the water out of the Guthega Dam higher up; and the Judge was on the far side of the Gutters when this happened and got into trouble trying to come back. His friend waded out chest-deep into the torrent and pulled him across with a stick. The worst thing about those floods was that the river, which had long before swept itself clean, swelled up around you with no discoloration and none of the debris of leaves and twigs you would expect, rising so swiftly that you were in bother before you noticed it.

If I didn't myself ever really do the Gutters justice, I did in that same year of the grasshoppers catch myself a nice fish about a mile further downstream; a three-pound brown; and if this was an absurdly simple feat it was also quite a pretty bit of fishing. There was a most curious piece of water where, sneaking back from the head of a long straight pool and lying shallow, narrow and motionless between the hillside and a sandbank, a backwater baked in the sun; and, as I was walking along the bank above the tail of it, where it wasn't more than a foot in depth, half a dozen grasshoppers plopped away from me into the water; and the big brown trout, which had been waiting for just such an event, rose from behind a snag and took one of them. There he was, to be caught. The problems were: how, without disturbing him, to move into concealment from that high bank; how to approach from the flat bare sandbank, without being seen; and how to drop the fly lightly and accurately exactly where he lay beyond the snag. That clear shallow water allowed no blundering. I should have changed my big wet Claret and Teal for a dry fly, which would have been more manageable, but I felt I couldn't spare the time. I thought only one cast with the wet fly would be possible; to withdraw it and cast again would almost certainly disturb him, and he would be off into the depths. Neatly, very neatly, the Claret and Teal, from where I lay prone on the sandbank, floated through the air and landed, like a small aeroplane, precisely where it was meant to. The fish rose, inspected it, and sank again below the snag. It was not, he decided, a grasshopper.

Woe. Agony. I pulled it out and cast again without hope. Inexplicably, he took it … I was just a little disconcerted when I bore back the three-pounder in triumph to the Creel, to learn that that very day the giant fisherman had chosen to bring home his four-pound rainbow from the Gutters; but a three-pounder is never to be sneezed at.

And I myself, in another year, caught a four-pounder just a couple of hundred yards further downstream; or at least I thought I did. It was in a fascinating big round pool among the hills, and the fish lay in a runnel between the shore and a granite reef. Racing over to Hiawatha after dinner to catch the last of the fishing in the dusk, I had hooked and lost him two or three times. I knew exactly where to go and how to fish for him. I knew how big he was; I had felt his weight on the line. And this night, dashing over to the river with David Campbell, I was determined to get him. And, while David perched himself on a slippery rock in midstream somewhere and hooked a nice little fish himself, I fished again for the monster, and I got him. He was fully six inches long and must have weighed about as many ounces. Small fish, hooked in the darkness, should really be lost in the darkness if they are to keep their weight up.

That was the pool where Percy Mathers, when I fished it with him in the year of the grasshoppers, gave me the worst fright he ever gave me. The track down to it, over the smooth granite rocks and the slides of rubble, was steep. The current, sinister in the dusk, ran deep and swift under a ledge at the end of it. Percy was never very good at balancing himself. His method of proceeding down a mountain was to walk straight into the air, head erect, boldly striding forward as if the slope wasn't there. And, if you walked it that way, it wasn't. Down came Percy, slithering erect, right to the brink of the torrent; and there, mercifully, paused swaying for an instant before taking the final plunge into limbo. 'This scramble fishing,' he said with a rare touch of testiness, 'is no good to me.'

Percy was a remarkable character. He was a naturalist of great renown in England, expert in the peculiarities of the chaffinch. He carried in his pocket, for light holiday reading, the odes of Pindar in Greek. He had been something at Oxford; he had been editor of a famous English quarterly. He had been something to do with elephants in Burma; and in Hitler's war, engaged in highly confidential diplomacy, he had spent a great deal of time dashing about under the oceans in a submarine. Heaven knows how he got to the Creel, in the wilderness of the Snowy Mountains, so many thousands of miles from his native haunts. He came there, he told me, because he loved mountains and fishing. There were plenty of both at the Creel; but they were both a little more rugged than he had anticipated.

He was a slight, rather frail-looking man, was Percy, with a peculiar kind of glitter about him. I think this was partly because of his horn-rimmed glasses, partly because of his enthusiasm, partly because of his wit. One way or another there was always a kind of twinkle coming from him, like sunlight on a small, eager rapid. His wit, naturally enough, was chiefly for after dinner. A hot shower and two dry sherries, and Percy came to the dinner table prepared to glitter. It was a tradition; it was a ritual; it was what one did while the red wine passed. Percy's wit was small and impish and punning – 'God have mercy upon them, miserable spinners!' was his great triumph, one night when we were talking about the spinner-fishermen then beginning to invade the sacred waters of the Snowy.

He was the absent-minded professor to perfection. Every morning as he stood on the steps of the fishing lodge ready for the day's excursion, his eager, bird-like face twinkling under his very small sola topee, he would, so to speak, count himself up to make sure nothing would be left behind. He had a most useful mnemonic which, patting his pockets and peering in his creel, he would carefully recite:

> *My rod, my reel,*
> *My flies, my creel.*

Very good; nothing could be forgotten. I use it now myself. But what about his tobacco? What about the wine? What about the scissors which, as a true dry-fly man, he regarded as essential for changing a fly in a hurry or poking into knots in his cast? What about a change of boots and trousers? What about lunch? What about getting all his precious belongings home again? Percy was not to be trusted. He left his fishing bag somewhere in the Thredbo and cleverly found a small wicker creel, left by some other absent-minded professor, on the banks of Spencer's Creek. He left his scissors on a rock at the Gutters. He left his entire stock of flies in their transparent box on that rather cow-trodden part of the Moonbah called the Banks and we used to call in regularly to look for it. If he put a cast down beside him in the grass it instantly vanished – as indeed does everybody's cast. If he put a fly down beside him while he was changing it, the fairies took it. Wisely he kept his spare pair of spectacles tied onto him with string; which, when he had bought some new ones in the store in Jindabyne – very special ones, 'made in *Germany*' – he also did with his scissors.

Beaming like a leprechaun under his sun-helmet, tied up and trussed with odd articles, soldierly in a windjacket and khaki trousers, complete with 'my rod, my reel, my flies, my creel', Percy, as he trudged that high country, was the most indomitable fisherman I ever saw. Once, I think, he had been a very good fisherman. But he cast his line now, for some reason of his own, with an unorthodox sideways motion that sent the fly swinging behind him in a half-circle. When, as was usually the case, there was a serried mass of tea-tree behind him, he hooked the tea-tree. When there was a clear space behind, he hooked himself. When he was not hooked up in the tea-tree or himself, he was usually to be found prostrate in the tussocks or the streams. He had a remarkable propensity for falling over, and could do it with equal ease on land or water. His way of marching straight forward, shoulders back, head erect, eyes front, in perfect military style, not only brought him slithering down slopes but got him into bother with any obstacles that might be on the most level ground. I see him now in my mind's eye striding across the high plain by Spencer's Creek in a thunderstorm, crashing over the holes and boulders in the heath, or, indelibly and immortally, falling headlong in the Snowy at Island Bend and rising up dripping and bleeding to go on fishing.

How he loved it all, in spite of his disabilities and his disasters! And how glad we were to see him rewarded in the end with a very nice fish from the Moonbah. 'But I *enjoy* it!' he used to say, whatever fate befell him; 'but I *enjoy* it!' His enthusiasm began at breakfast and continued all day. 'Spencer's Creek – *lovely!*' he would say if that was where we had decided to go for the day. 'Island Bend – *lovely!*' and above all, for it was the most manageable of the streams, 'Moonbah – *lovely!*'

And that was, indeed, the great advantage of fishing at the Creel: not merely that the Thredbo was just off the veranda and the Snowy only about half a mile away, but that there were so many fishable streams all within easy reach if you had a car. East, west, north and south, everywhere there were trout-streams.

If you followed the Thredbo up for a full day's fishing, through the gorge where it tumbled through the walls of granite and on past the rocky bends and the Sandy Pool where one day I thought I had lost my sister when she wandered off looking at the wildflowers, you came to the deep still waters of Paddy's Corner where Charlie Collins, an old-timer of the mountains, lived alone with his horses and an old blind bitch that used to make nasty little runs at your legs; and where, if I never caught any of the enormous fish that were reputed to lurk there, I used to enjoy the company of two large and very slithery lizards, speckled like the granite, who lived in a chink in the rocks and made a sinister rasping noise as they slid into it. They were Cunningham's skinks, I think.

Up from Paddy's the river lost itself in the wilderness, only to be reached by intrepid souls who rode it on horseback with Charlie Collins, and did very well there, too; but, if you drove round through Jindabyne and up the Alpine Highway, you could meet it again at the Eel Hole. There were supposed not to be any fish worth talking about at the Eel Hole, but one beautiful maddening sunny afternoon they rose all round me and I

caught none while some clever stranger who was fishing the same water landed five quite respectable
rainbows. I don't know whether it was just that I was
having an off day, or whether it was because he was fishing with the very fine 4X cast, while I was using a 3X.
It was beautiful water, wide and green and deep.

On and up, a little trampled by Thredbo Village but
memorable for a gang-gang that came and watched me
one wet day, raising his red crest in astonishment while
I fished hopelessly in the yellow floodwaters, the
Thredbo at last lost itself in the rocks by Dead Horse
Gap; but over the top and down the Victorian side, in
that hot, lush valley of the tall timber, other rivers sprang
up to replace it. The Indi and the Geehi ran clear and
cold and shallow over their slippery round stones; and
the Murray too, somewhere in a ferny glade, began to
think about moving down the country … You could, if
you chose, have wandered on fishing for ever.

But then, not nearly so far to travel, branching off
the Alpine Highway back near Jindabyne, was that
lovely little stream, the Moonbah: rough and rocky and
snaky below the bridge; flat, tussocky and a little too
domesticated, but with some really good fish in it, in the
cow-paddocks around the Banks; offering a curious
diversion in its tiny tributaries, Grassy Plains Creek and
Rendezvous Creek, mere runnels through deep tussock,
where the best fish of all were caught early in the
season; exquisite in its upper reaches where, fringed
with black sallies, it bubbled at the foot of the mountains
or meandered across the wide swampy plain where the
red and white Hereford cattle used to feed. *'Ah, the
Moonbah!'* said Percy …

There was a gorge away up there where the fishing
was said not to be worthwhile; but I never saw grey

rocks so beautifully patterned with green lichens and moss as down in that fishless gorge; I never knew a piece of water more interesting and exasperating to fish as it twisted and turned and hid itself among its tangle of tea-tree and briers; and once, when I was fishing it with David Campbell, I saw a spiny ant-eater, the echidna, stumbling and rasping its way along a landslide of broken granite and, when I called out to David to come and see it, he told me that he had just seen 'the biggest, reddest fox I ever saw in my life.'

Once, too, surprisingly, I took a good fish out of it, a two-pounder which lay just where I thought it might lie, in a most impossible place under the tea-tree. And once, just where the gorge comes up into the open again, I met with another large and interesting fish who rose just in front of a rock in mid-stream, so that one had to stand below him in the water and drop the fly just over the top of the rock, a difficult and intriguing feat to accomplish. That was the day when a fisherman who was camping under the sally-trees told me that the only fly that was any use up there that season was – either the Royal Coachman with the crimson belly or the ordinary plain white Coachman … Only the right one was any good and I could never afterwards remem-ber which of the two to use. But whichever it was, if the tip is of any use to anyone, that was the fly which caught the three-pounder that day in front of the rock.

Then, upstream among the roaring Herefords, was that nice flat manageable piece of water where Percy Mathers achieved his triumph; and beyond that, the narrow, ever dwindling but still remarkably fishable streamlet, sparkling in the sun and bubbling over weedy shallows. Every now and again it dropped into surpris-ingly deep pools where, wading pool and shallow alike to avoid the snakes in the tussocks, my daughter and I once had a great day's fishing and caught, between us, eleven takeable trout. And beyond that, still dwindling but still with its fishable pools, the high remote waters through the last green farmlands and the wild mountains ... ah, the Moonbah, indeed!

Jacob's River, the Eucumbene, the MacLaughlin green with frog's blanket, the Gungahleen teeming with little fish as it tumbled through the gorge from the Snowy Plains to fall headlong into the Snowy – the Gungahleen where once I met a man who had caught a six-pounder three years before, and who had spent all his holidays on it ever afterwards, trying to catch another – everywhere, not to mention the Eucumbene Dam, there were fishable waters.

Far up on Kosciuszko where the mountains rolled down in slow green waves from the granite-scarred ridges to the high plain golden with buttercups and billybuttons and rosy with trigger-flowers, you could try out Spencer's Creek. There were millions of fish in Spencer's. All day long, even in the first big pool by the bridge and on up into the winding reaches where it slid under granite boulders or banks of heath, they rose for the little green grasshoppers that leapt into the air from your boots and sprinkled the water in front of you. Perhaps they ate too – and we hoped the big sluggish March-flies that settled on you every time you paused to rest and meditatively sucked your blood. At any given moment, anywhere along that clear shallow creek with its round granite boulders, its heathy channels and its sands glinting golden with pyrites, you could see a dozen fish rising.

But the size of them! If they grew eight inches long

they were monsters. They were mostly about six inches, and often you hooked them smaller. It was not fishing; it was massacre. You could catch a dozen or twenty of them in a morning if you liked, but what was the use of that? We did sometimes eat a few of the larger specimens for lunch, wrapped in wet newspapers and grilled over the embers of the campfire in the orthodox manner, and very nice they were too, prised gently away from their bones when they were cooked and laid on slices of bread and butter; but they were not fish you could be seen with.

Years and years ago, so the old hands say, respectable fish lived in Spencer's; but there, and in all the Kosciuszko waters, they seemed to have dwindled by the time I made their acquaintance. Once I tried out Spencer's neighbour, Betts' Creek. It looked very tempting, winding through bogs of wildflowers at the foot of the stony hillsides and opening into broad shallow pools quite deep enough in odd corners to hold a good fish. But the fish, though sometimes a six-incher took the fly with such a rush that you thought you had really got something at last, were as small as in Spencer's. Some looked young and some – the mighty seven-inchers looked dark and old. Summer's brief showers of grasshoppers and March-flies couldn't have been enough to fatten a fish that had to live – how did they live? – through the long bleak winters up there, when the streams were buried in snow. Sensible fish, presumably, all migrated downstream when they grew up.

Once, too, I fished those enticing billabongs that, apparently unconnected with any stream, lay glittering in the heath above Spencer's; big, round, icy-clear pools, naked to the mountains' reflections and the winds. I saw nothing in them except the tiniest trout and, not exactly helping the fishing, a solitary wild duck that swam ahead of me as I walked.

There were just two occasions in Spencer's when I saw good fish; and they were very good fish indeed; and both, I think, cannibals. One was enormous. I saw it chasing the small fish about in the pool above the bridge; they leapt into the air to escape from it, like small fry from a killer in the sea. Its back jutted out of the water as if it was too big for the pool it swam in. It showed no interest whatever in the big salmon-fly I put on to engage its attention. The other big fish, down-stream among the rocks in the gorge, struck, so far as I could make out, at a small fish which had just taken my fly. I really don't know what happened. There was a commotion in the water; the impression of a heavy weight on my line; then a very small fish on the end of it, and a fine two-pound rainbow darting away again to his fastness under the cliff. Maybe there would still have been good fish to be caught there, as there are said to have been in the old days, if one could have stayed for the evening rise; but Spencer's Creek always seemed very cold and a long way from home in the dusk, and long before then we had usually been chased out by a thunderstorm. They came pouring through a gap in the mountains, lilac and mauve with the burden of far-off dust-storms, and lashed us with hail and lightning. If we didn't particularly object to such weather — and Percy enjoyed it — the trouble was that in no time at all the river came up in flood and that was the end of the fish-ing.

There was one surprising thing you could do when the storms had driven you out from Spencer's, and that was to drop a fly in the lake that lay in the hollow by the old Kosciuszko Hotel. It seemed vaguely immoral, and possibly illegal, but it was very interesting to squelch through those snaky-looking reed-beds to the point where Betts' Creek ran in, and there drop a fly to a rising trout, and pull out, if not a large fish, a brownie at least worth taking home.

And so, back to the Snowy. One wet day when we had been stormed out from Spencer's and even the big river was coming up in flood, I fished the Snowy upstream from the junction with the Thredbo, and remember it for a small lean brown trout which was a triumph in the circumstances, and for a large kangaroo which hopped through the undergrowth towards me and stood up very tall and menacingly said 'Oof!' It was a half-tame creature which had come down out of the snow one winter and had been befriended by someone living on the river-bank. Higher up was the big Horse-shoe Pool where, between fishing in vain one sunny morning for a very small fish that rose over a rock-ledge in about six inches of water, we watched a great flock of gang-gangs — twenty-two of them there were — enjoy-ing themselves in a huge old ribbony-gum over the river; and higher up still, to be reached by driving along a jeep-track through the bush, then slithering down a mountainside, was a rough and noble stretch of water which I chiefly remember because, fishing it one day with Percy, I lost my car in the bush … at such times there always seems to be a great deal of bush in Australia. And then, higher still, was Island Bend, beginning then to be invaded by the Snowy Mountains Authority, but still with some beautiful water upstream from it. One lovely day there, when the sun shone on the broad stream and the thrushes called high and piercingly sweet in the tall timber, I hooked the most handsome three-pound rainbow. He was rising in a deep pool for small green beetles that I could see floating down the stream to him. So I sagaciously put on a fly that looked like a small green beetle; and lo, he took it! And lo, he dashed towards me at full speed; and dashing backwards over the slippery rocks to keep pace with him, I fell flat on my back in the water … and goodbye fish.

I thought once I would have a look away up under the summit of Kosciuszko to see where all this water came from: I would seek out the source of the Snowy. But that was easier said than done.

The great problem was, first of all, to find the Snowy. There, under the concrete bridge on the road to the summit, it was unmistakeable: wide and shallow, and of that absolute pure clarity which only new-born rivers have, a surprisingly big stream for one that had only just gathered itself together out of the snow. Upstream, too, for a little way, round those first bends where it lay in its great blue pools under the snowbanks, it was still unmistakably itself. But then the trouble began. The river divided. There were two Snowys. The only thing you could do was choose one of them, and call that the Snowy; so I took the stream to the right, which came down more directly from the ramparts of Kosciuszko. But soon it too divided. It was not one stream, but a hundred. It was a patch of bog and buttercups. It was a hole in the heath, filled with clear water, beside which lay the claws of a long-dead yabbie, still purple and green despite the weathering by sun and snow. It was a wide watery shallow, unconnected so far as you could see with any direct movement of the stream, lying aimlessly among speckled boulders and the dark-green carpet of heath as if the country could not make up its mind whether to be land or water.

All you could do in this maze of water and flowers
– the shiny yellow buttercups, the giant dandelions, the
purple eyebright, the silver snow-daisies, the billybuttons, the creamy sprays and green fronds of the alpine
parsley, the exquisite mauve-flowered dwarf mint-bush
– was to pick one trickle and follow it. On went the
trickle through the heath, straight to the final wall; and
there, in the little sunlit pool where the snow thrust over
the boulders and turned into water before your eyes,
surely lay the source of the Snowy. But no; five yards or
so beyond it, lay another little pool; and another again
beyond it. There was no saying which was the source.
Far up the mountainside soaks of melted snow lay
hidden among the moss; water gleamed on the granite.
The whole mountain was the source. But in and out of
the sunlight and the shadowy caverns of the snow in
those final crystalline pools, climbing up the mountain
as far as a fish could well climb, darted tiny rainbow
trout. What a long way they had to go before they grew
into four-pounders at the mouth of Wollondibby Creek!

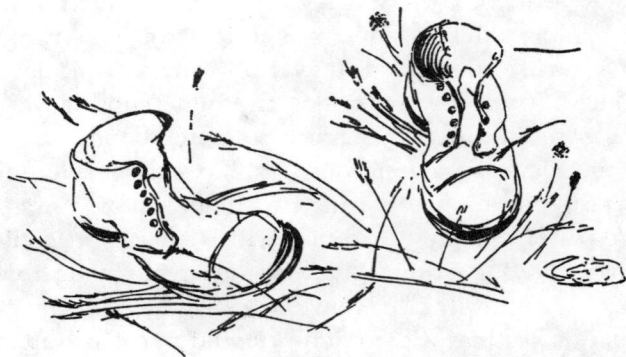